# Discourse

This new and engaging introduction offers a critical approach
to discourse, written by an expert uniquely placed to cover the
subject for a variety of disciplines. Organised along thematic
lines, the book begins with an outline of the basic principles,
moving on to examine the methods and theory of CDA (critical
discourse analysis). It covers topics such as text and context,
language and inequality, choice and determination, history
and process, ideology and identity. Blommaert focuses on how
language can offer a crucial understanding of wider aspects of
power relations, arguing that critical discourse analysis should
specifically be an analysis of the *effects* of power, what power
does to people, groups, and societies, and how this impact
comes about. Clearly argued, this concise introduction will
be welcomed by students and researchers in a variety of disciplines involved in the study of discourse, including linguistics,
linguistic anthropology, and the sociology of language.

JAN BLOMMAERT is Professor of African Linguistics and
Sociolinguistics at Ghent University. He has undertaken fieldwork in East and Southern Africa, and in 2002–2003 he was
awarded the *Emile Verhaeren Chair* at the Free University of
Brussels. He is the author of *State Ideology and Language in
Tanzania* (1999), co-author of *Debating Diversity* (1998), editor of
*Language Ideological Debates* (1999), and co-editor of the *Handbook of Pragmatics* (1995–2002). He has also published in a wide
variety of journals.

KEY TOPICS IN SOCIOLINGUISTICS

This new series focuses on the main topics of study in sociolinguistics today. It consists of accessible yet challenging accounts of the most important issues to consider when examining the relationship between language and society. Some topics have been the subject of sociolinguistic study for many years, and are here re-examined in the light of new developments in the field; others are issues of growing importance that have not so far been given a sustained treatment. Written by leading experts, the books in the series are designed to be used on courses and in seminars, and include useful suggestions for further reading and a helpful glossary.

Already published in the series:

*Politeness*, by Richard J Watts

*Language Policy*, by Bernard Spolsky

Forthcoming titles:

*World Englishes*, by Rakesh Bhatt and Raj Mesthrie

*Analyzing Sociolinguistic Variation*, by Sali Tagliamonte

# Discourse
## A Critical Introduction

JAN BLOMMAERT

CAMBRIDGE UNIVERSITY PRESS
Cambridge, New York, Melbourne, Madrid, Cape Town, Singapore, São Paulo

Cambridge University Press
The Edinburgh Building, Cambridge, CB2 8RU, UK

Published in the United States of America by Cambridge University Press, New York

www.cambridge.org
Information on this title: www.cambridge.org/9780521535311

First published 2005
Fourth printing 2007

Printed in the United Kingdom at the University Press, Cambridge

*A catalogue record for this publication is available from the British Library*

*Library of Congress Cataloging in Publication data*
Blommaert, Jan.
Discourse : a critical introduction / Jan Blommaert.
    p.   cm. – (Key topics in sociolinguistics)
Includes bibliographical references and index.
ISBN 0 521 82817 1 – ISBN 0 521 53531 X (pbk.)
1. Discourse analysis – Social aspects.   I. Title.   II. Series.
P302.84.B585   2004
401'.41 – dc22   2004045825

ISBN 978-0-521-82817-8 hardback
ISBN 978-0-521-53531-1 paperback

For Dell H. and John G.

# Contents

# Preface

It is a wonderful opportunity to be able to produce a synthesis of work which in the present economy of academic publishing is dispersed over too many fragmented little bits. The opportunity was offered to me by Andrew Winnard of Cambridge University Press, to whom I express my gratitude. This is indeed a synthesis of thoughts and approaches developed over many years, and evidently too many people were involved in this process of development to even attempt to thank them all. I shall (have to) restrict myself here to those who directly influenced the genesis of this particular book.

There are, first, a number of intellectual partners who will undoubtedly find many echoes in this book of conversations I had with them over the years. My close friends in the Flemish National Science Foundation network on Language, Power, and Identity are prominent among them. Jim Collins, Monica Heller, Ben Rampton, Stef Slembrouck, and Jef Verschueren have not only discussed almost all the issues treated here repeatedly and at great length with me, they have also read drafts of the book and provided extremely important comments and suggestions. Dell Hymes, John Gumperz (to whom I dedicate this book), Michael Silverstein, and Ron Scollon are all great sources of inspiration for my approach and also provided tons of illuminating comments and useful suggestions on the manuscript. From slightly further afield, I am sure that people such as John Haviland, Kit Woolard, Sue Gal, Brian Street, Bob Hodge, Nik Coupland, Johannes Fabian, and Judy Irvine will find numerous traces of their own work here, either because of the usual technique of reading and adopting, or because of direct contacts I had with them.

I was able to write the draft of this book in the excellent and generous environment provided to me by the Department of Anthropology of the University of Chicago during the Winter Quarter of 2003. With the astonishing Regenstein Library as my working instrument, Paige Davis and Anne Ch'ien ensuring that I could work without being bothered by administrative or organisational details, and weather cold enough to lock me behind my writing table, the writing conditions were just ideal. Add to this the exceptionally stimulating intellectual environment provided by people such as Michael Silverstein, Sue Gal, Marshall Sahlins, George Stocking, Rob Moore, Flagg Miller, Sali Mufwene, Mara Tapp, and many others. And add to this, finally, a group of excellent students who were eager to serve as the first-line audience for the ideas I was developing in my writing cell. Some of them don't know it, but a number of the ideas in this book emerged directly from talks I had with them (Gretchen, Matt, Elif, Christie, Jaclyn, Cassie, and the others: thanks). It was a treat.

The same goes for my colleagues and students at home. I have had outstanding groups of students all along, totally committed to what they do and not afraid of explorative and innovative work, a privilege to work with but far too numerous to thank individually. May it suffice to say that almost all of this was developed as a result of my teaching work with them and my involvement in their individual projects which provided me with rich and widely varied empirical data. People such as Chris Bulcaen, Karel Arnaut, Michael Meeuwis, Katrijn Maryns, and Annelies Verdoolaege have been inspiring collaborators and critical, but always supportive, readers of my work. Thanks to all of them.

Nothing can work, of course, without a family supporting such adventures and tolerant enough to suffer the long physical and mental absences that were part of this writing process. Therefore: Pika, Fred, and Alex, thanks and sorry. I am also sorry that my father, Paul Blommaert, did not live to see the completion of this book. This book is therefore also tied to memories of loss.

# Acknowledgments

Various parts of this book have been previously published, sometimes in co-authorship with colleagues, all of whom I wish to thank for allowing me to re-use the product of our collective efforts. Thus, the groundwork for chapter 2 was laid in Jan Blommaert and Chris Bulcaen (2000) 'Critical discourse analysis' (*Annual Review of Anthropology* 29: 447–466). Large parts of chapter 3 are drawn from Jan Blommaert (2001), 'Context is/as Critique' (*Critique of Anthropology* 21/1: 13–32). The section on 'inequality and the narrative order' in chapter 4 analyses data originally discussed in Jan Blommaert, Kay McCormick, and Mary Bock (2002), 'Narrative inequality and hearability in the TRC Hearings' (*LPI Working Paper 8*, Ghent, London, Toronto, Albany). And in the same chapter, the section on 'inequality, literacy and globalisation' partly recapitulates an analysis presented in Jan Blommaert (2003) 'Commentary: a sociolinguistics of globalization' (*Journal of Sociolinguistics* 7/4: 607–623). In chapter 6, section 6.5 was originally presented in Jan Blommaert (1997) *Workshopping: Notes on Professional Vision in Discourse Analysis* (Antwerp: UIA-GER). And finally, section 7.5 originally appeared as Jan Blommaert (1997) 'The slow shift in orthodoxy (re)formulations of "integration" in Belgium' (*Pragmatics* 7/4: 499–518). I am grateful to Annual Reviews, Inc., Sage Publications, and Blackwell for permission to include these materials in this book.

# 1 Introduction

## 1.1 WHAT ARE WE TALKING ABOUT?

Power is not a bad thing – those who are in power will confirm it. They will argue convincingly that power is necessary in every system, for it is often that which allows the system to function in particular ways, without which the system would disintegrate or cease to operate effectively. Yet, power is a *concern* to many people, something that is easily translated into topics of discussion or narration. Power, its actors, its victims, and its mechanisms are often the talk of the town, and our everyday conversations, our mass media, our creative arts gladly use power as themes or motifs in discourses on society at large. Few stories are juicier than those of a president brutally abusing his power for his own personal benefit or for his own personal wrath against competitors for power – *All the President's Men* was a great movie. Few individuals are more fascinating than those who embody and emanate absolute power and are not afraid of wielding it in unscrupulous ways – Stalin, Napoleon, Mobutu, W. R. Hearst, and Onassis were all culture heroes of some sort in their days and afterwards. And scores of scholars ranging from Plato over Hobbes, Machiavelli, Marx, Gramsci to Foucault and Althusser have all theorised on the nature of power. Thus, we seem to have a strangely ambivalent attitude towards power: it attracts as well as repels; it fascinates and abhors at the same time; it has a beauty as well as an ugliness to it that match those of few other phenomena.

This book intends to offer a proposal for critical reflection on, and analysis of, discourse, and right from the start I wish to establish that a critical discourse analysis should not be a discourse analysis that reacts against power *alone*. It is a commonplace to equate 'critical approaches' with 'approaches that criticise power'. My point of view is that we need to be more specific. The suggestion I want to offer is that it should be an analysis of power *effects*, of the outcome of power, of what power

1

*does to* people, groups, and societies, and of *how* this impact comes about. The deepest effect of power everywhere is *inequality*, as power differentiates and selects, includes and excludes. An analysis of such effects is also an analysis of the conditions for power – of what it takes to organise power regimes in societies. The focus will be on how language is an ingredient of power processes resulting in, and sustained by, forms of inequality, and how discourse can be or become a justifiable object of analysis, crucial to an understanding of wider aspects of power relations. I situate my argument in a particular environment: that of the present world system, that of so-called 'globalisation'. A critical analysis of discourse, I shall argue, necessarily needs to provide insights in the dynamics of societies-in-the-world.

In order to substantiate this, three central notions require clarification. The first one is the concept of *discourse*, our object of analysis; the second is the *social nature* of discourse; and the third is the *object of critique* in a critical analysis of discourse.

## Discourse

In this book, discourse will be treated as a general mode of semiosis, i.e. meaningful symbolic behaviour. Discourse is language-in-action, and investigating it requires attention both to language and to action (Hanks 1996). There is a long tradition of treating discourse in linguistic terms, either as a complex of linguistic forms larger than the single sentence (a 'text') or as 'language-in-use', i.e. linguistic structures actually used by people – 'real language' (Brown and Yule 1983; and de Beaugrande and Dressler 1981). This conception of discourse, broadly speaking, underlies the development of contemporary linguistic pragmatics. It has informed numerous studies in which, little by little, old and well-established concepts and viewpoints from linguistics were traded for more dynamic, flexible, and activity-centred concepts and viewpoints (Verschueren 1995, 1998; Verschueren *et al.* 1995; Mey 1998). This development was fuelled, on the one hand, by developments within linguistic theory itself, which called for more activity-centred approaches to analysis, the recognition of language-in-use as a legitimate object of analysis, and the discovery of grammatical and structural features of language operating at levels higher than the single sentence – coherence and cohesion (Halliday and Hasan 1976; Tannen 1984). On the other hand, it was fuelled by intensified interdisciplinary contacts between linguists and scholars working in fields such as literary analysis, semiotics, philosophy, anthropology, and sociology, where conceptions of language were used that derived from Boas, Sapir, Bakhtin, Saussure, and Jakobson (Hymes 1983). It was the (re)discovery of a radically different parallel stream of conceptions of language and analytical tools of analysing them that led to more mature approaches to discourse (Jaworski and Coupland 1999 provide a useful overview; see also Hanks 1989, 1996).

I intend to follow this pragmatic stream, but I also intend to widen it by including conceptions of discourse that could be called fully 'non-linguistic', in the sense that they would not be acceptable to most linguists as legitimate objects of inquiry. Discourse to me comprises all forms of meaningful semiotic human activity seen in connection with social, cultural, and historical patterns and developments of use. Discourse is one of the possible names we can give to it, and I follow Michel Foucault in doing so. What is traditionally understood by language is but one manifestation of it; all kinds of semiotic 'flagging' performed by means of objects, attributes, or activities can and should also be included for they usually constitute the 'action' part of language-in-action. What counts is the way in which such semiotic instruments are actually deployed and how they start to become meaningful against the wider background mentioned above. Recent semiotic work has shown how rather than single objects and instruments, intricate connections between all kinds of semiotic modes and media make up contemporary semiosis (Kress and van Leeuwen 1996). A typical newspaper advertisement nowadays contains written text in various shapes and formats, ranging from headlines to small print, with differences in shape or colour that are meaningful. It also contains images, pictures, logos, symbols, and so on; it is of a particular size and it displays a particular architecture – the overall makeup of such signs is visual rather than textual, or at least, the textual (content) cannot be separated from the visual (form). It occurs in a space–time frame: advertisements that are printed only once are different from those that appear every day over a period of time; those that appear on the front page have a different status from those that occur on page 6 of the paper. None of the components of the advertisement is arbitrary, but none of them is meaningful in itself: the object we call 'discourse' here is the total layout of the advertisement, the total set of features – in short, it is *the advertisement*, not the text or the images. Contemporary discourse analysis has to account for such complex signs and needs to address them, first and foremost, as contextualised *activities* rather than as objects (Scollon 2001). So, though this book will offer primarily 'linguistic' materials, examples, and arguments, the wider set in which such items belong should not be lost out of sight. This is not a linguistic book.

## The social nature of discourse

A second item that requires clarification is the *social nature of discourse*.
Does discourse matter to people? Yes it does, and the clearest evidence
for it is the simple fact that we use it all the time. It has been stated
over and over again: the use of language and other meaningful symbols
is probably what sets us apart from other species, and what accounts
for the peculiar ways of living together we call society or community.
There is no such thing as a 'non-social' use of discourse, just as there
is no such thing as a 'non-cultural' or 'non-historical' use of it. But all
of this is truistic; the full story is obviously far more complex and will
require the remainder of this book to start being told. What concerns
us here is how discourse can become a site of meaningful social differences, of conflict and struggle, and how this results in all kinds of
social-structural effects. The fact is: it can, and does so all the time.
The reason for this is that we have to use discourse to render meaningful every aspect of our social, cultural, political environment: an
event becomes 'a problem' as soon as it is being recognised as such
by people, and discursive work is crucial to this; a mountain becomes
a 'beautiful' mountain as soon as someone singles it out, identifies
it and comments on it to someone else. In short, discourse is what
transforms our environment into a socially and culturally meaningful
one. But this kind of meaning-construction does not develop *in vacuo*,
it does so under rather strict conditions that are both linguistic (never
call a mountain a 'bird' or a 'car') and sociocultural (there are criteria for calling something 'beautiful' or 'problematic'), and this set of
conditions cannot be exploited by everyone in the same way. This is
where social differences in discourse structure and usage emerge as
a problem, something that invites investigation and precision. Again,
this will make this book less 'linguistic' than social-scientific.

## The object of critique

We need to specify what our object of critical investigation will be. My
suggestion is that a critical analysis of discourse in contemporary societies is an analysis of *voice*. Voice is a complex concept with a considerable history of use in the works of, for example, Voloshinov (1973);
Bakhtin (1981 1986); Ducrot (1996); and Hymes (1996) (see Thibault
1989; Roulet 1996), and with widely different definitions and modes
of application. The way in which I shall use it in this book can be summarised as follows. Voice stands for the way in which people manage
to make themselves understood or fail to do so. In doing so, they have
to draw upon and deploy discursive means which they have at their

disposal, and they have to use them in contexts that are specified as to conditions of use. Consequently, if these conditions are not met, people 'don't make sense' – they fail to make themselves understood – and the actual reasons for this are manifold. They will be the topic of the best part of this book. My point of departure is: in contemporary societies, issues of voice become ever more pressing, they become more and more of a problem to more and more people. Voice is the issue that defines linguistic inequality (hence, many other forms of inequality) in contemporary societies. An analysis of voice is an analysis of power effects – (not) being understood in terms of the set of sociocultural rules and norms specified – as well as of conditions for power – what it takes to make oneself understood. This will be my object of investigation; and needless to say this object is only partially linguistic in nature.

I am not saying anything new here; in fact, I align myself with a long and very respectable tradition in the study of language in society – we shall turn to this tradition below. I see my own contribution to this field as synthetic, as an attempt to bring together a number of insights and approaches that are dispersed over time, place, and subdisciplinary audiences. Bringing them together, however, may result in something new and perhaps more useful or more applicable. It is my firm belief that a wide variety of social-scientific disciplines could benefit from structured, disciplined attention to language and discourse (and, to be sure, I am not alone in this). But it is up to us, scholars of language, to do our jobs and to provide sound, tested, and practical tools for analysis to others (just as we may expect similar efforts from scholars in other disciplines). What follows is a modest attempt at providing such a tool.

## 1.2 THE CRITICAL POOL

Before moving on, I need to mark the space in which I shall situate myself. It is a space of ideas and scholarship that I find useful and relevant for this project: the critical pool from which I shall draw material and inspiration.

In recent years, Critical Discourse Analysis has become a household name in the social sciences, and the term – abbreviated as CDA – has come to identify a 'school' of scholarship led by people such as Norman Fairclough, Ruth Wodak, Teun van Dijk, Paul Chilton, and others. Largely grounded in a European tradition of scholarship, CDA has become a popular and firmly established programmatic approach to language in society with some institutional muscle. CDA was groundbreaking in establishing the legitimacy of a linguistically oriented discourse analysis firmly anchored in social reality and with a deep interest in actual problems and forms of inequality in societies. It also broke ground in its proclaimed attempt at integrating social theory in the analysis of discourse (see especially Fairclough 1992a; Chouliaraki and Fairclough 1999). And it produced a discourse about itself which was perceived by many as liberating, because it was upfront about its own, explicitly left-wing, political commitment. Consequently, many would now view CDA as synonymous with the critical study of language and discourse at large.[1]

Obviously, this is a mistake. CDA has done much to revitalise socially committed analysis of language after a long period in which the study of language was, and apparently had to be, a purely academic endeavour in the sense that problem-orientedness, let alone political agendas, were taboo if one were a linguist. And CDA has certainly done much to re-open the issue of how studies of language can, and should, be studies of society. Chapter 2 will expand on this. But CDA is one out of many attempts towards the development of critical approaches to language, culture, and society. In fact, it needs to be set against the background of a whole stream of such attempts throughout the twentieth century.

A comprehensive survey of such traditions would require a book of its own; it would also be burdened by terminological and ideological issues over what constitutes 'critical' and what does not. But to the extent that 'critical analysis' stands for performing analyses that would expose and critique existing wrongs in one's society – analyses that should be 'brought home' – there are quite a few candidates for that status. I would like to single two out because of their immediate relevance to the purpose of this book: American linguistic anthropology; and mainstream sociolinguistics. I am selecting these two not to create a contrast with CDA and even less as a suggestion of 'more and better' than CDA, but because it offers us two things. First, they will show us that CDA is part of a wider landscape of critical approaches to language and society, and will thus make our view of the contribution of CDA sharper and clearer. Second, they will offer us a number of theoretical principles of respectable age which we can use in the remainder of the book.

## American linguistic anthropology

It is a commonplace to begin the story of American linguistic anthropology with Franz Boas, and, in fact, the move by Boas from the margin to the centre of American anthropology in the late nineteenth and early twentieth centuries marked the beginning of scientific anthropology as we now know it (Darnell 1998, 2001; Stocking, 1974; Hymes 1983). Central to the Boasian anthropological paradigm was cultural relativism, as we know. Boas and his students set out to investigate the 'Native point of view'; culture as seen, lived, and experienced by its members, and they underpinned this endeavour with epistemological and methodological arguments that deserve reiterating, even if they should by now be common knowledge.[2] Two arguments in particular deserve our attention here.

First, Boas and his students saw the discovery (or, better, the (re)construction) of the 'Native point of view' as something that would provide, explicitly and implicitly, a critique of their own society. There was among the Boasians a widespread dissatisfaction with the way in which contemporary American society worked and lived. Providing descriptions and interpretations of alternative points of view articulated by Native American groups was sensed to contribute to the necessary revision of American mainstream culture. The superiority of this American culture was called into question by means of examples from cultural practices by groups whose culture was, in the climate of the time, defined as far inferior. Thus Edward Sapir (1924) would oppose the 'spurious' American culture witnessed in the 'efficient' but meaningless and unfulfilling routine practices of a phone operator to the 'genuine' culture of Native fishermen from the north-west coast, characterised by complex, meaningful, and culturally as well as individually satisfying practices. To Sapir (in a way remarkably applicable to present-day concerns), the uniformising tendencies of social values such as efficiency were devastating to 'genuine' culture (Darnell 2001: 119).

Second, the Boasians would emphatically abstain from passing value judgements on the cultural practices they observed, claiming that groups were fully operational, effective systems and that differences between groups were merely differences in 'standpoint' (Darnell 2001: 111ff.). Such differences represented different ways in which societies came to terms with their lives in a particular environment. This sense of completeness and efficacy, famously articulated in Boas' introduction to the *Handbook of American Indian Languages* (Boas 1911), extended to all aspects of a culture, from its religion to its linguistic system. Research into this internally coherent and homogeneous system involved a standpoint in its own right: anthropological research was biased by the position of the observer, and the Native point of view had to be distinguished from the anthropologist's point of view.

Thus, thinking about other cultures and languages could no longer rely on presumed 'standards' or universal needs for all cultures, and '[a]nthropology offered its fellow social sciences a view from outside standpoints that otherwise were likely to persist without awareness of ethnocentrism' (Darnell 2001: 113).

What this amounted to was, in effect, a problemisation of difference *as inequality*. Ethnocentrism, as a standpoint deeply ingrained in scholarship and everyday thinking, was a denial of equivalence of standpoints that were functionally equivalent when observed in their particular environments. Anthropology emerged as a critically reflexive tool capable of exposing the dynamics of disqualification of alternative solutions to similar problems. Anthropology was as much about us as it was about Native American groups: the so-called Sapir–Whorf hypothesis, which claimed that groups saw, dissected, and acted upon reality very much in terms of the categories provided by their native languages, was not only about the Hopi but also about mainstream Americans, equally held in captivity by their own categories and ways of acting upon them.

What this amounted to, as well, was the foregrounding of *contextual* studies of cultural forms – what we would now call an *ecology* of cultural forms. An understanding of culture and language requires setting culture and language firmly in the whole of the system in which a group operates, and explaining culture and language not by reference to a universal standard but by reference to the particular environment in which this culture and language occurs. The principle of relativity entails contextualisation, a focus on concrete, actual ways of functioning of cultural forms.

Despite the gradual move from a holistic agenda towards more specialised forms of anthropology, there is a direct line in the American tradition of scholars emphasising these critical concerns, from Franz Boas, Edward Sapir, Ruth Benedict, Benjamin Lee Whorf, and Paul Radin over post-Second World War scholars such as Dell Hymes (e.g. Hymes 1996, 1969) and John Gumperz (e.g. Gumperz 1982) and later to anthropologists such as James Clifford (e.g. 1988), Johannes Fabian (e.g. Fabian 1983, 1986), Charles Briggs (e.g. Briggs 1996 1997; Bauman and Briggs 2003), James Collins (e.g. 1998), William Hanks (e.g. 1996), and many others. In the field of linguistic anthropology, this tradition has witnessed a growing concern for inequality and ideology in language, reflexivity in research, and the capacity of linguistic-anthropological research to address questions of immediate relevance to disenfranchised or vulnerable groups in society (see the collections by Brenneis and Macaulay 1986 and Duranti 2001; let it be noted that both John Gumperz and Dell Hymes actively contributed to this trend). Crucially important work has been done on the status of linguistic varieties, language variation, and language shift (Gal 1979; Hill and Hill 1980; Kulick 1992; Woolard 1989), on authority in language (see Bauman and Briggs 2003; the collections by Schieffelin, Woolard, and Kroskrity 1998; Kroskrity 2000; Gal and Woolard 2001; compare Milroy and Milroy 1985 and Cameron 1995), on narrative, literacy and schooling (Heath 1983; Collins and Blot 2003), on identity, discourse, and hegemony (Jaffe 1999), on discourse practices as constitutive of social identities (e.g. Conley and O'Barr 1990; Jacquemet 1996; Hall and Bucholtz 1995) and so on – concerns that sound familiar to those acquainted with CDA and indeed echo the programmatic concerns of CDA (e.g. Gumperz 1982; Woolard 1985; Irvine 1989; Gal 1989; Bauman and Briggs 1990). By anyone's standards, this tradition is critical, and I shall come back to it in various places in the next chapters.

There has not been much interaction between scholars from CDA and American linguistic anthropology, despite the fact that their programmes may very well be compatible and their agendas partially overlapping (Blommaert *et al.* 2001). Both traditions have nourished themselves on similar social-theoretical complexes (notably those developed by Foucault, Bourdieu, Bakhtin, and Voloshinov), as well as on similar technical-analytic paradigms such as conversation analysis or interactional sociolinguistics (compare e.g. Fairclough 1989 and Heller 1994). Yet, a few 'crossover' exceptions notwithstanding (e g Ron Scollon 1998, 2001), the general picture is one of two (or more) separate worlds – and a lot of untapped sources of mutual inspiration.[3] There is far more critical work available than that which goes under the label of 'critical'.

## Sociolinguistics

Sociolinguistics has produced a remarkable body of such critical work and, in fact, one could argue that sociolinguistics arose out of a concern with differential distribution patterns of language varieties and forms of language use in societies – with difference and inequality in other words. There have been, and still are, various branches of sociolinguistics. One pole would be formed by a branch that has close affinities with the linguistic-anthropological tradition mentioned above (e.g. Gumperz and Hymes 1972; Bauman and Sherzer 1974; Hymes 1974a; Gumperz 1982) and focuses on interactional patterns in small communities and/or particular types of social encounters. The other pole would be a quantitative paradigm of variation studies, focused on the discovery of correlations between linguistic varieties and social variables such as race, class, or gender (e.g. Labov 1972; Sankoff 1980, 1988; Dittmar 1996). In between, there are branches that are strongly oriented towards sociology (Fishman 1972; Bernstein 1971) and branches that are very much linguistics-oriented (Halliday 1978), as well as several creative mixtures of various approaches (e.g. Eckert 2000). Closely related to sociolinguistics as a theoretical and descriptive paradigm are more applied branches such as, for example, studies of language planning (Fishman 1974) and bilingualism (Romaine, 1989; Hoffman 1991; Heller 1995) (see Meshtrie 2001 for a survey).

What ties these very diverse approaches together is a shared concern with the *nature and distribution of linguistic resources in societies*. And just like in the case of American anthropology, we can distil from sociolinguistics some general insights without which any critical endeavour in the field of language would be futile.

First, as for *the nature of linguistic resources*, sociolinguistics has demonstrated that 'languages' as commonly understood (i.e. things that have names such as 'English', 'French', 'Hindi', 'Zulu') are sociolinguistically not the most relevant objects. These 'languages' are, in actual fact, complex and layered collections of *language varieties*, and the study of language in society should not be, for instance, a study of *English* in society, but a study of all the different varieties that, when packed together, go under the label of 'English'. These varieties can be categorised on the basis of a set of parameters, including at least: (a) varieties identified on the basis of the modes or channels of communication: spoken versus written, direct versus indirect (mediated) communication, etc.; (b) geographically identified varieties – 'dialects', regional accents; (c) socially identified varieties often called 'sociolects' – class varieties, professional jargons, peer-group talk, age-, gender-, or ethnically marked varieties, etc.; (d) situationally or domain-identified varieties, i.e. varieties used on particular occasions or in particular social domains, such as peer-group talk, dinner table conversations, doctor–patient interactions, classroom interactions etc.; (e) styles, genres, formats of communication – formal versus informal varieties, storytelling, jokes, casual chat, public speech, media discourse, etc.

It is clear that every chunk of real language will carry *all* these features at the same time. As already said, there is no such thing as 'non-social' language: language manifests itself in society always and simultaneously in the shape of a package containing all of the diacritics mentioned above. Any utterance produced by people will be, for instance, an instance of oral speech, spoken with a particular accent, gendered and reflective of age and social position, tied to a particular situation or domain, and produced in a certain stylistically or generically identifiable format. And the point is: all of these diacritics are not only linguistic diacritics but also *social* ones. They reflect speakers' identities, expectations as to what speakers intend to accomplish in a particular act of communication, elements of the wider social structure in which speakers are caught, and so on.

It is one of sociolinguistics' great accomplishments to have replaced a uniform and homogeneous notion of 'language' – 'English', 'French' etc. – by a fragmented one, and to have explained why this fragmentation is necessary. The central argument is about the nature of meaning. The Saussurean and Chomskyan traditions in linguistics focused on the fact that sentences produced by widely different people – men and women, all ages, all professions, all regions of a particular linguistic area – could still be understood by all of these widely different people. Consequently, it was argued, underlying this enormous variability was a 'stable' core of pure meaning, a 'deep structure' which made sure that sentences had similar meaning regardless of how they were produced, by whom, in what context, and so on. To quote Silverstein's description of this assumption (1977: 140): '[s]urface structures are "the same" at the underlying level when they achieve "the same" referential effect in all of these instantiations'.

The problem, however, is that referential or denotational, 'pure' meaning is only one part of the effects of language use. Apart from referential meaning, acts of communication produce *indexical* meaning: social meaning, interpretive leads between what is said and the social occasion in which it is being produced. Thus the word 'sir' not only *refers* to a male individual, but it *indexes* a particular social status and the role relationships of deference and politeness entailed by this status, and thus shapes *indexical* contrasts between 'sir' and other *referentially* cognate terms (for general discussions, see Hanks 1990, 2000; Mertz and Yovel 2000; Sidnell 1998; Scollon and Scollon 2003: chapter 2; Duranti 1997: 17–20; a fine case analysis is Spitulnik 1996). Through indexicality, every utterance tells something about the person who utters it – man, woman, young, old, educated, from a particular region, or belonging to a particular group, etc. – and about the kind of person we encounter – we make character judgements all the time, and labels such as 'arrogant', 'serious', 'funny', 'self-conscious', or 'businesslike' are based almost exclusively on how people communicate with us. Every utterance also tells us something about the utterance itself. Is it serious or banter? Is this an anecdote, a joke, an order, a request? Is the speaker sure/sincere/confident of what s/he says? What kind of relationship between the speaker and the hearer is articulated in this utterance – is this a friendly or a hostile utterance? And every utterance tells us something about the social context in which it is being produced: is this a formal or an informal occasion? Are things such as social class, gender, ethnicity, or professional status played out in the utterance? Are social roles reinforced or put up for negotiation? Are social rules being followed or broken? And so on. Indexical meaning is what anchors language usage firmly into social and cultural patterns.

The fact is that people give off and pick up all of this information while engaging in communication, and that the diacritics mentioned above are the signals triggering such interpretations. Consequently, a sociolinguistic notion of meaning is one that embraces all of these 'meaning effects' and looks for the way in which 'pure' meaning comes alongside 'social meaning'. This is a far richer concept of meaning, a *communicative* or *semiotic* one that is fundamental to any discourse-analytic enterprise. It is not an unproblematic notion of meaning, however, for it displays the tendency to move the analysis away from the linguistic aspects of communication to its contextual aspects. As we shall see in chapter 3, this invites complex forms of analysis and exposes the limits of linguistic technique. But, at the same time, it is the point where discourse analysis becomes necessarily an interdisciplinary field of scholarship.

The second main concern of sociolinguistics is *the distribution of linguistic resources in society*. William Labov's path-breaking studies on sociolinguistic variation in New York (Labov 1966, 1972) demonstrated that seemingly unimportant features of speech such as the pronunciation or absence of pronunciation of the [r] sound in words such as 'fourth (floor)' systematically differed according to the social background of speakers. The tiny features thus became indexes of large patterns of social stratification in society. Two things were clear: first, not everyone in New York City spoke the same 'English'; and second, *it mattered*, it provided all sorts of clues about the social background of people, it pointed towards their identity and towards the organisation of social structure in general.

Basil Bernstein almost simultaneously developed a thesis identifying two different 'codes' in education, understood as structured patterns of language use (Bernstein 1971): an 'elaborate' code, and a 'restricted' code. The former was said to convey primarily abstract, 'decontextualised' propositional meanings, while the latter articulated more relational, involved forms of meaning. The precise nature and dynamics of this difference is highly debatable (and was, in fact, hotly debated), but Bernstein's main point was that the distribution of codes corresponded to social class differences, and that this had real effects on education performance. Children from privileged backgrounds would typically control the 'elaborate' codes, while children from less privileged social backgrounds would control the 'restricted' codes, and the education system would systematically tend to attribute higher value to the elaborate codes. Success in education, Bernstein argued, was dependent on the particular set of linguistic resources to which pupils had access, and this pattern of access was unequal and tended to privilege the privileged. This aspect of Bernstein's thesis remains valid; Pierre Bourdieu's work on economies of symbolic forms and systems of reproduction in society expanded the same theme and arrived at broadly similar conclusions (Bourdieu 1982, 1984, 1991; Bourdieu and Passeron 1977).

The principle we need to distil from this is that 'it is a fallacy to equate the resources of a language with the resources of (all) users' (Hymes 1996: 213). Connecting to what we said earlier, 'language' needs to be seen as a collection of varieties, and the distribution of such varieties is a matter of analysis in and of itself, for no two human beings, even if they speak the same 'language', have the same complex of varieties. Their *repertoire* is different; they will each control a different complex of linguistic resources which will reflect their social being and which will determine what they can actually do with and in language. The repertoires allow people to deploy certain linguistic resources more or less appropriately in certain contexts. To quote Hymes (1996: 33; see also Hymes 1974b and Gumperz 1972):

> A repertoire comprises a set of ways of speaking. Ways of speaking, in turn, comprise *speech styles*, on the one hand, and *contexts of discourse*, on the other, together with *relations of appropriateness* obtaining between styles and contexts.

And this is where inequality enters the picture: not everyone will have the same means of communication and, consequently, not everyone will be able to perform the same *functions* of communication. People are restricted as to what they can do with and in language, depending on the range and composition of their repertoires. In that sense, apart from what people do to language, there is a lot that language does to people.

## 1.3 FIVE PRINCIPLES

In trying to sketch my own intellectual space I have deliberately gone back in history, all the way to the classics of our branches of scholarship. The reason is that concepts, methods, and viewpoints come with a history of use and interpretation, and this history matters: 'we must think historically while we think theoretically' (Darnell 2001: 1). The history of concepts sometimes provides us with new opportunities for employing them, stretching them, connecting them to other concepts and methods – opportunities often seemingly impossible when one accepts a synchronic hegemony over the interpretation or 'allowable use' of a concept. We can, and should, sometimes take fresh looks at old and dust-covered concepts and approaches, for they often underlie a contingent history of further development often partially realising the original agenda of the approach.

Let me now try to summarise what has been said so far. In developing a critical science of language, we should at least take stock of what is around. One can be eclectic (and this book will surely be an exercise in eclecticism) but, even so, a number of basic theoretical principles will have to be used in order to provide sufficient coherence in the argument. The building-blocks for my attempt are rooted in the critical pool provided by linguistic anthropology and sociolinguistics, and they define in my view the intellectual history of these traditions to such an extent that they should not require much empirical substantiation anymore. I can safely use them as fundamental points of departure. They can be defined as follows.

1. In analysing language-in-society, the focus should be on *what language use means to its users*. We can, and must, start from the observation that language matters to people, that people make investments in language, and that this is a crucial part of what they believe language does for them and what they do with language. Consequently, we need to find out *how* language matters to people. The 'insiders' view' of Boasian anthropology is a crucial tool in understanding the dynamics of language in society, and it is the cornerstone of ethnography.

2. We have to be aware that *language operates differently in different environments*, and that, in order to understand how language works, we need to contextualise it properly, to establish the relations between language usage and the particular purposes for which and conditions under which it operates. Every 'model' offered as a blanket explanation should be critically checked against the specifics of the case we are investigating. This goes for language, its structure, and functions, but also for society, power, history, and so on. This, like the first principle, is a principle derived from Boasian anthropology and, like the first principle, it is fundamental to ethnography.

3. Our unit of analysis is not an abstract 'language' but *the actual and densely contextualised forms in which language occurs in society*. We need to focus on varieties in language, for such variation is at the core of what makes language and meaning social. Whenever the term 'language' is used in this book, it will be used in this sociolinguistic sense. One uneasy by-effect of this sociolinguistic use is that we shall often be at pains to find a name for the particular forms of occurrence of language. The comfort offered by words such as 'English', 'Zulu', or 'Japanese' is something we shall have to miss. We shall have to address rather complex, equivocal, messy forms of language.

4. Language users have *repertoires* containing different sets of varieties, and these repertoires are the material with which they engage in communication; they will determine what people can do with language. People, consequently, are not entirely 'free' when they communicate, they are constrained by the range and structure of their repertoires, and *the distribution of elements of the repertoires in any society is unequal*. Such inequality of repertoires requires us to use a sociolinguistic backdrop for discourse analysis because what people actually produce as discourse will be conditioned by their sociolinguistic background. The notion of 'voice' must be situated at the intersection of sociolinguistics and discourse analysis.

To these four principles I shall add a fifth, one that derives from very different sources but which I believe is indispensable for an analysis of discourse in the modern world.

5. We have to conceive of communication events as ultimately influenced by *the structure of the world system*. In an era of globalisation, the threshold of contextualisation in discourse analysis or sociolinguistics can no longer be a single society (or even less a single event) but needs to include the relationships between different societies and the effect of these relationships on repertoires of language users and their potential to construct voice. The world system is characterised by structural inequality, and this also counts for linguistic resources (Wallerstein 1983, 2001; Blommaert 2003a). This fifth principle is a perspective on the four other principles: it adds a new dimension to the various foci of attention derived from the critical pool.

The well-informed reader will notice very few similarities between the principles formulated here and those used in mainstream CDA (compare, for example, Fairclough 1992a; Wodak 1995; Chouliaraki and Fairclough 1999). I shall use a very different angle to approach the same topics and issues, in an attempt to widen the range and punch of a critical analysis of discourse. The ethnographic bias in my approach is clear; yet, equally clear should be the larger scale, sociolinguistic, and world-systemic framing of ethnography. If a conventionally worded label should have to be stuck on the collection of principles, it could be an 'ethnographic-sociolinguistic analysis of discourse'. A less conventionally worded label, however, could be just 'ethnography': it is a common misunderstanding that ethnography is an analysis of 'small things', local, one-time occurrences only. It is, and always has been, an approach in which the analysis of small phenomena, is set against analysis of big phenomena, and in which both levels can only be understood in terms of one another (Hymes 1972, 1974a are recommendable; see also Burawoy 2001). The reduction of ethnography to a study of local, small-scale events is an illustration of what I mentioned above: the contingent histories that only realise part of the original agenda.[4]

To this set of principles I shall add a very eclectic theoretical, methodological, and technical-analytic apparatus, drawing mainly on sources from (different branches of) linguistics, anthropology, cultural studies, sociology, and history. This eclectic apparatus should enable me to look at language in society in ways that allow *simultaneously* to focus on linguistic form and on social environment, and to avoid a discontinuity between various levels of explanation. The target of such explanations will be *language-in-society* – a notion which I have already used several times in this chapter, and which I take to be an object in its own right referring to the intrinsic interrelatedness of language and society, in fact, of the irrelevance of their separation as different terms. The shape in which language-in-society comes to us is discourse, as outlined above. In arriving at such explanations I shall undoubtedly violate all kinds of disciplinary orthodoxies and I shall allow myself the freedom to use whatever can be useful for solving my analytical problems. I beg the guardians of disciplinary orthodoxies for forgiveness – it is my deep belief that science has everything to gain from consciously exploring the margins of its own system.

## 1.4 CENTRAL PROBLEMS: THE ORGANISATION OF THE BOOK

I shall have to address several general problems in this book and a discussion of these problems will provide the main architecture of the book. Over the course of several chapters, I shall appear to move gradually away from 'micro', i.e. textually focused, issues to 'macro' issues, such as inequality and history, and then return to the textual level. Every chapter can, to some extent, be seen as a relatively self-contained discussion of a particular theoretical and methodological domain. But connections and overlaps between the different chapters are obvious, and particular data sets – material typical of modern globalisation processes – will no doubt provide coherence across the different chapters. Imagine these materials are a Coca-Cola can on a table; if you walk around the table while watching the can, stop every now and then and describe the can as you see it. The description will each time be partly similar and partly different. Yet it is the same can, and no single description of it is comprehensive, since every single description is biased by the particular position from which we described it. My aim here is not to provide a comprehensive analysis, but to identify and illustrate various positions from which we can analyse social facts of globalisation.

The discussion of the various problems will, to some extent, be put in perspective by the way in which they are being treated (or fail to be treated) in contemporary CDA. Consequently, I shall devote chapter 2 of this book to a detailed discussion of the origins and contemporary preoccupations of CDA. At the same time, the aim of the discussions is not so much a critique of CDA as an independent attempt to come to terms with the central problems in our field of inquiry. Consequently, whereas CDA will receive pride of place in this book, it is definitely not the key in which the various discussions of the central problems should be read.

Perhaps the most crucial problem in our field is that which defines our tradition: the relationship between linguistic forms – 'text' – and *context*. This will be the topic of chapter 3, but will, at the same time, be the pervasive motif throughout the book. The reason for this is obvious and has already been emphasised repeatedly here: whenever the analysis of language aspires to be critical, it needs to engage the world in which language operates. Analysis in CDA as elsewhere almost invariably focuses on text–context relations as the site of power or inequality, on connections between linguistic occurrences and social relations or structure – and it very often claims that communication actually constructs context or social structure. Such claims need to be examined, and an examination of them will open up a whole set of different problems, which will be the topics of the chapters that follow. My examination of the problem of context will lead us through the ways in which context is being used in CDA and in another prominent branch of discourse analysis, Conversation Analysis. I shall argue that both approaches use problematic notions of context, and I shall suggest a number of 'forgotten' contexts, crucial for our understanding of language in society in the current world system characterised by processes often qualified as globalisation. Globalisation and the world system will be recurrent themes throughout the book, for they constitute the highest-level (determining) context for language usage in any society, at any time.

On the basis of these insights into necessary and forgotten contexts I shall engage with another central problem in chapter 4: *inequality*. As noted above, inequality is the central target of a critical analysis of discourse and we need adequate understandings both of the nature of inequality in contemporary societies and of its actual dynamics and modes of occurrence. The discussion of context will have offered us some guidelines as to where and how we can situate inequality. In this chapter, I shall offer a general framework for looking at inequality from a discursive and semiotic point of view, a theory of voice so to speak. I shall also suggest different analytical approaches that may shed light on important sites of linguistic inequality such as, for example, narrative and literacy, again using features of globalisation and the present world system as my backdrop. This discussion will lead us into the problem of *choice and determination*, which will be the topic of chapter 5. Much work in discourse analysis, and, in fact, in the social sciences in general, starts from the assumption that social life is governed by choices made by individuals. There is a long intellectual and ideological history to this, of course, but the argument developed in this chapter will produce a view in which choice is an object of inequality and consequently, a matter that needs to be investigated, not posited. We shall go back to theories of 'determination' – the absence of choice or the way in which choice becomes a structured, regimented field governed by constraints. In the context of globalisation, such constraints on choice must be taken seriously if for nothing else because all available evidence suggests that people are not becoming more free by becoming more mobile.

The connection with the next chapter is again a rather organic one. In chapter 6 we shall address the problem of *historicity and process*. When we talk about determination, we talk about the historical conditions under which particular forms of communication become meaningful or not. Consequently, we need to conceive of all instances of language usage as intrinsically historical, that is, as bearers of both immediate conditions of use and perduring conditions of use. Part of these conditions are invisible, they do not show themselves in the line-by-line deployment of meaningful practices in human interactions. But they are there, and they condition what can be done by whom, how, and when. In this chapter, we shall engage with the age-old issue of how to connect 'micro'-instances of social practice with 'macro'-levels of social structure and history. This will feed into the discussion in chapter 7 on *ideology*, a much-used topic of investigation in CDA. Ideology, I shall argue, constitutes the historical layer in everyday conduct, while at the same time it provides immediate, on-the-spot social meaningfulness to such conduct. Analytically, this offers us some opportunity, for it accounts both for the sharedness of language and for power and inequality in its use. At the same time, ideology is the gate through which we are forced to leave the strictly linguistic analysis and move into an interdisciplinary field.

The last problem in this series is that of *identity*, which is the topic of chapter 8. Building on the material gathered in the previous chapters, and again keeping the framework of globalisation and the world system in mind, I shall offer some suggestions as to how we might conceive of identities as layered and multiple, and then expand the discussion to issues of ethnolinguistic identities and of spatially organised identities. Thus, we get a context which is both material and cultural, again extending the field of analysis into an interdisciplinary arena in which discourse becomes inescapably social, cultural, historical, and political. A summary of this view will be offered in the concluding chapter 9. I shall try to provide a synthesis of the various theoretical comments dispersed over the different chapters, not, as I said above, to offer a definitive analysis, but rather to describe the walk around the can on the table as a single journey.

It is my ambition to produce a set of suggestions for how to organise an interdisciplinary field of Critical Discourse Analysis, one that offers input to, and receives input from, a wide variety of social-scientific approaches. This is why I organise the book around problems that I know are shared by scholars in other branches of the social sciences. While writing the book, I keep such people in mind. Often they are individuals I know personally, and it is my desire to make this book an accessible and stimulating text for them. As for the conditions under which such an interdisciplinary programme can develop: the main condition is a shared concern for genuine problems in the world and a desire to contribute to their solution. This I know is there.

The main thrust of this book is theoretical, in the sense that I hope to offer reflections on theory and methodology organised in one coherent perspective on my topic of inquiry. This, to me, causes some discomfort, for I see myself primarily as an empirical analyst passionately engaged in solving analytical problems. This empirical bias will be manifest in the sometimes long and substantial illustrations I shall offer in almost every chapter. These illustrations will elaborate theoretical points made in the chapters, but they will also show a wide variety of analytical approaches and a range of different data, from spoken narratives over bits of handwritten materials to public and internet discourses. I hope in this way to provide evidence of the wealth of analytical practices that (can) go under the label of discourse analysis. When taken literally – as the 'analysis of discourse' – discourse analysis can allow itself to treat any chunk of any type of semiosis in very eclectic ways. The last thing this book intends to do is to offer a codex of discourse analysis; what it hopes to accomplish is to offer a range of problem-solving tactics.

Many of the examples I shall give are African. Partly this is due to my own scholarly background and academic place as an Africanist, but partly it is done to demonstrate how different certain forms of analysis become as soon as we face materials from societies (very) different from our own. For reasons spelled out above, in the age of globalisation, it is worth having a look at materials from the peripheries of the world system. It compels us to abandon so many unspoken assumptions of sharedness – they do not work anymore – and to look more closely and more deeply into our own interpretive repertoires and practices – they have to be revised in order to produce the kinds of understandings we are after. The argument in this book, I hope, will benefit from it.

## SUGGESTIONS FOR FURTHER READING

Books that treat discourse in the sense outlined here are Hanks (1996) and Scollon (2001). Both start from the necessarily contextualised nature of discourse and focus on discursive/semiotic practices rather than discursive artefacts. The volume edited by Jaworski and Coupland (1999) provides essential classic papers and articulates an interestingly wide scope. I find Hymes (1996) the most forceful statement on critique in the field of language studies, and Gumperz (1982) is equally indispensable reading. The history of American anthropology is admirably documented in Darnell (2001) and in a whole series of studies compiled by George Stocking (e.g. 1974). Sociolinguistics is too wide a field to be covered appropriately by one single book, though the *Concise Encyclopaedia of Sociolinguistics* (Meshtrie 2001) does a remarkable job. People interested in World Systems Analysis should read Wallerstein (1983), an excellent introduction.

# 2 Critical Discourse Analysis

## 2.1 INTRODUCTION

Critical Discourse Analysis (CDA) is undoubtedly the most visible 'school' in the field under scrutiny in this book. At the same time, it would be a mistake to see CDA as the *only* possible critical perspective on language in society. This chapter offers a discussion of the emergence and development of the 'school' of CDA, as well as a survey of its main areas of inquiry: political discourse, media, advertisement, ideology, racism, institutional discourse. I shall also offer a brief survey of the main theoretical and methodological assumptions in CDA, and a glimpse of its major theoretical and empirical shortcomings. These shortcomings will be addressed more fully in some of the chapters that follow.

An obvious warning to be extended at this point is that whenever we make reference to a 'school', we find ourselves on thin ice. People identified as 'members' of this school may not always perceive themselves as such, and many observers would emphasise the incoherence and internal contradictions in what I am presenting here as a more or less unified and streamlined movement. What we are facing when we talk about CDA is a group of leading scholars, each with a background of their own, who agree on certain principles of analysis, who agree to address similar issues, and who have developed some institutional tools for doing so. The leading scholars are usually seen as the quartet of Norman Fairclough, Ruth Wodak, Teun van Dijk, and Paul Chilton, with people such as Margaret Wetherell, Michael Billig, Christina Schäffner, Theo van Leeuwen, Gunther Kress, and others also quite closely associated. Rather than a group, we are dealing with a network of scholars with very different backgrounds and predilections. Norman Fairclough has a background in systemic-functional linguistics; Teun van Dijk in text linguistics and cognitive linguistics; Ruth Wodak in interactional studies; Paul Chilton in linguistics, semiotics, and communication studies. Their work and approaches develop fast.

21

So there is always a danger of objectification when we discuss a dynamic and developing movement such as CDA as a 'school', locked in time and space.

A second danger is that of isolation and intellectual-historical closure. As we shall see below, CDA historically emerged out of Hallidayan linguistics, but this, in turn, needs to be contextualised. Post-Second World War developments in the study of language included the Chomskyan revolution and a number of strong reactions against this revolution, often focusing on the exclusion of social and cultural dimensions from the Chomskyan programme of linguistics. The emergence of sociolinguistics in the early 1960s was a reaction in this sense, as well as the result of an interdisciplinary dynamics in the social sciences of the day. Hallidayan linguistics, in turn, was inspired by a desire to incorporate social semiotic functions into a theory of grammar (Butler 1985, 1995; Kress 1976). In literary analysis, the (re)discovery of Bakhtin's work turned scholars towards voice and social layering in communication. Social theorists such as Foucault, Bourdieu, and Habermas addressed language from a broadly social-semiotic viewpoint and offered new foundations for sociolinguistic and discourse-analytic work. Applied linguistics took hold and focused, among other things, on education as a field where social and linguistic forces met and often clashed. CDA was founded on the premises that linguistic analysis could provide a valuable additional perspective for existing approaches to social critique, and it attempted to combine (at least a number of) these post-Second World War developments. In that sense, the intellectual history of CDA is far wider and deeper than often suggested.[1]

With these *caveats* in mind, we can now turn to a discussion of the main features, advantages, and disadvantages of CDA.


## 2.2 CDA: ORIGINS AND PROGRAMME

### The origins of CDA

In historical surveys such as Wodak (1995), reference is made to the 'critical linguists' of the University of East Anglia, who, in the 1970s, turned to issues such as the use of language in social institutions and relations between language, power, and ideology, and who proclaimed a critical (in the sense of left-wing) and emancipatory agenda for linguistic analysis. The works of Kress and Hodge (1979) and Fowler, Hodge, Kress and Trew (1979) are seminal in this respect (see Fowler

1996; Birch 1998 for surveys). The work of these critical linguists was based on the systemic-functional and social-semiotic linguistics of Michael Halliday, whose linguistic methodology is still hailed as crucial to CDA practices (notably by Fairclough) because it offers clear and rigorous linguistic categories for analysing the relations between discourse and social meaning (see, for example, Chouliaraki and Fairclough 1999; Hodge and Kress 1988). Martin (2000; Martin and Wodak 2003) reviews the usefulness of systemic-functional linguistics for CDA, suggesting that CDA should apply systemic-functional notions more systematically and consistently, and Fairclough (1992b) reviews CDA work in light of the amount of (Hallidayan) textual analysis they offer.

Apart from Hallidayan linguistics, Slembrouck (2001) identifies another profound influence on CDA: British Cultural Studies. The Birmingham Centre for Contemporary Culture Studies (headed by Stuart Hall) had a noticeable influence because it systematically addressed social, cultural, and political problems related to transformations in late capitalist society in Britain: neo-liberalism, the New Right headed by Thatcher, racism, diaspora, the end of the welfare state, and so on. Some of these topics have become foci of intense activity within CDA. The Birmingham school of Cultural Studies also introduced French post-structuralist theory in its analyses, and together with the delineation of a domain of analysis, this pool of theories was adopted by, for example, Fairclough.

While the influence of Halliday's social-semiotic and grammatical work is acknowledged and verifiable, references to other discourse-analytic precursors (such as Michel Pêcheux, e.g. 1982) often seem more *post hoc* and motivated rather by a desire to establish a coherent authoritative lineage than by a genuine historical network of influences. One can note, in general, that the universe of mobilised sources invoked to support the CDA programme is rather selective. As mentioned in the previous chapter, references to work done in American linguistics and linguistic anthropology are very rare (with the exception of some research on literacy, see below), as are references to some precursors who have had a manifest influence on many other 'critical' approaches to language (e.g. Rossi-Landi 1983; Mey 1985; Bolinger 1980) and to critical work in other strands of language studies (e.g. in sociolinguistics, notably the works of Gumperz and Hymes). The potential relevance of these largely overlooked traditions will be discussed below.

Fairclough's *Language and power* (1989) is commonly considered to be the landmark publication for the 'start' of CDA. In this book, Fairclough engaged in an explicitly politicised analysis of 'powerful' discourses in Britain (Thatcherite political rhetoric and 'new economy' advertisements) and offered the synthesis of linguistic method, objects of analysis, and political commitment that have become the trademark of CDA. Despite the presence of such landmark publications and of some acknowledged leading figures, the boundaries of the CDA movement are rather fuzzy. Scholars identifying with the label CDA seem to be united by the common domains and topics of investigation, an explicit commitment to social action and to the political left wing, a common aim of integrating linguistic analysis and social theory, and – though in more diffuse ways – by a preference for empirical analysis within a set of paradigms, including Hallidayan systemic-functional linguistics and social semiotics, conversation analysis, cognitive-linguistic approaches to metaphor, argumentation theory, text linguistics, and discursive social psychology.

There is a tendency within CDA to identify itself as a 'school', and a number of writings are programmatically oriented towards the formation of a community of scholars sharing the same perspective and, to some extent, also sharing similar methodologies and theoretical frameworks. Fairclough (1992a: chapter 1) surveys a variety of discourse-analytic approaches, qualified as 'non-critical', in contrast with his own critical approach. Such boundary-shaping practices are worded in such resolute terms that they result in suggestive divisions within discourse analysis – 'critical' versus 'non-critical' – that are hard to sustain in reality (a comment also made by Widdowson 1998; cf. Verschueren 1999).

CDA has enjoyed a remarkable success with students and scholars. It has major fora of publication in the journals *Discourse and Society* (edited by Teun van Dijk), *Critical Discourse Studies* (edited by Norman Fairclough), and *Journal of Language and Politics* (edited by Ruth Wodak and Paul Chilton) as well as in several book series. A European interuniversity exchange programme devoted to CDA is now in place; various websites and electronic discussion groups offer contacts and information on CDA projects and viewpoints. This active pursuit of institutionalisation has an effect on what follows. To some extent, the 'school' characteristics of CDA create an impression of closure and exclusiveness with respect to critique as a mode, ingredient, and product of discourse analysis.

## The CDA programme

In general, power, and especially institutionally reproduced power, is central to CDA. The purpose of CDA is to analyse 'opaque as well as transparent structural relationships of dominance, discrimination, power and control as manifested in language' (Wodak 1995: 204). More specifically,

> [CDA] studies real, and often extended, instances of social interaction
> which take (partially) linguistic form. The critical approach is
> distinctive in its view of (a) the relationship between language and
> society, and (b) the relationship between analysis and the practices
> analysed. (Wodak 1997: 173)

CDA states that discourse is socially constitutive as well as socially conditioned. Furthermore, discourse is an instrument of power, of increasing importance in contemporary societies. The way this instrument of power works is often hard to understand, and CDA aims to make it more visible and transparent:

> It is an important characteristic of the economic, social and cultural
> changes of late modernity that they exist as discourses as well as
> processes that are taking place outside discourse, and that the
> processes that are taking place outside discourse are substantively
> shaped by these discourses. (Chouliaraki and Fairclough 1999: 4)

In that sense, CDA sees its own contribution as ever more crucial to an understanding of contemporary social reality, because of the growing importance in the social order of discursive work and of discourse in relation to other practices.

CDA focuses its critique on the intersection of language/discourse/ speech and social structure. It is in uncovering ways in which social structure relates to discourse patterns (in the form of power relations, ideological effects, and so forth), and in treating these relations as problematic, that researchers in CDA situate the critical dimension of their work. It is not enough to uncover the social dimensions of language use. These dimensions are the object of moral and political evaluation, and analysing them should have effects in society: empowering the powerless, giving voices to the voiceless, exposing power abuse, and mobilising people to remedy social wrongs. As part of critical social science, CDA

> may subvert the practices it analyses, by showing proto-theories to be
> miscognitions, and producing scientific theories which may be taken
> up within (and enter struggles within) the practices. (Chouliaraki
> and Fairclough 1999: 33)

But apart from (passive) subversion, CDA also advocates (active) intervention in the social practices it critically investigates. Toolan (1997) even opts for a prescriptive stance: CDA should make proposals for change and suggest corrections to particular discourses. CDA thus openly professes strong commitments to change, empowerment, and practice-orientedness.

CDA's preference for work at the intersection of language and social structure is manifest in the choice of topics and domains of analysis.[2] CDA-practitioners tend to work on applied topics and social domains such as:

- *Political discourse*: i.e. the discourse of politicians (e.g. Wodak 1989; Chilton, Mey, and Ilyin 1998; Fairclough 1989, 1992a, 2000; Chilton and Schäffner 2002; Schäffner and Wenden 1995).
- *Ideology*: discourse is seen as a means through which (and in which) ideologies are being reproduced. Ideology itself is a topic of considerable importance in CDA. Kress and Hodge already set the tone with their *Language as ideology* in 1979. More recently, van Dijk has produced a socio-cognitive theory of ideology (van Dijk 1998).
- Particular attention within this study of ideology is given to *racism*. Van Dijk stands out as a prolific author (1987, 1991, 1993b), but the topic has also been covered by many others (see Wodak and Reisigl 1999 for a survey; see also the special issue on racism of *Discourse and Society*, 11/1, 2000). Related to the issue of racism is a recent interest in the discourse on immigration (e.g. Martín-Rojo and van Dijk 1997; van Leeuwen and Wodak 1999).
- *The discourse of economics* (e.g. Fairclough 1995: chapters 5 and 6). In relation to this, the issue of globalisation has been formulated as an important preoccupation for CDA (Slembrouck 1993; Chouliaraki and Fairclough 1999: 94).
- *Advertisements* and *promotional culture* (e.g. Fairclough 1989, 1995; Slembrouck 1993; Thornborrow 1998).
- *Media language* (e.g. Fairclough 1995; van Dijk 1991; Kress 1994; Martín-Rojo 1995; Bell and Garrett 1998).
- *Gender*: especially the representation of women in the media (e.g. Talbot 1992; Caldas-Coulthard 1993, 1996; Wodak 1997; Clark and Zyngier 1998; Walsh 1998; Thornborrow 1998).
- *Institutional discourse*: the role of language in institutional practices such as doctor–patient communication (e.g. Wodak 1997), social work (e.g. Wodak 1996; Hall, Sarangi, and Slembrouck 1997), bureaucracy (Sarangi and Slembrouck 1996).
- *Education* (e.g. Kress 1996; Chouliaraki 1998). Education is seen as a major area for the reproduction of social relations, including representation and identity-formation, but also for possibilities of change. Fairclough and associates have developed a Critical

Language Awareness approach that advocates the stimulation of critical awareness with students of pedagogical discourses and didactic means (cf. Clark *et al.* 1990, 1991; Fairclough 1992; Ivanic 1998).

There is also some interest among CDA-practitioners in *literacy*, though literacy cannot be seen as a 'pure' CDA-field of study. CDA studies of literacy have linked up with those anthropological and sociolinguistic analyses that view literacy as 'situated practices' (the so-called New Literacy Studies, e.g. Heath 1983; Street 1995; Collins and Blot 2003), for example, in the context of local communities (Barton and Hamilton 1998) or education (Baynham 1995; New London Group 1996; Cope and Kalantzis 2000).

## 2.3 CDA AND SOCIAL THEORY

CDA conceives discourse as a social phenomenon and seeks, consequently, to improve the social-theoretical foundations for practising discourse analysis as well as for situating discourse in society. Fundamental to CDA is that it claims to take its starting-point in social theory. Two directions can be distinguished. First, CDA displays a lively interest in *theories of power and ideology*. Most common in this respect are the use of Michel Foucault's (e.g. 1975, 1982) formulations of 'orders of discourse' and 'power/knowledge'; Antonio Gramsci's (1971) notion of 'hegemony'; Louis Althusser's (1971) concepts of 'ideological state apparatuses' and 'interpellation'. Works in which connections between discourse and power processes are being spelled out are also widely cited, such as Ernesto Laclau and Chantal Mouffe (1985) and John Thompson (1990). In Fairclough (1992a) these theories and concepts are given a linguistic translation and projected onto discourse and communicative patterns in an attempt to account for the relation between linguistic practice and social structure, and to provide linguistically grounded explanations for changes in these relations.

The second direction that can be distinguished is an attempt to *overcome structuralist determinism*. Inspiration here is usually found in Anthony Giddens' (1984) theory of structuration, where a dynamic model of the relation between structure and agency is proposed. Giddens serves as the theoretical background to CDA's claim that actual language products stand in a dialectic relation to social structure, i.e. that linguistic-communicative events can be formative of larger social processes and structures. Obviously, when the relation between linguistic-communicative (or other semiotic) action and social processes is discussed, frequent reference is also made to the work of Pierre Bourdieu (in particular his *Language and Symbolic Power*, 1991) and Jürgen Habermas (*Theory of Communicative Action*, 1984, 1987). Bourdieu's work is also influential in studies on educational practices.

The use of these theories can be partly traced back to the influence of Cultural Studies on CDA. CDA still holds pace with Cultural Studies in that it continually but critically engages with new research trends in, for example, postmodern, feminist, postcolonial, and globalisation studies (see especially Chouliaraki and Fairclough 1999, a 'rethinking' of CDA that intends to ground it more firmly in social theory). It is nonetheless important to realise that, despite the input from a variety of social-scientific angles, CDA should primarily be positioned in a linguistic milieu, and its successes are measured primarily with the yardstick of linguistics and linguistically oriented pragmatics and discourse analysis (see Fairclough 1992b).

## 2.4 THEORY AND METHODOLOGY: NORMAN FAIRCLOUGH

On the methodological level, CDA presents a diverse picture. For historical reasons mentioned earlier, the use of systemic-functional linguistics is prominent, but categories and concepts have also been borrowed from more mainstream pragmatics, discourse analysis and text linguistics, stylistics, social semiotics, social cognition, rhetoric, and Conversation Analysis. Ruth Wodak and her associates have developed a discourse-historical method intent on tracing the (intertextual) history of phrases and arguments (see, for example, Wodak 1995; van Leeuwen and Wodak 1999; Martin and Wodak 2003). The method starts with original documents (e.g. Wehrmacht documents on war activities in the Balkans), augmenting these with ethnographic research about the past (e.g. interviews with war veterans), and proceeding to wide-ranging data collection and analysis of contemporary news reporting, political discourse, lay beliefs, and discourses.

Whereas some practitioners of CDA explicitly encourage and welcome the diversity of methodology (Chouliaraki and Fairclough 1999: 17), others strive for a systematic and focused framework, based, for instance, on concepts of genre and field and on the socio-semantic representation of social actors (van Leeuwen 1993, 1996). And whilst scholars such as Kress and van Leeuwen (1996; Kress 1996; also Slembrouck 1995) emphasise the importance of incorporating visual images in concepts of discourse and move towards broader multimodal conceptions of semiosis, the general bias in CDA is towards *linguistically defined text-concepts*, and linguistic-discursive textual structures are attributed a crucial function in the social production of inequality, power, ideology, authority, or manipulation (van Dijk 1995).

The most elaborate and ambitious attempt towards theorising the CDA programme is undoubtedly Fairclough's *Discourse and Social Change* (1992a), later followed by Chouliaraki and Fairclough's *Discourse in Late Modernity* (1999). Fairclough (1992a) constructs a social theory of discourse for which he claims affinity with Foucault, and he provides a methodological blueprint for Critical Discourse Analysis in practice.[3] Fairclough sketches a three-dimensional framework for conceiving of, and analysing, discourse. The first dimension is *discourse-as-text*, i.e. the linguistic features and organisation of concrete instances of discourse. Choices and patterns in vocabulary (e.g. wording, metaphor), grammar (e.g. transitivity, modality), cohesion (e.g. conjunction, schemata), and text structure (e.g. episode marking, turn-taking system) should be systematically analysed. The use of passive verb forms or nominalisations in news reporting, for instance, can have the effect of obscuring the agent of political processes.

The second dimension is *discourse-as-discursive-practice*, i.e. discourse as something which is produced, circulated, distributed, consumed in society. Fairclough sees these processes largely in terms of the circulation of concrete linguistic objects (specific texts or text-types that are produced, circulated, consumed, and so forth). Remarkably little time is spent, however, on the issue of (socio)linguistic resources – the language varieties, for instance – and other 'macro' conditions on the production and distribution of discourse such as literacy. Approaching discourse as discursive practice means that after the analysis of vocabulary, grammar, cohesion, and text structure, attention should be given to speech acts, coherence, and intertextuality – three aspects that link a text to its wider social context. Fairclough distinguishes between 'manifest intertextuality' (i.e. overtly drawing upon other texts) and 'constitutive intertextuality' or 'interdiscursivity' (i.e. texts are made up of heterogeneous elements: generic conventions, discourse types, register, style). An important aspect of 'manifest intertextuality' would be discourse representation: how quoted utterances are selected, changed, contextualised (see Baynham and Slembrouck 1999 for recent contributions to the study of discourse representation).

The third dimension is *discourse-as-social-practice*, i.e. the ideological effects and hegemonic processes in which discourse is seen to operate. Hegemony concerns power that is achieved through constructing alliances and integrating classes and groups through consent, so that 'the articulation and rearticulation of orders of discourse [i.e. the Foucaultian regimentation and disciplining of and through discourse] is correspondingly one stake in hegemonic struggle' (Fairclough 1992a: 93). It is from this third dimension that Fairclough constructs his approach to social change: hegemonies change and this process can be witnessed in discursive change when the latter is viewed from the angle of intertextuality. The way in which discourse is being represented, re-spoken, or re-written sheds light on the emergence of new orders of discourse, struggles over normativity, attempts at control, and resistance against regimes of power.

To these three dimensions, Fairclough adds a threefold distinction in research methodology. CDA, according to Fairclough, should make a progression from *description*, to *interpretation*, to *explanation* (1989: 26). In the phase of *description*, CDA focuses on the textual-linguistic features of the material. Description is an activity similar to that of participants in the sense that the researcher adopts the participants' categories in his description, but the researcher (in contrast to the participant) needs to make his/her interpretive framework explicit. *Interpretation* is concerned with the way in which participants arrive at some kind of understanding of discourse on the basis of their cognitive, social, and ideological resources. The interpretive phase already requires a degree of distancing between the researcher and the participant, but the interpretation is still done by means of categories and criteria provided by participants. Often, Fairclough argues, such interpretations display ideological framings – participants 'reproduce' elements of social ideologies through everyday interactionally organised interpretive procedures. That is why CDA requires a third analytical phase: *explanation*. In the explanatory phase, the researcher draws on social theory in order to reveal the ideological underpinnings of lay interpretive procedures. Social theory creates the distance necessary to move from 'non-critical' to 'critical' discourse analysis. It provides the larger picture in which individual instances of communication can be placed and from which they derive meaning. It also provides grounds for transcending the limitations of lay consciousness about the ideological dimensions of discourse.

Fairclough is explicit with regard to his ambitions: the model of discourse he develops is framed in a theory of ideological processes in society, for discourse is seen in terms of processes of hegemony and changes in hegemony. Fairclough successfully identifies large-scale hegemonic processes such as democratisation, commodification, technologisation on the basis of heteroglossic constructions of text genres and styles. Modern political discourse, for instance, operates through a blending of formal and informal, authoritative and congenial, declarative and conversational styles and genres, and this heteroglossic blend makes it harder to criticise political discourse or to voice dissent (Fairclough and Mauranen 1997). He also identifies the multiple ways in which individuals pass through such institutionalised discursive regimes, constructing selves, social categories, and social realities. At the same time, the general direction is one in which social theory is used to provide a metadiscourse on linguistic phenomena, and in which the target is a refined and more powerful technique of text analysis. I shall come back to this below.

## 2.5 THE PROS AND CONS OF CDA

CDA has received its share of flak from other researchers. I shall distinguish between two kinds of criticisms that can be, and are, levelled against CDA: first, specific critical comments on method, methodology, and analytical approaches; and second, more general criticisms relating to the potential offered by CDA for becoming a critical study of language. In the first part, I shall let others speak; the second part, however, reflects my own points of view on CDA in light of the aims of this book.

### Theoretical and methodological defects

Critical reactions to CDA centre on issues of interpretation and context. More specifically, critics focus on what they see as bias in the analyses and argue against particular research tactics and methodological shortcomings.

In a series of review articles, Henry Widdowson (1995, 1996, 1998) accused CDA of blurring important distinctions between concepts, disciplines, and methodologies (for reactions, see Fairclough 1996; Chouliaraki and Fairclough 1999: 67). First, Widdowson notes the vagueness of many concepts as well as the vagueness of the analytical models in CDA. This general fuzziness is not helped by what Widdowson perceives as the merely rhetorical use of popular or fashionable concepts from social theory. Secondly, Widdowson argues that in its actual analyses, and despite its theoretical claims to the contrary, CDA provides biased interpretations of discourse under the guise of critical analysis. CDA does not analyse how a text can be read in many ways, or under what social circumstances it is produced and consumed. The predominance of biased interpretation begs questions about representativeness, selectivity, partiality, prejudice, and voice (can analysts speak for the average consumer of texts?) (cf. also Stubbs 1997).

The most fundamental problem to Widdowson is that CDA collapses semantics and pragmatics: pragmatics is, in fact, reduced to semantics. Texts are found to have a certain ideological meaning that is forced upon the reader; the function of a text can be deduced from its meaning, and whatever is ill-intended will also be ill-received (see also Pennycook 1994). In a similar vein, Verschueren (2001) notes how CDA often demonstrates the obvious, and does so from a particular analyst's point of view which does not differ in substance from that of the participants. One ideological frame is replaced by another – a capitalist framing of meanings is 'criticised' by substituting it with an anti-capitalist one. This framing can be gauged from metapragmatic qualifications used in Fairclough's analyses and attached to particular moves in talk: terms such as 'standard' versus 'alternative' interactional practices invoke an evaluative stance, a distinction between (objectively) 'good' and 'bad', which is often not supported by the evidence in the data. Thus, particular images of society and social structure are projected onto stretches of discourse, and CDA becomes 'symptomatic' analysis, an analysis aimed at proving the (predefined) presence of a disease on the basis of an analysis of its symptoms.

Another critical debate on CDA was initiated by Emanuel Schegloff (1997) and continued in *Discourse and Society* (Wetherell 1998; Billig and Schegloff 1999; see also Chouliaraki and Fairclough 1999: 7). In Schegloff's opinion, there is a tendency to assume the a priori relevance of aspects of context in CDA work: analysts project their own political biases and prejudices onto their data, and analyse them accordingly. Stable patterns of power relations are sketched, often based on little more than social and political common sense, and then projected onto (and into) discourse. Schegloff's own solutions are those of his own orthodox version of Conversation Analysis: relevant context should be restricted to those elements to which participants in a conversation actively and consequentially orient (a position equally vulnerable to critique, see, for example, Duranti 1997: chapter 8, and the next chapter of this book).

Finally, a substantial problem for CDA was raised by Slembrouck (2001). Slembrouck questions the 'explanatory' level in CDA. The analyst, according to Fairclough, moves from ideology-dominated interpretation to 'absolute' or 'pure' explanation by drawing on social theory.[4] So, whereas Fairclough himself would emphatically stress the fact that no discourse or social activity is ideology-free, a level of analysis is proposed on which no such forces operate. Social theory provides an Archimedean point of view on social reality, and a different kind of knowledge can be constructed by taking this point of view. The argument is, of course, reminiscent of Althusser's insistence on 'pure' knowledge as generated (only) by taking recourse to Marxist theory (see Thompson 1978 for a devastating critique). And, according to Slembrouck, apart from a danger of 'social-theoretical reductionism' as dangerous as the linguistic reductionism against which CDA militated (Slembrouck 2001: 42), it creates several important problems for CDA. One clear problem is that of reflexivity. The process of analysis is necessarily dialogical, and so is the interpretation eventually effected by the analyst. But through the withdrawal to a higher level and exclusive realm of theory-as-truth, the dialogic process is closed and the analyst becomes the ultimate arbiter of meanings. This, then, produces a problem of voice, and CDA risks producing a view from above rather than from below (a point also made by Rampton 2001). The participant is pushed out of the analysis, so to speak, as soon as the explanatory phase of the analysis is entered. To the extent that CDA aspires to the empowerment of subjects through critical analysis, this is a serious problem, the more since, as many critics claim, CDA tends to project specific (and often analytically unmotivated) interpretations onto discourse data. Less than careful CDA may thus result, not in an empowered subject speaking with a more audible voice, but in a stentorian analyst's voice.

## The potential and limitations of CDA

In view of the agenda set in this book, CDA offers considerable potential, but some big problems remain. To start with the potential, it is hard to disagree with the basic paradigmatic principles underlying CDA. Discourse analysis should result in a heightened awareness of hidden power dimensions and its effects: a *critical language awareness*, a sensitivity for discourse as subject to power and inequality. Language to CDA is never a neutral object, it is subject to assessment, value-attribution, and evaluation, and consequently it is subject to deep cleavages, forms of in- and exclusion and of oppression. The emancipatory potential of work on such inequalities in and through language deserves emphasis – a preoccupation CDA shares with several other scholars and schools (see, for example, Hymes 1996: chapter 10). Second, one can also easily join the call for increased *dialogue between linguistic analysis and other social-scientific endeavours* – again something forcefully advocated by several other scholars. This book will explore precisely this space of interdisciplinarity, accepting that our very object of study – socially situated and contextualised discourse – is intrinsically interdisciplinary. Third, CDA rightly focuses on *institutional environments* as key sites of research into the connections between language, power, and social processes. It thus reacts against the 'mundanisation' of discourse, the reduction of everything to 'normal' discourse, often observed in many other branches of language studies (Briggs 1997b) and manages to identify 'special' discourses, discourses that belong to centres of power and the reproduction of social structure. A certain naïveté with respect to such manifest forms of institutional power, characterising some other discourse analytic branches, is thus avoided. And finally, at a more technical level, I also share some of Fairclough's views on the layering of discourse and on its multiple but simultaneously occurring functions, and both themes will be central to much of the argument in the remainder of this book. It is precisely in breaking down the old idea that a chunk of discourse has only *one* function and *one* meaning that the critical dimension may prove to reside.

So CDA offers us considerable potential, and it can show substantial accomplishments in its field of research. But I see three main problems.

1. The first one is *the linguistic bias in CDA*. It has been noted several times above: CDA (and Fairclough in particular) puts a very high price on linguistic-textual analysis, more specifically on systemic-functional linguistics. This emphasis is articulated repeatedly, and it is used as an important criterion for the assessment of work aspiring to be 'critical' (e.g. Fairclough 1992b). We shall see further on how Fairclough uses the absence of attention to linguistic detail as a point of critique against Foucault. There is also closure when the issue is debated; witness how Chouliaraki and Fairclough (1999: 139) causally relate CDA's presumedly unique critical capacity to Hallidayan systemic-functional linguistics:

> It is no accident that critical linguistics and social semiotics arose
> out of SFL [systemic-functional linguistics] or that other work in CDA
> has drawn upon it – SFL theorises language in a way which
> harmonises far more with the perspective of critical social science
> than other theories of language.

Thus, there seems to be only one theory of language that offers good opportunities for converting research into critical research. This, of course, begs the question as to where other undisputably critical scholars got their theoretical ammunition, as well as why by no means all work within SFL can qualify as critical – why, in fact, a lot of it is aridly grammatical. Perhaps what is meant here by 'theory of language' is *linguistic* theory of language. And perhaps in that world, Hallidayan linguistics would offer more than, for instance, Chomsky's Government and Binding or Minimalist programme. But it should be clear from what has been said in the previous chapter that linguists have no monopoly over theories of language, and that as soon as one accepts that, far more candidates for critical potential offer themselves than SFL.

But the problem is more substantial. The emphasis on linguistic analysis implies an emphasis on *available* discourse, discourse which is there. There is no way in which we can linguistically investigate discourses that are absent, even if such analyses would tell us an enormous amount about the conditions under which discourses are being produced (by whom? when? for what purpose?) and circulated (who has access to them and who doesn't?). It also means that discourse analysis starts from the moment that there is linguistically encoded discourse, bypassing the ways in which society operates on language users and influences what they can accomplish in language long before they open their mouths, so to speak. It means that analysis stops as soon as the discourse has been produced – while, as we shall see in the chapters to follow, a lot happens to language users long after they have shut their mouths. In short, the linguistic bias restricts the space of analysis to textually organised and (explicitly) linguistically encoded discourse, not to where it comes from and goes to. The argument I shall develop in the remainder of this book will strongly centre on such conditions for, and constraints on, discourse. My point will be that if we wish to understand contemporary forms of inequality in and through language, we should look inside language *as well as outside it*, in society, and both aspects of analysis are not separable.

2. A second big problem I see in CDA is its *closure to particular kinds of societies*. Fairclough, Wodak, van Dijk, and Chilton have produced magnificent analyses of discourse in their countries of origin and other countries from what we could call the core of the world system. Fairclough (1989) is probably the best description of a Foucaultian order of discourse in Great Britain during the Thatcher era. It is by all standards a very good book, which makes many accurate observations about discourse in society. The problem is that it makes such observations only about that one, very particular, society. There is no reason to restrict critical analyses of discourse to highly integrated, Late Modern, and post-industrial, densely semiotised First-World societies. There is even less reason to assume that descriptions of such societies can usefully serve as a model for understanding discourse in the world today, for

the world is far bigger than Europe and the USA, and substantial differences occur between different societies in this world.

The self-evident way in which features of the First World are projected onto the globe and attributed to all mankind is perplexing. We can already see this projection from the social-theoretical 'canon' invoked in CDA: Foucault, Bourdieu, Giddens, Habermas, Žižek, Baudrillard: all of them scholars who have described developments and features of First-World societies, and have done so with considerable brilliance. We shall look in vain, however, for social theory that addresses north–south relations or the structure and development of the world system. I have never encountered a reference to, for example, Immanuel Wallerstein, Giovanni Arrighi, Samir Amin, or André Gunder Frank in CDA work, despite the fact that these scholars have produced bodies of theory of indisputable importance for understanding societies outside the First World as well as transnational and global processes of interconnectedness, inequality, and value-differentiation. And when reading statements such as:

> [social changes in Late Modernity] have also profoundly affected our sense of self and place, causing considerable confusion and what has been widely referred to as a loss of meaning. (Chouliaraki and Fairclough 1999: 3)

I keep wondering how I could find evidence for such processes in a village in Central Tanzania. I also wonder how I shall find such typical discourse products of supposedly universal Late Modernity as highly intricate multimedia messages and websites or complex advertisement campaigns and TV commercials in that same village where more than 75 per cent of the inhabitants are illiterate and where no single house has electricity. The fact is: the particular shapes taken by Late Modernity, including its semiotic shapes, are very different across the world; the shape it has taken in First-World societies is very particular, and a majority of the people in the world live in conditions closer to those of villagers in Central Tanzania than to those of inhabitants of Manchester or Vienna. Any general approach to discourse, especially one that aspires to address discourse in an era of globalisation (like Chouliaraki and Fairclough 1999), needs to take that into account and needs to account for that. In scholarship that aspires to a critique of the present system, it would be very unwise to assume universal validity for our ways of life. CDA takes far too much sharedness for granted when it comes to discourse in contemporary societies across the world. One could say, by way of summary, that CDA overlooks sociolinguistics.

3. The third problem I see with CDA is its *closure to a particular time-frame*. There is hardly any analysis of historical developments in CDA, and no inspiration is drawn from authors who could contribute to such a historicising move (but see Martin and Wodak 2003). The absence of historical CDA is not so much the issue here – it is the absence of a *sense of history* in CDA. This has to do, obviously, with the two previously mentioned problems: a focus on the linguistic artefact, which almost invariably forces temporal closure on the analysis, restricting it to the here-and-now of communication; and a focus on contemporary developments in one's own society again forcing one's eyes to look for the present and to see very fast developments as 'historical' (e.g. the differences between the political rhetoric of Macmillan and Thatcher described by Fairclough and Mauranen 1997 and separated by three decades). The fact is that the historical horizon of CDA, much like its geographic one, is very restricted. And to the extent that CDA attempts to launch a critique of *systemic* features of contemporary societies and focuses on issues of power in doing so, a synchronic approach will not do. Neither will an expression of interest in historical backgrounds or intertextuality serve as a substitute for a genuine historical analysis of the ways in which power regimes come into place.

This too will be a key point in my argument: a critical analysis of discourse necessarily needs to transcend the present and address history in and through language. Power and inequality have long histories of becoming; so have the linguistic repertoires of people; so too have social structures and systems such as capitalism and its many transformations. We need to take history seriously, for part of the critical punch of what we do may ultimately lie in our capacity to show that what looks new is not new at all, but the outcome of a particular process which is systemic, not accidental. It may help us to avoid looking at symptoms and to expose causes – an ambition I share with Fairclough and all other CDA practitioners.

So the remainder of this book will offer suggestions to solve some of the problems mentioned here. In the next chapter, I shall continue the critique of existing approaches to discourse, focusing on deficient notions of context. At the same time, this is the point of departure for the work of construction I intend to do in this book. Starting from a critique of notions of context, I shall move on in later chapters to define several aspects and dimensions of discourse and suggest ways of studying it. Let it be clear that although my approach will differ substantially from what can be found in CDA literature, I have drawn a lot of inspiration from it. Our goals are the same; our instruments may differ somewhat.

## SUGGESTIONS FOR FURTHER READING

Fairclough (1992) and Chouliaraki and Fairclough (1999) are the most impressive theoretical statements on CDA. It is worthwhile, though, to confront it with some precursors, notably the (still very interesting) classics by Kress and Hodge (1979); Bolinger (1980); and Mey (1985). The recent collection edited by Martin and Wodak (2003) attempts to move CDA into the field of history. The special issues of *Critique of Anthropology* on 'Discourse and Critique', edited by Blommaert *et al.* (Vols. 21/1 and 21/2, 2001) contain a series of critical essays on CDA and related approaches.

# 3 Text and context

## 3.1 INTRODUCTION: CONTEXT IS/AS CRITIQUE

Critical trends in discourse analysis emphasise the connection between discourse and social structure. They locate the critical dimension of analysis in the interplay between discourse and society, and suggest ways in which features of social structure need to be treated as context in discourse analysis. For instance, in analysing doctor–patient interaction, the facts that one participant is a doctor and another is a patient, and that this interaction consequently develops in an institutional environment, are crucial elements in understanding the power balance in that interaction. There will be a particular power dynamic *because* one is a doctor and another is a patient, and *because* this turns the particular interaction into an instance of an institutionalised genre. Critical analysis is thus always and necessarily the analysis of situated, contextualised, language, and context itself becomes a crucial methodological and theoretical issue in the development of a critical study of language.

There is a vast and significant literature on context (see, for example, Auer and Di Luzio, 1992; Duranti and Goodwin 1992; Auer 1995), and the most general way of summarising it is to say that it addresses the way in which linguistic forms – 'text' – become part of, get integrated in, or become constitutive of larger activities in the social world (see also Scollon 2001). To some extent, this is self-evident: language is always produced by someone to someone else, at a particular time and place, with a purpose and so forth. But, given the history of linguistics as the study of an object defined as necessarily non-contextual and autonomous, attention to the context-sensitive dimensions of language was something that required substantial argument. We are beyond such arguments now, fortunately, and we can turn to a whole complex of approaches to text–context relations. We can now accept without having to go into detailed discussion that the way in which language fits into context is what creates meaning, what makes it (mis)understandable to others.

Context comes in various shapes and operates at various levels, from the infinitely small to the infinitely big. The infinitely small would be the fact that every sentence produced by people occurs in a unique environment of preceding and subsequent sentences, and consequently derives part of its meaning from these other sentences. The infinitely small can also pertain to one single sound becoming a very meaningful thing – 'yes' pronounced with a falling intonation is declarative and affirmative; spoken with a rising intonation it becomes a question or an expression of amazement or disbelief. The infinitely big would be the level of universals of human communication and of human societies – the fact that humanity is divided into women and men, young and old people, and so on. In between both extremes lies a world of different phenomena, operating at all levels of society and across societies, from the level of the individual all the way up to the level of the world system. Context is *potentially* everything and contextualisation is *potentially* infinite. But, remarkably, in actual practice it appears to be to some extent predictable. People seem to have rather clear (though not necessarily accurate) ideas about how they have to make language fit into activities and how they have to create meaning out of this blending.

I shall address some of the main challenges posed by context for a critical analysis of discourse, reviewing the ways in which context has been used so far in mainstream CDA and Conversation Analysis – two contenders for leadership in the critical analysis of discourse. After that, I shall survey a number of 'forgotten' contexts of discourse and illustrate their potential usefulness as critical tools. But before embarking on that discussion, I shall offer some general guidelines for addressing context as conceived here.

A warning is in place. My discussion will be very selective, focusing on issues that are directly relevant for the remainder of this book. I shall not address the linguistic and cognitive aspects of context and contextualisation, for instance, but that does not mean that I deny the contribution made by scholars in these fields.

## 3.2 CONTEXT: SOME GENERAL GUIDELINES

Interpretation and contextualisation

Perhaps the most basic principle we have to use is that we cannot do without context, that we absolutely need it in any kind of analysis. This sounds self-evident, but it is not, it has considerable implications. In order to clarify this, I need to start from John Gumperz's (1982, 1992) seminal concept of 'contextualisation'. Contextualisation 'comprises all activities by participants which make relevant, maintain, revise, cancel . . . any aspect of context which, in turn, is responsible for the interpretation of an utterance in its particular locus of occurrence' (Auer 1992: 4).

Gumperz developed the notion of contextualisation to account for the ways in which people 'make sense' in interactions and, taking on board both broad ethnographic concerns as well as narrower conversation-analytic ones, he observed that people pick up quite a few 'unsaid' meanings in such interaction. These are the indexical meanings mentioned in chapter 1: the connections between language form and social and cultural patterns. People detect these indexical meanings because speakers provide verbal and nonverbal, behavioural 'cues' that suggest a fit between utterances and contextual spaces in which they become meaningful:

> I argue that conversational interpretation is cued by empirically detectable signs, contextualization cues, and that the recognition of what these signs are, how they relate to grammatical signs, how they draw on socio-cultural knowledge and how they affect understanding, is essential for creating and sustaining conversational involvement and therefore to communication as such. (Gumperz 1992: 42)

The pivot of this process is the utterance itself: 'it is the linguistic form itself which serves to signal the shift in the interaction' (1992: 43). And the target of contextualisation consists of complexes of presupposable knowledge in which utterances are made coherent (contextualised):

> all understanding is framed understanding, . . . it ultimately rests on contingent inferences made with respect to presuppositions concerning the nature of the situation, what is to be accomplished and how it is to be accomplished. (1992: 43–44)

Such forms of framing are linguistic and cognitive, to be sure, but also eminently social and cultural. They have a perduring, conventional, normative character: 'we can speak of *systems of contextualization conventions* in terms of which individual cues are related.' (1992: 51, italics added). Relatively little work on interaction has focused on this *systemic dimension of contextualisation*, most analysts having concentrated their efforts on analyses of the contingent conversational deployment of contextualisation practices (but see Gumperz 2003; Eerdmans 2003; I should also note that systemic aspects of contextualisation are central in 'poetics' as conceived by Jakobson 1960). This conventional,

perduring dimension will be central in my treatment of contextualisation, here as well as in the next chapters.

Of course, contextualisation is not unproblematic, and all kinds of
things can go dramatically wrong. Gumperz and his associates devoted
enormous efforts to demonstrating the perils of contextualisation in
everyday interactions, especially in situations where power asymmetries prevailed and/or sociopolitically sensitive categories such as race,
gender, or ethnicity were involved (Gumperz 1986; Gumperz and Cook-
Gumperz, 1982; Jupp, Roberts, and Cook-Gumperz 1982; Gumperz and
Roberts 1991). 'Misplacing' utterances in contexts – intentionally or
not – results in misunderstandings, conflicts, or breakdowns of communication. Let me give an innocent (though embarrassing) autobio-
graphic example.

Some time ago, I went to a conference together with a young female
research associate of mine. We had just checked into our hotel and
upon entering my hotel room, I had discovered that it had a very nice
balcony overlooking part of the city. Half an hour later, we met in the
hotel lobby and went off to have dinner. As we walked out of the hotel,
I asked her 'do you have such a nice balcony too?' The term for 'balcony'
in our native language Dutch, *balkon*, is among other things a rude,
deeply sexist male term used to refer to female breasts – the rough
equivalent of what in American English is known as 'a rack'. While
asking this question, I had failed to spot a woman who was walking in
the opposite direction to us, wearing a deeply cut summer top exposing parts of her breasts. Unfortunately, my young female research associate had noticed this woman – she had picked up a contextualisation
cue – and the term 'balcony' suddenly acquired a very suggestive, sex-
ually offensive, meaning, which called for extensive explanation and
damage repair afterwards. My words had been placed in (or made to
'point to', to index) a context which had altered their meaning, triggering a shift from a descriptive, neutral meaning for 'balcony' to an
implicit, male sexist slang meaning. In this contextualisation process,
our identities had shifted as well from a friendly, professional, and
organisational-hierarchical sphere to a sexualized, masculine, power-
laden sphere. My female associate had been pictured as an object of
lust, and I had become an abusive male chauvinist. All of a sudden,
we found ourselves in a threatening, embarrassing, sexualised situation. Thus, meanings of words as well as the identities of those who
exchanged them, and indeed the whole situation, had been affected
by a mismatch between text and context.

The point to all of this is: what we often call 'interpretation' or
'understanding' (as in 'I *understand* what you are saying') is the result

of contextualisation processes in which text (utterances, statements, oral as well as written) are indexically 'made to fit' a particular (set of) context(s) by participants in the interaction. We understand something because that something makes sense in a particular context.

This obviously entails that what we understand here by 'meaning' is rather different from what many others understand by it – and this is where contextualisation becomes a fundamental theoretical instrument. As we have seen in the example above, the denotational, lexical meaning of 'balcony' shifted from 'building balcony [standard, neutral]' to 'bodily balcony [vernacular, sexist]' because of the way in which the utterance fitted a particular context. The existence of these lexical meanings *and* their attached indexicalities offered opportunities for (mis)contextualisation. So when looking into how my colleague and I ultimately construed this episode – in other words, how we understood its 'meaning' – not only lexical meanings were involved but also identity categorisations and the structure of the whole event.

Our first guideline is therefore: if we want to explain the way in which people make sense socially, in real environments, we need to understand the contexts in which such sense-making practices develop.

## Contextualisation is dialogical

The second principle is an elaboration of something that should already have become clear from the example given above. Context and contextualisation are dialogical phenomena. It is not the speaker alone who offers context to statements and generates context, but the other parties in the communication process do so as well. And often what counts or what is most consequential is the contextualisation performed by the one who receives and decodes the message – the *uptake*. In Gumperz's words, 'signs have meaning only by virtue of being taken to stand for an object *by some interpreter*' (Gumperz 2003: 113, italics added). In the example above, it was my colleague who spotted the possible contextual fit between my use of the term 'balcony' and the *décolleté* of the woman walking in our direction. My words received an unexpected uptake, taking them into directions of meaning and social effect I had (honestly) not intended. Note that there is an important temporal dimension here: the process of uptake is part of a temporal sequence in interaction, and uptake can only occur when utterances have been offered for uptake.

Most discourse analysts would subscribe to the dialogic nature of communication, and would very often refer to the classic formulations by, for example, Bakhtin (1981, 1986); Voloshinov (1973); or Kristeva

(1986, 1989) that meaning is always a meeting of (at least) two minds and consciousnesses, creating results that cannot be reduced to either one of them. People have contextualisation universes: complexes of linguistic, cognitive, social, cultural, institutional, etc. skills and knowledge which they use for contextualising statements, and interaction involves the meeting of such universes. Bakhtin captures this process under the term 'responsive understanding': meaning is 'contextual', i.e.

> integrated meaning that relates to value – to truth, beauty and so forth – and requires a *responsive* understanding, one that includes evaluation (Bakhtin 1986: 125, italics in original)

This responsive meaning is active and transformative, it is not just a 'reception' of meaning, but a process in which meaning is changed in the sequence of interaction and made dialogical, i.e. a product of two (or more) minds.

In spite of this consensus on the importance of the dialogic nature of meaning, there are three general problems which can be encountered over and over again in published work and which lead to a reduction of the scope of dialogicity. I shall mention them briefly here and they will be discussed and illustrated at greater length elsewhere in the book.

a *Dialogue does not presuppose co-operativity.* It is very often assumed in much discourse analysis that the dialogic nature of communication involves exchange of meanings between co-operative, willing, and bona fide partners, who offer large spaces for negotiating meanings (see, for example, Grice 1975 for a classic discussion). The term 'dialogue' connects to a folk category of human interaction which may be characterised by such features, and it therefore suggests this category – friendly, co-operative conversation and exchange of views (i.e. intentionalities) – as the archetype of 'dialogue'. This is, of course, unjustified: dialogue is the meeting of different contextualisation universes, and very often this meeting is a clash and a conflict rather than a friendly encounter (Sarangi and Slembrouck 1992). Co-operativity is a *variable* in dialogue, not a rule.

b *Dialogue does not presuppose sharedness.* Similarly, it is very often assumed that participants in communication share lots of common ground – language or language variety, referential and indexical meanings attributed to words, utterances or speech events, and so on. Again, this is a mistake: the meeting of contextualisation universes is not necessarily a meeting of *similar*

contextualisation universes. On the contrary, it may be more productive to take the non-sharedness of contextualisation universes
as our point of departure.

c *Dialogue does not presuppose symmetry in contextualising power.* The
assumption of negotiability of meaning, derived from Gricean
pragmatics, suggests symmetry in contextualising power, the fact
that all the participants in communication have equal access and
control over contextualisation universes. We should not forget,
however, that precisely this degree of access and control is a
feature of power and inequality, and that power and authority
in societies depend, among other things, on *exclusive* access to
particular contextual spaces (Briggs 1997a; see also Barthes 1957).
Lawyers, doctors, judges, politicians, academics, etc. can all be
characterised as professional and social-status groups by their
exclusive access to specific, powerful, contextualising spaces –
the law, medicine, intelligence reports, scientific canons – and
the fact is that non-members of these groups have no (or less)
access to such spaces. (Think also of gender, ethnicity, and class
as critical features in this respect.) Consequently, very often the
process of contextualisation is not negotiable but unilateral, with
somebody *imposing* a particular contextualisation on somebody
else's words.

Thus, I believe we need to be more careful in the ways in which we actu
ally use the dialogic principle in analysis. My suggestion is to exploit it
fully, turning it into a general awareness that what we call 'meaning'
in communication is something which is, on the one hand, produced
by a speaker/writer, but still has to be granted by someone else. This
can be done co-operatively and on the basis of sharedness and equality,
but it need not, it can also be done by force, unilaterally, as an act of
power and an expression of inequality. The concept of voice which we
introduced earlier is all about that: it is about the capacity to cause an
uptake close enough to one's desired contextualisation. What people
do with words – to paraphrase Austin (1962) – is to produce *conditions
for uptake*, conditions for voice, but as soon as these conditions are
produced, uptake is a fully social process, full of power and inequality.
Consequently, context is not something we can just 'add' to text – it *is*
text, it defines its meanings and conditions of use.

## Context is local as well as translocal

A third guideline is that we should not restrict the notion of context to what happens in specific communicative events. As we have
seen above, Gumperz already insisted on the systemic character of

contextualisation conventions. But there is another simple reason: a lot of what we perform in the way of meaning-attributing practices is the *post-hoc* recontextualisation of earlier bits of text that were produced, of course, in a different contextualisation process, at a different time, by different people, and for different purposes. This is clearest in the field of literacy: whenever we read a book, we recontextualise what we read and add or change meanings. The book is re-set in a new contextualising universe and becomes a new book – but we do drag along with us the baggage of the history of contextualisation/interpretation of the text. There is no reason to restrict this observation to literate text, for similar processes occur in all fields of communication, and several useful concepts have been developed to address these phenomena. Erving Goffman's concept of *frames* (Goffman 1974) comes closest to the concept of contextualisation used here. Goffman, like Gumperz, assumed that people construct interpretive universes in which utterances are set and offered for interpretation, and Goffman added to this the idea of multiple frames operating at the same time – different potential sets of interpretive universes, between which the interlocutors can choose or shift *footing*. In the space of one conversation, for instance, something that was a 'serious' utterance can be re-framed as a joke by a change in footing. We shall come back to this notion of frames at several places in the book.

Two other concepts deserve some more detailed comments. The first, and well-known, concept is that of *intertextuality*, a concept often ascribed to Bakhtin (and usefully developed by, for example, Kristeva 1986; Thibault 1989 and Fairclough 1992b; Slembrouck 2002 provides an overview). In its simplest form, intertextuality refers to the fact that whenever we speak we produce the words of others, we constantly cite and re-cite expressions, and recycle meanings that are already available. Thus every utterance has a history of (ab)use, interpretation, and evaluation, and this history sticks to the utterance. It accounts for the fact that the term 'balcony', in the example given above, suddenly acquired the offensive and sexist meaning it had in the particular context: this attribution of meaning is an effect of the tradition-of-use of terms such as 'balcony' by male groups in a particular society to derogatively describe female breasts. Intertextuality grounds discourse analysis firmly into histories of use – histories that are social, cultural, and political, and which allow the synchronic use of particular expressions to acquire powerful social, cultural, and political effects. It invites us to look beyond the boundaries of particular communicative events and see where the expressions used there actually come from, what their sources are, whom they speak for, and how they relate to traditions of use. To illustrate the latter: terms traditionally having extremely negative connotations such as 'nigger' and 'bitch' can acquire positive, even self-celebrating, meanings central to identity pride when used by individuals or groups negatively described by the terms, because of their peculiar inverted relationship with the (negative) tradition of use of the terms. Intertextuality accounts for a lot of what we understand by the 'normative' or the 'standard' in language use, and Gumperz (2003: 117) rightly emphasises the value of intertextuality in uncovering the indexical ties between signs and interpretations.

A second concept is *entextualisation* (Bauman and Briggs 1990; Silverstein and Urban 1996). It has considerably less currency than intertextuality, but adds important qualifications and turns intertextuality into an empirical research programme. Entextualisation refers to the process by means of which discourses are successively or simultaneously decontextualised and metadiscursively recontextualised, so that they become a new discourse associated to a new context and accompanied by a particular metadiscourse which provides a sort of 'preferred reading' for the discourse. This new discourse has become a 'text': discourse lifted out of its interactional setting and transmitted together with a new context (cf. Bauman and Briggs 1990: 73). Silverstein and Urban (1996: 1) specify:

> The text idea allows the analyst of culture to extract a portion of ongoing social action – discourse or some nondiscursive but nevertheless semiotic action – from its infinitely rich, exquisitely detailed context, and draw a boundary around it, inquiring into its structure and meaning. This textual fragment of culture can then be re-embedded by asking how it relates to its 'context', where context is understood as nonreadable surround or background (or if the context is regarded as readable, by asking how the text relates to its 'co-text').

Entextualisation is part of what Silverstein and Urban call the 'natural history of discourse'. 'Original' pieces of discourse – socially, culturally, and historically situated unique events – are lifted out of their original context and transmitted, by quoting or echoing them, by writing them down, by inserting them into another discourse, by using them as 'examples' (or as 'data' for scientific analysis). This decontextualisation and recontextualisation adds a new metadiscursive context to the text; instead of its original context-of-production, the text is accompanied by a metadiscursive complex suggesting all kinds of things *about* the text (most prominently, the suggestion that the discourse is indeed a *text*).

Entextualisation builds further on notions of the reflexive nature of language usage (for the latter, see Lucy 1993). Every utterance not only says something *in* itself (i.e. about the world, about an extralinguistic referent of some kind), but it also says something *about* itself, and hence, every 'pragmatics' (every way of handling language) goes hand in hand with a 'metapragmatics' (comments about, and references to, the way of handling language). At the same time and through this reflexive dimension, it amends overly linear or static views of context, adding an important praxis-related dimension to text–context relationships. In the eyes of Bauman and Briggs (1990: 69):

> Contextualization involves an active process of negotiation in which participants reflexively examine the discourse as it is emerging, embedding assessments of its structure and significance in the speech itself.

In other words, while talking, participants themselves mark those parts of speech that are 'text' and those that are 'instructions about how that discourse is to be approached as a text, through replication or with some form of response' (Urban 1996: 33) (e.g. by means of self-corrections, hedges, hesitations, interjections, false starts, explicit qualifications such as 'what I really mean is . . .', 'I don't want to say that . . .'). A very fine illustration of these processes is Urban's (1996) description of the ways in which fieldwork informants provide clues as to what parts of discourse are 'replicable'. In a structured way, informants treat and modify 'traditional' or 'original' material so as to make it a culturally and textually adequate 'replication' of the original text. Needless to say, the replication involves a whole set of transformations and is thus not a mere 'copy' of the original. Replicating itself is entextualisation *par excellence*, an 'attempt at reproducing, at relocating the original instance of discourse to a new context – carrying over something from the earlier to the later one' (Urban 1996: 21). In other words, it is a phase in the history of discourse and not just a seemingly atemporal projection of discourse from one 'stable' context onto another.

If we take intertextuality and entextualisation together, we have instruments that allow us to set unique communicative events within larger historical frames, both those of the text itself and of the interpretations given by the text. This provides us with bridges between the micro-local events and the macro-patterns of which they are part (either by insertion in these patterns or by departing from them), and it allows us to understand individual discourse events as eminently social, cultural, and political.

## The danger of ethnocentrism in context

A final guideline for treating context is to be aware of the danger of ethnocentrism. Many of the problems identified above, notably the tendencies to assume co-operativity, sharedness, and equality/negotiability in the analysis of communication, are based on often untheorised, intuitive generalisations of communication patterns in one's own society, even one's own immediate peer group. Unsurprisingly, in such familiar surroundings communication may be characterised by an enormous degree of sharedness (of language/language variety/code, contextualisation universes, cultural routines, meanings, and so forth), a willingness to arrive at friendly consensus, a tolerance for deviations from norms, and so on. But this is not the rule – it is an observation of a particular collection of clearly contextualised events – and even less a model of communication that can be projected onto every instance of communication.

The problem fits in a larger one, one that characterises the genesis of the social sciences as sciences taking their own societies as the object of study. In Immanuel Wallerstein's (2001: 20) words, the emerging social-scientific disciplines of the nineteenth century

> were concerned empirically primarily, almost exclusively, with the core countries of the capitalist world-economy – indeed, primarily with just a few of them. . . . [A]lmost all scholars worked on empirical materials concerning their own countries

To a large extent, this is still true in the sense that most of what we now accept as significant social theory supporting discourse analysis is based on reflections of First-World societies. The inclusion of First-World models in particular empirical efforts does not, of course, preclude a reformulation of their theses so as to fit other realities than those of the First World, but the fact remains that the direction of projection is still one that starts from First-World societies to other societies. Neither do we see much attention paid to anthropological theory, a phenomenon which Wallerstein understands as an effect of the separation of scientific disciplines that study 'our' societies from those that study 'other' societies in the late nineteenth century, with 'our' society as a model for 'other' societies.

As noted in chapter 2, one of the problems I have with CDA is the self-evidence with which it adopts the First-World highly integrated, Late Modern and post-industrial, densely semiotised societies as its model for explaining discourse-in-the-world. We have to be aware of the fact that the world is divided into a wide variety not only of linguistic systems – languages, dialect continua, and so on – but also of *sociolinguistic systems* (Hymes 1996) which define the ways in which texts and contexts relate to one another. It is also wise to remind ourselves of the fact that the world is big, and that there are many such sociolinguistic systems. Our own environments, from which we so often deduct principles of human communication, may well be (and probably are) highly peculiar environments with norms, codes, and conventions for understanding that are not present in most other parts of the world. We shall see below as well as in later chapters how important this basic observation becomes as soon as we address communication phenomena that are often captured under the umbrella term of 'globalisation'. In such cases, little of what we are familiar with on the basis of our own experiences as locally socialised communicating beings can be taken for granted. When we think of context, we need to think of *different* contexts in *different* environments, and of highly problematic processes of interpretation occurring as soon as text from one environment is transported to another one.

## 3.3 TWO CRITICAL CONCEPTIONS OF CONTEXT

With the main lines of our approach to context now sketched, we can turn to a discussion of the treatment of context in two schools of discourse analysis. On the one hand, and expanding some remarks made in the previous chapter, I shall discuss CDA; on the other hand, I shall discuss critical claims in Conversation Analysis – an equally popular school of discourse analysis focused on the examination of procedures and methods of interactional behaviour. It so happens that both schools occasionally engage in debates over 'critique' in their respective approaches (see Schegloff 1997; Wetherell 1998; Billig and Schegloff 1999).[1]

### The backgrounding of context: Critical Discourse Analysis

One of the most important methodological problems in discourse analysis in general is the *framing* of discourse in particular *selections of contexts*, the relevance of which is established by the researcher but is not made into an object of investigation. Part of this problem appears to be unavoidable: one always uses all sorts of presuppositions and assumptions, real-world and commonsense knowledge in analysis (see Verschueren 2001; Blommaert 1997a). But this problem is especially pressing in the case of CDA, where the social situatedness of discourse data is crucial, and where context is often taken to include broad systemic and institutional observations. Not just discourse is analysed, but *political* discourse, *bureaucratic* discourse, *doctor–patient* discourse. In CDA, discourse is accompanied by a narrative on power and institutions, large portions of which are just copied from rank-and-file sources or inspired by received wisdom.[2] Charles Briggs observes that

> the question of what is 'ordinary' or 'everyday' involves more than simply which data we select but crucially depends on how we frame and analyze them. By severing indexical links to broader social, political and historical parameters we can give even the most historically compelling discourses the look and feel of the mundane. (Briggs 1997b: 454)

I would add: and vice versa, even the most mundane talk can be transformed in an instance of vulgar power abuse if framed properly. It all comes down to establishing the indexical links referred to by Briggs, identifying them, and specifying their precise structure and function. In this respect, a lot of a priori contextualisation goes on in work qualified as CDA which I find objectionable. Thus, in much CDA work, a priori statements on power relations are being used as perspectives on discourse (e.g. 'power is bad', 'politicians are manipulators', 'media are ideology-reproducing machines'), and social-theoretical concepts and categories are being used in off-hand and seemingly self-evident ways (e.g. 'power', 'institutions', also 'the leading groups in society', 'business', and so on). This leads to highly simplified models of social structures and patterns of action – politicians *always* and *intentionally* manipulate their constituencies; doctors are *by definition* and always the powerful party in doctor–patient relations, etc. – which are then projected onto discourse samples. Power relations are often predefined and then confirmed by features of discourse (sometimes in very questionable ways – see Verschueren 2001).

Of particular interest here is the use of what could be called *prima-facie ethnographies*: dense descriptions of contexts and institutions used as framing devices in analyses. Let us turn to a concrete example: Ruth Wodak's (1997) classic paper 'Critical discourse analysis and the study of doctor-patient interaction'. In the beginning of her paper she brings to our attention that

> In modern societies [socially important] domains are embodied in institutions which are structured in terms of social power relationships and characterised by specific divisions of labour . . . Within institutions, elites (typically consisting of white males) occupy the dominant positions and therefore possess power. They determine what Bourdieu . . . calls the 'symbolic market' . . . ,

> i.e. the value and prestige of symbolic capital (or certain
> communicative behaviour). This can be seen most readily in the
> technical registers used by all professional groups . . . but it also
> manifests itself less obviously in the form of preferred styles and
> certain communicative strategies. (Wodak 1997: 174)

And some pages further, she introduces her research in the hospital
in the following way:

> For an understanding of the context, it is important to realise that
> the outpatients' ward has very low status and prestige in relation to
> the rest of the hospital. It is a type of outpost and . . . serves as a
> training ground for young doctors, which results in inexperienced
> insiders working where experienced ones are arguably most
> necessary. Hierarchy, knowledge, experience and gender are
> interlinked in a strange and unique way in the outpatients' ward. . . .
> (Wodak 1997: 179)

We are not informed about where such crucial ethnographic information comes from. Neither do we see any questioning here of whether
'contextual' features such as the low prestige of the outpatients' ward
may precisely *be discursively produced, as a result of systemic interactional
patterns* within the hospital. In other words, the possibility that the
general status-rank of the locus of fieldwork may be related to the
object of fieldwork – discourse patterns – is not addressed (while this
reality-creating dimension of discourse is openly professed as part of
the CDA agenda). This is the 'context' for the rest of the analysis,
and this context is offered as an unquestionable, untheorised set of
'facts' contradicting part of the methodology of discourse analysis.
The source of such contextual accounts is often obliquely referred to
as on-site observation and interviewing (again, untheorised and without any explicitised procedures). Their function, however, is crucial:
they are central contextualising features that facilitate claims about an
'insiders' perspective' on the communication patterns studied in CDA
(Wodak 1997: 178). The ethnographic basis of these claims is placed
outside the scope of CDA, and one will rarely encounter discussions of
fieldwork procedures and approaches in CDA writings. Analysis starts
as soon as the data 'are there'.

    In the sort of CDA examined here, it is through such a priori con-
textualisations that talk is socially situated and that distinctions are
established between instances of communication that are potential
topics for Critical Discourse Analysis and others that are not. The distinction usually has to do with the presence and salience of power
relations. The problem is that such power relations are often already

established before the actual analysis of discourse can start, by means of – all in all often very 'uncritical' – contextual narratives.

This then leads to a number of methodological claims guiding the work of interpretation. Let us once more take Wodak's (1997) paper as an example. Her research team was called in to investigate and to remedy certain institutional and organisational weaknesses in the outpatients' ward. Wodak's analysis shows that certain beliefs of hospital staff (what she calls the 'myth of efficiency', and ideas about an economy of time) are instances of false consciousness. In her view, the reasons for organisational failure lie elsewhere (in the 'opaque aspects' of reality). She concludes therefore:

> Only an exact analysis of the context, an understanding of everyday life in the institution, and the sequential analysis of the discourse permit a full interpretation of events and the discovery of contradictions and of the ways in which power is exercised. (Wodak 1997: 197)

Strictly speaking, the only analysis offered in her paper is an analysis of the 'sequential analysis of discourse'; neither the 'context', nor 'everyday life in the institution' have been analysed. Yet, *discourse analysis* is supposed to explain and clarify the 'hidden' power relations, the structure of which has already been given in the contextualising accounts. So what does discourse analysis actually do? Often it (unsurprisingly) confirms the forms of inequality and asymmetry already given in the description of the context of talk. In a lot of CDA work, context is often a mere background to rather orthodox (linguistic or interactional) discourse analysis, with some connections running between text and context, while both 'blocks' remain distinct units. Critique thus becomes too often and too much a matter of the credibility of the researcher, whose account of power in contextual narratives is offered not for *inspection* but for *belief*.

## Talk in-and-out-of interaction: Conversation Analysis

The overt bias and the projection of 'relevant' context on discourse has also been noted by scholars in Conversation Analysis (CA), notably by Emanuel Schegloff. When it comes to identifying text–context relations and locating critique in analysis, Schegloff advocates the primacy of 'internal analysis':

> even where critical analysis is wanted, is justifiable, and can have its basic pre-conditions met, what it should properly be brought to bear on is an internally analyzed rendering of the event, the episode, the exchange, the 'text' . . . You need to have technical analysis *first*, in

order to constitute the very object to which critical and sociopolitical analysis might sensibly and fruitfully be applied. And then you may find it no longer in point. (Schegloff 1997: 174)

Schegloff offers a methodological argument for that claim: talk-in-interaction is an object 'with a defensible sense of its own reality' (Schegloff 1997: 171). Hence, no analyst's imputations are required, as the sociopolitical dimension is provided by the speakers themselves and observable in the deployment of their interaction. Schegloff says: 'talk-in-interaction does provide . . . an Archimedean point . . . internal to the object of analysis itself' (Schegloff 1997: 184).

CA displays an intense respect for the density and complexity of human interaction; its accomplishments in demonstrating the richness of human talk are enormous (see, for example, Goodwin 1981; Psathas 1995). At the same time, due to a number of principles and self-imposed restrictions in its methodological programme, there are limits to the relevance of Schegloff's brand of CA for the agenda I wish to pursue here. I see two main problems here: one that has to do with analysis as entextualisation practice; and one that has to do with the location of the sociopolitical aspects of context in concrete stretches of talk (see also Duranti 1997: 264–275).

To start with the first point, conversation-analytical interpretations of speakers' opinions, ideas, political positions, etc. are based on observations of interactional regularities. The argument appears to proceed along these lines: if participants make the expected moves, legitimate the things brought about by their interlocutors, establish validity for certain claims, and respond to and co-construct identities, then analysts are not 'mind reading' but 'virtually mandated to analyze it that way' (Schegloff 1997: 175). Schegloff's CA thus becomes the analytical *replication* of what participants said and did. This core methodological argument – the 'naturalness' of data – is circular because the notional erasure of the analyst's voice depends on the analyst's observations of speakers' regularities in behaviour. These regularities have been established by CA by means of analytically focused and empirically grounded claims, i.e. by using the analyst's voice. Note, for the sake of clarity, that observed regularities can, of course, be valid as claims about the object of investigation; my point is not to claim that they are false or that they are not vindicated, for instance, by speakers' own judgements of behaviour. My problem is that this recognition of analytically established regularities in talk is lifted to the level of a replica of talk: what CA identifies in talk *is* talk. The mediating link between thing and description – analysis – is elided.

Analysis is entextualisation. Despite the fact that the extremely rigid and uniformised conversation-analytical transcription procedures are a clear case in point (Bucholtz 2000), CA – or at least the brand of CA discussed here – fails to recognise the sheer existence of the entextualising practices it applies to text, insisting instead on an isomorphism between 'original text-and-context' and 'analytic text-and-context'. In other words, socially situated events and the analytic artefacts representing them are seen as one and the same object. The metapragmatic framing (and hence remodelling) involved in *all* analysis is denied or, if it is acknowledged (as some CA practitioners do with regard to, for example, transcription procedures), it is not applied in the work of interpretation. Talk is defined and remodelled – 'textualised' – in the professional tactics of CA (perhaps more so, and more radically so, than in most other branches of discourse analysis), and there is a belief that '[s]uch a maximally transparent strategic interactional text can be studied transcriptionally *in vitro* with confidence that the *in vivo* reality is close to hand' (Silverstein 1992: 74).

This brings us to the second problem. In Schegloff's view, as a matter of methodological principle, the social is seen to pertain only to the level of co-participants in specific stretches of talk. Thus, for instance, gender is not a priori relevant in conversations: 'understanding . . . along gender lines, can also, in principle, be shown in any particular case to be the understanding of the participants, but this needs to be *shown*' (Schegloff 1997: 180). The methodological principle underlying this could be labelled the 'mundanisation' of talk (cf. Briggs' 1997b comments above). Gendered, racialised talk needs to be treated in first instance as 'normal', orderly talk. 'Special' contexts are in principle contexts like any other whose 'specialness' needs to be established by internal analysis of talk, which is, in turn, restricted to momentary, very brief, sequences of talk. The latter is important: in contrast to, for example, linguistic-anthropological ethnography, CA tends to prefer small and well-delineated instances of talk, disregarding *post-hoc* accounts of interaction or the way in which single instances can be embedded in larger patterns of interaction across events.

Yet, as Briggs (1997b) argues, not all talk is the same, not all categories in social conduct are equivalent. It is one thing to characterise people as 'speakers' and 'hearers', another to characterise them, as in CA, as 'members' (of what?), and still another to categorise them in terms of institutionalised categories based on macro-sociological differentiations in societies such as race, gender, ethnicity, sexual preference, age, and so forth, the political and ideological importance of which has been established by other kinds of research. In Schegloff's

and related work, a reduction of context is performed to a stereotypical, neutral, and self-contained context, in which *everything* seems to
happen. But, as mentioned earlier, talk can (e.g. in institutional set-
tings) be understood along gender lines by *other* participants, later, and
in consequential ways for the 'original' participants (Ochs 1992). Antici-
pating the discussion in the next section, this is precisely one of the
key critical issues: the fact that talk may *not* have certain implications
to the ('direct') participants, that certain matters are not 'demonstrably relevant', but that *they are made relevant by later re-entextualisations
of that talk by others.*

The option taken by Schegloff is clear: 'interaction' is equated with
(single-instance) 'context'. Automatically, in terms of CA's research
agenda, the relevant context is idealised as being the interaction, and
social roles and functions (including 'distal', i.e. non-immediate, features such as institutional or political-ideological elements) are only
relevant in as far as they are 'procedurally consequential', i.e. in as
far as they actually show up *demonstrably in the interactional practices.*
Schegloff posits that 'social structure' (including power relations) is
produced in (single instances of) interaction, since the same conversational 'mechanic' can be found across instances. In fact, the sociological ambition of CA is 'to show how the parties are embodying for one
another the relevancies of the interaction and are thereby producing
the social structure' (Schegloff 1999: 113), and CA attempts to show
how social structure appears 'in that actual conduct *to which it must
finally be referred*' (1999: 114, emphasis added).

The problem lies in the association between 'talk-in-interaction' –
the object of CA – and the qualification of such instances of talk as
'an activity in its own right' (Schegloff 1999: 109), thus calling for
some kind of 'context in its own right'. Unfortunately for those who
subscribe to this credo, talk is very often an activity that only *appears*
to be 'in its own right', but which in fact is *at the same time* an activity that can be appropriated and made subject to interpretations and
relevance assessments that are far beyond the (direct) participants'
concerns. 'Talk-in-interaction' is very often accompanied by 'talk-out-
of-interaction'.

## 3.4 FORGOTTEN CONTEXTS

The two approaches discussed above both offer views and accounts
of contexts as a locus for deploying critical analysis, focusing
strongly upon simple relationships between individual instances of

text/discourse and context(s). The question is generally that of '(a) context for (a) (particular) text'. In both cases, I hope to have shown that the connection between discourse and social structure leaves much to be desired. In both cases, the relevance of contexts is generally based on judgements of demonstrability (involving connotations of explicitness, outspokenness, denotational aspects of language, and so on): in so far as a text is believed to show *identifiable traces of social structure* (demonstrated or not, which is another matter), social structure serves as a critical context for a text.

This view is partial, and it fails to explain quite a bit of what happens in interaction. I want briefly to present some other contexts – or better, present some phenomena of discourse and suggest that they might be seen as 'contexts' to 'texts'. In all the cases, the contexts I shall offer will give us additional – accumulatively refining – inroads into social structure. In other words, their contextualising function will consist in *merging* discourse and social structure, thus offering better prospects for critical analysis. In all the cases, the contexts are not features of single texts but of larger economies of communication and textualisation. They are not adequately dealt with in either CDA or CA; they are often 'forgotten' contexts.

To substantiate this claim, I shall use a particular type of data: data reflecting globalisation processes. I shall illustrate my arguments with material drawn from research on African asylum seekers' narratives in the asylum application procedure in Belgium (Blommaert 2001a, 2001b; Maryns and Blommaert 2001). These data, collected through long narrative interviews in 1998 at the height of a political crisis on asylum seekers in Belgium, are prime targets for 'traditional' critical analysis. The people who perform them belong to a marginalised group in Belgian society whose rights and opportunities in life are fragile, and who are the object of repression and administrative control. They are faced with huge institutional pressure to tell stories in specific ways – the outcome of the asylum procedure is almost completely based on (perceptions of) the cogency and coherence of the stories they tell. But the telling and interpretation of their stories involves complex contextualisation work – more complex than can be captured by the context conceptions discussed in the previous section, because we are dealing with communication events that can only be understood against the background of globalisation, or, more precisely, of structural inequalities within the world system. Such features of communication do not occur when one studies material from (the perspective of) one's own society; yet, in the present world such data become more and more frequent. They have one big advantage: they compel us to accept that the world is not an abstract thing somewhere 'out there' but that it is right at our doorstep.

## Resources as contexts

The first forgotten context I wish to discuss is the complex of linguistic means and communicative skills usually identified as resources. And, right from the start, that means that we are addressing macrocontexts, contexts that have to do with the structure of the world system and that create situations over which individuals have hardly any control. Speakers can/cannot speak varieties of languages, they can/cannot write and read, and they can/cannot mobilise specific resources for performing specific actions in society. And all these differences – different degrees of proficiency ranging from 'not at all' to 'full mastery' of codes, language varieties, and styles – are socially consequential. Resources are hierarchised in terms of functional adequacy, and those who have different resources often find that they have unequal resources, because access to some rights and benefits in society is constrained by access to specific communicative (e.g. narrative) resources (cf. Hymes 1996).

Asylum seekers in Belgium are confronted with a complex set of administrative procedures, involving and presupposing access to various genres (e.g. legal texts, welfare regulations), various languages (Dutch, French, English), language varieties and channels (written, spoken, visual, electronic). Apart from what they need for the asylum procedure, they also need to be able to lead a life in a Belgian village or town. The approximately fifty asylum seekers we interviewed all used English, French, and Dutch for conducting their daily business. Many of them did, however, display considerable difficulties in expressing themselves in these languages. Restricting ourselves to spoken discourse here, the degrees of proficiency ranged from very poor to sophisticated, and these differences obviously affect the structure and content of narratives. Shifting and mixing of codes, varieties, and styles was a crucial ingredient of the stories as well (see Maryns and Blommaert 2001). Let us take a look at example (1), a brief fragment from a narrative by an Angolese man told in French.[3]

*Fragment (1)*

> oui/l'autre président . . . (xxxxxx)/ on l'a empoisonné/ c'est le
> président Mobutu/ qui a mis le poison retardé/ il est parti au russe /
> l'URSS/ pour traîter/ il a retourné/ il est mort/ mais on a abandonné
> son corps hein/ oui/ {{*Question: c'était un président de MPLA?*}} c'était le
> même mouvement MPLA/ dans le temps / année septante-cinq/ quand

il est mort on dit/ comme on =il est marxisme/ on a pris on a choisi
=on= on a fait faux testament/ cette testament c'était au temps du
russe qui a fait ça/ comme toi tu =le= le président il est mort/ il a
décidé Eduardo qui va me remplacer/ sans vote/ parce que il est
toujours du même parti/ Eduardo il est d'origine angolais/ mais il est
des Cap Verdiens/ parce que ce sont des anciens prisonniers/ et
Portugais il a mis à l'île hein/ nous sommes à l'océan/ et on a mis
une prison là-bas/ parce qu'il est venu pour commander
l'indépendance/ c'était une petite ville=une petite=une petite village/
on a mis au pouvoir/ maintenant le président/ c'est on dit/ il dit que
non/ tous les gens/ qui parlent Lingala/ les gens du Nord/ ce sont des
gens plus malins/ plus intelligents/ par rapport au gens du Sud/ en
Angola nous sommes quatre couleurs/ comme le Bré=le Brésil.

Translation

yes/the other president . . . (xxxxxx)/they have poisoned him/ it's
president Mobutu/ who put the delayed poison/ he has left to
Russian/ the USSR/ to treat/ he gave back/ he died/ but they have left
his corpse, right/ yes/ {{*Question: it was a president of the MPLA?*}}/ it
was the same movement MPLA/ in those days/ year seventy-five/
when he died they say/ like they=he is Marxism/ they took they
chose=they=they have made false testament/ those testament it was
in the time of Russian that has made it/ since you you=the=the
president is dead/ he decided Eduardo who is going to replace me/
without vote/ because he is always of the same party/ Eduardo he is
of Angolan origin/ but he is of the Cape Verdians/ because they are
former prisoners/ and Portuguese has put on the island, right/ we are
at the ocean/ and they have put a prison over there/ because he had
come to command the independence/ it was a small town=a small=a
small village/ they have put to power/ now the president/ that is what
they say/ he said that no/ all the people/ who speak Lingala/ the
people from the north/ they are more clever people/ more intelligent/
in relation to the people from the south/ in Angola we are four
colours/ like Bra=Brazil

The Angolese man is at pains to explain the wider political context in
which his escape from Angola should be set. In doing so, he is forced
to provide detailed information about the political regime in Angola,
including digressions into the Portuguese colonial practices (sending
MPLA fighters into exile on the Cabo Verde islands), and into linguistic and ethnic divisions in the country. The story is highly complex
and detailed, and apparently all these details count for the narrator. Such detailed and complex digressions on the home country feature in almost all the narratives we recorded, to the extent that they
can generically be identified as 'home narratives' (Blommaert 2001b).
Home narratives fulfil often crucial contextualising functions in the

larger stories: without them, a precise understanding of the causes
and motives for the escape cannot be reached. Narrators often explicitly flagged the importance of these dense contextual accounts for
an understanding of who they were and why they came to Belgium.
The point is that this complex and important package of information
has to be transmitted by means of a very 'broken' variety of French,
informally acquired during sojourns in Congo and during his stay in
Belgium (and bearing traces of this migration itinerary). The French
used by the Angolese man is, like the English and Dutch of many others, a product of refugee life and it mirrors the marginality in which
they find themselves wherever they go.

The shape of narratives cannot be separated from their content: stories such as this one are shaped to a large extent by the resources
people have for telling them, *what* can be told depends on *how* one can
tell it. Complex stories become even more complex when they are told
in uncomfortable varieties of languages. The way in which the temporal sequentiality of events is organised in fragment (1), for instance, is
highly problematic (e.g. where do we have to situate the 'parce qu'il est
venu pour commander l'indépendance' in the passage on Cabo Verde?);
the same goes for crucial qualifications given by means of less than
adequate lexical choices (e.g. 'il est *marxisme*' instead of 'il est *marxiste*');
deixis and reference are another domain of problems (see the 'il' in
'parce qu'il est venu pour commander l'indépendance'). The struggle
with the medium of narration also has an effect on the rhythm and the
prosody, causing disruptions in the flow of narration and the loss of an
important range of contextualisation cues. Told to Belgian interlocutors who are either native speakers (in the case of Dutch and French)
or non-native speakers commanding a sometimes equally problematic
variety of English, the potential for being misunderstood is obviously
very high. And, in the punitive atmosphere of application interviews,
'rambling' stories are quickly turned into 'bad' stories, qualified as
'unreliable' or full of 'unclear elements' and 'contradictions'. Parts of
the stories that are difficult to understand during the interaction are
often *not* understood at all. The resources controlled by the narrators
and their interlocutors are part and parcel of the interpretations given
to their stories, and given the central role of the stories in the asylum
procedure matters of resources may influence the outcome of their
asylum application.

Resources and the way in which they feature as elements of social
structure are often 'invisible' contexts in discourse analysis. Illiterates
will not show up in analyses of written discourse; their perceptions of
'news' and 'politics' do not feature in analyses of newspaper reporting.

There is no conversation analysis possible when people don't converse because they do not share resources. Such analyses are not about, nor *for* them. The errors in discourse of people who lack access to 'high' standardised varieties of a language are often edited and corrected, and thus disappear as indexes of social structure and inequality-as-identity for those people. Their utterances are usually transcribed in standard orthographies of languages, so that social stigmas in accents and 'small' discourse features are being effaced and a homogenisation of such language users with 'average' features of the speech community is accomplished (Ochs 1999). However, the importance of resources lies in the deep relation between language and a general economy of symbols and status in societies – we shall come back to this in later chapters. The point is that one does not just 'have' or 'know' a language. Such seemingly innocuous phrases hide a complex and highly sensitive political-economic dynamics of acquisition and differential distribution. Words, accents, intonation contours, styles all come with a history of use and abuse (Bakhtin's intertextuality); they also come with a history of assessment and evaluation. This is where language leads us directly to the heart of social structure: an investigation into language becomes an investigation into the systems and patterns of allocation of power symbols and instruments, and thus an investigation into basic patterns of privilege and disenfranchisement in societies (see Bourdieu 1991; Gumperz 1982; Heller 1994). Looking at issues of resources makes sure that any instance of language use would be deeply and fundamentally socially contextualised; connections between talk and social structure would be *intrinsic*.

At the same time, the context-shaping role of resources extends beyond the occurrence of single texts or instances of discourse. They are not strictly features of texts, but of societies and social structures, and in the final instance, of worldwide relations between parts of the globe. Hence, the chances that they would emerge from doctrinaire (linguistic) discourse analysis are very slim – often, they belong to the realm of the 'normal' and of the 'usual', they *condition* interactions in society, and they make sure that some interactions will simply never occur. Hymes accurately notes:

> There is a fundamental difference . . . between what is not said because there is no occasion to say it, and what is not said because one has not and does not find a way to say it. (Hymes 1974a: 72)

In a critical study of language, the absence of certain discourse events and the particular shape of others *because of matters of resource allocation* should be a major preoccupation. Why cannot everyone speak or write in certain ways? Why is some discourse the privilege of some people because it is based on exclusive usages of rare resources? For an understanding of what language does in society, I believe these are fundamental questions.

## Text trajectories

A second 'forgotten' context has already been briefly mentioned above when we discussed the importance of translocal contexts. One of the features of, for instance, institutional communication processes is the shifting of discourse across contexts: talk finds its way into notes, summaries, case reports, citations, discussions of others. Briggs (1997a) and Silverstein and Urban (1996) have argued that precisely this shifting of texts between contexts – re-entextualisation practices – involves crucial questions of power. To recapitulate briefly what we said above, not every context is accessible to everyone, and re-entextualisation practices depend on who has access to which contextual space. Access here also depends on resources: re-entextualisation often involves a technology of contextualisation, a degree of expertise that is very exclusive and the object of tremendous inequality in any society (e.g. legal re-entextualisations require access to legal expertise, see Philips 1998). The dynamics of entextualisation clearly leads us back into issues of differential access to power resources, and thus again leads us directly to social structure.

In the Belgian asylum procedure, the story of the applicant is the central ingredient, and obviously a number of things happen to these stories. The long interview on their motives for seeking asylum in Belgium is followed by a number of administrative text-making procedures: a case report, quotation of fragments in notes and letters exchanged between the administration and lawyers or welfare workers, official interpretations and summaries in verdicts from the asylum authorities, and so forth. Consider the following fragment from an official letter to the Angolese man whose home narrative we discussed above. In this letter, he was notified of the rejection of his asylum application. The rejection is motivated by means of interpretive summaries of parts of the story of the man (Dutch original, my translation):

*Fragment (2)*

> The concerned was interrogated on November 23, 1993 at the Commissariat-General [for Refugees and Stateless Persons], in the presence of [name], his attorney.

He claimed to be a 'political informant' of the MPLA. On October 18, 1992 however, he passed on information to UNITA. At the UNITA office, however, he met with Major [name], who works for the MPLA. Two days later, Major [name] had the concerned arrested. Fearing that the concerned would give the Major away at the trial, [name of the Major] helped the concerned to escape. The concerned fled to [locality] where a priest arranged for his departure from Angola. The concerned came, together with his wife [name and register number] and three children, through Zaïre and by plane, to Belgium. They arrived on May 19, 1993.

It has to be noted that the concerned remains very vague at certain points. Thus he is unable to provide details about the precise content of his job as 'political informant'. Furthermore the account of his escape lacks credibility. Thus it is unlikely that the concerned could steal military clothes and weapons without being noticed and that he could subsequently climb over the prison wall.

It is also unlikely that the concerned and his wife could pass the passport control at Zaventem [i.e. Brussels airport] bearing a passport lacking their names and their pictures.

Furthermore, the itinerary of the concerned is impossible to verify due to a lack of travel documents (the concerned sent back the passports).

The statements of the concerned contain contradictions when compared to his wife's account. Thus he declares that the passports which they received from the priest [name] were already completely in order at the time they left Angola. His wife claims that they still had to apply for a visa in Zaïre.

Two comments are in order. First, the asylum application is not constructed in one act of communication; it is constructed through a sequence of re-entextualisations, involving far-reaching reinterpretations of the story, summarising and rewording practices, and the reframing of a story in a legal and procedural framework containing criteria for 'truth' and 'plausibility' (Blommaert 2001b). This sequence is fixed: the text trajectory is a uniform administrative procedure. The 'procedurally consequent' context, to adopt CA terminology, involves a series of individual events as well as the relations between these events: the fact that talk is translated, written, summarised, and put into a legal/procedural framework, in sum, that every step in the systematically and uniformly performed process involves not replication but far-reaching transformations of the 'original' story. Yet, throughout this series of transformations, the story is still said to be that of the asylum applicant (cf. phrases such as 'the statements of the concerned'). So, what is 'the story of the applicant'? The story is the whole text trajectory.

Second, in light of the remarks on resources made above, the salience of text trajectories becomes even greater. Every step in the trajectory involves inequalities in resources. The story told either in a native language and translated (usually into French or English) by an interpreter, or in the sort of varieties of French, English, or Dutch illustrated in fragment (1) is put into a standard, written variety of Dutch or French. It is filtered in the way discussed above: parts that were hard to understand while the story was being told are either deleted from the story or misinterpreted. The administrator has selected those parts of the story that appear to be of consequence for the outcome of the asylum application, using criteria of coherence and consistency that are directly fed into legally consequential assessments of truth and reliability. The story is measured against legal criteria and evaluated as either 'truthful' or 'unreliable'. Inequalities in linguistic-communicative resources in the asylum procedure accrue as the story is processed along the text trajectory.

Attention to this type of shifting of discourse across contexts involves issues of control and power in each of the phases of recontextualisation. These features of analysis can obviously not be accommodated by CA. In CDA, some attention to such phenomena is given by Fairclough (1992b), though the focus is on textual flows rather than on the shifting between contextualising universes and resources that determine recontextualisation work. My approach is derived from ethnography – an awareness that text is contextualised in each phase of its existence, and that every act of discourse production, reproduction, and circulation or consumption involves shifts in contexts (Silverstein and Urban 1996; Philips 1998). In studying discourse and social structure, such shifting of discourse across contexts containing important power features appears to be a crucial critical enterprise, if for nothing else because in the context of globalisation processes one can only expect enormous intensifications of such shifts.

## Data histories

A third 'forgotten context' is directly related to the foregoing: the history of discourse data. As said above, analysis is entextualisation – it is, in other words, also part of a text trajectory. Hence, some sensitivity to what professionals do with discourse samples as soon as they call them data can be useful. I have noted above that, especially in CDA, the ethnographic origin and situatedness of data are hardly treated; similar remarks can be made with regard to CA (Duranti 1997: 267–270). In ethnography, however, the history of data is acknowledged as an important element in their interpretation. It is recognised that the way in which data have been gathered, recorded, and treated by the analyst influence what these data tell us (e.g. Bauman 1995; Silverstein 1996a; Haviland 1996; Urban 1996). The time, place, and occasion at which data are being gathered have an effect on the data: they are what they are because they occurred in that shape in that context. The question 'Why do we investigate *this now*?' is an important question, for it points towards the social situatedness of our own research.

This is important, for it is often either overlooked as a factor in research and interpretation or treated as a self-evident matter and given little prominence. I intend to foreground it, for it is again a case of often invisible context determining what can happen how and at what time. Some things can only be said at certain moments, under certain conditions. Likewise, and very often as a correlate of this, some things can only be researched at certain moments and under certain conditions. I mentioned at the beginning of this section that our data were collected in 1998. A few weeks prior to the start of our fieldwork, an important political crisis erupted over matters of asylum in Belgium. The cause of the crisis was the violent death of a Nigerian female asylum seeker in the hands of police officers. As a reaction to this incident, there was a spontaneous outburst of sympathy for the predicament of asylum seekers among large sections of the Belgian population; asylum seekers organised themselves and demonstrated in large numbers for the first time in history. They occupied churches and schools and were eager to tell their stories. Suddenly, and for a brief period of just a couple of months, we found ourselves in unique, unprecedented, research conditions. Prior to this incident it was very difficult actually to locate asylum seekers, most of them being clandestine and preferring not to disclose the locations where they lived. And after a few months the protest movement lost momentum and the asylum seekers went underground again. During this brief period, we recorded the stories of people who wanted to tell the stories of their miserable lives back home, on the road, and in Belgium. People told their stories eagerly and repeatedly to anyone who cared to listen. One important feature of this period was *contact*: the public outcry after the death of the Nigerian girl created a forum for debate between Belgians and asylum seekers – a forum in which stories about asylum and asylum seekers' lives could be circulated. Consequently, the stories changed and many of the stories in our corpus display features of what Hymes (1998) calls 'fully-formed narratives': narratives that display growing tightness in narrative structure due to repeated instances of narrating, 'rehearsals' so to speak. Thus, the concrete context of the fieldwork had an impact on our data on at least two levels: (1) the fact that people could be interviewed at all and were willing to disclose their identities and 'cases' to us; (2) the particular structural characteristics of some of the stories, bearing traces of repeated narrating.

The narratives only exist as research objects because their sheer genesis is a matter of context: the stories were only available during that period and because of the political upheaval which foregrounded the issue of asylum in public debate. It was a crisis phenomenon, an effect of one of these moments when chaos and acceleration seem to take over and force all kinds of 'hidden transcripts' to the surface (Scott 1990). After this brief period, the stories disappeared together with the people who told them. So they can only be researched as instances of inequality because they were recorded at a moment in which such inequality had become visible and salient and had become accessible for research.

The fact that certain discourse forms only become visible and accessible at particular times and under particular conditions is in itself an important phenomenon, which tells us a lot about our societies and ourselves, and which necessarily situates particular discourses in the wider sociopolitical environment in which they occur. The stories have a particular 'load' which relates to (and indexes) their place in a particular social, political, and historical moment. Removing this load from the narratives could involve the risk of obscuring the reasons for their production as well as the fact that they are tied to identifiable people and to particular, uniquely meaningful, circumstances that occasioned them.

## 3.5 CONCLUSIONS

Conceptions of context can be critical to the extent that, rather than as direct referential contributions to text-meaning, they are seen as *conditions* for discourse production and for looking at discourse, both from lay and professional perspectives. We should be looking at how the linguistic generates the economic, social, political, as well as how the economic, social, and political generate the linguistic. The problems I have identified with treatments of context in CDA and CA all had to do with the centrality of text in both traditions. Despite claims voiced in both traditions about the mutually constitutive relationship of discourse and society, the ultimate ambition remains explaining discourse, not explaining society through the privileged window of discourse. My own suggestions were informed by the opposite strategy: using discourse as a social object, the linguistic characteristics of which are conditioned and determined by circumstances that are far beyond the grasp of the speaker or user, but are social, political, cultural, and historical. It is remarkable that whenever we say that text is 'situated' in discourse-analytical terms, we seem to refer to forms of strict locality: the unique, one-time, and micro-situatedness of text. From this individual situatedness, larger structures, patterns, or 'rules' can then be deduced, but these generalisations do not involve higher-level situatedness: discourse seems to lose context as soon as it is raised above the single-text level. This different degree of situatedness – large, general, supra-individual, typical, structural, and higher than the single society – should have a place in any form of critical study of discourse.

To the extent that critical approaches to discourse should be concerned with power, they cannot be concerned exclusively with either predefined power – power of which text is only illustrative or symptomatic, as in CDA – nor with explicitised, visible, and event-centred power within the grasp of individual practices, as in CA. It must also be concerned with invisible, hegemonic, structural, and normalised power sedimented *in* language and not only *through* language. As we all know, language itself is an *object* of inequality and hegemony; revealing the power effects of language cannot overlook this dimension of how language and speech themselves have been 'molested', to use Hymes' (1996) term. That simple phenomenon in itself – people talking and writing, using language for specific functions – is not an unquestionable given, and analysis should not start, so to speak, as soon as people open their mouths. It should have started long before that. This is the topic of the next chapter.

## SUGGESTIONS FOR FURTHER READING

Two outstanding collections of essays on various kinds of context are essential reading: Auer and Di Luzio (1992), and Duranti and Goodwin (1992). Peter Auer's (1995) survey paper is a *tour de force*, and nobody should forget to read Gumperz on the topic (1982, 1992, 2003). The dialogical nature of interpretation is defined in Bakhtin (1981), while I find that everyone should have read Voloshinov (1973) at least once in life. A full understanding of the layered nature of context is impossible without reading Goffman on frames (1974). A very good survey paper on intertextuality is Slembrouck (2002), while the papers by Bauman and Briggs (1990) and Silverstein and Urban (1996) define and illustrate entextualisation.

# 4   Language and inequality

## 4.1   THE PROBLEM: VOICE AND MOBILITY

I announced in the introductory chapter that this book would address power effects in the field of language in society, and that, more in particular, inequality would be my central concern. Furthermore, I said that issues of voice would be identified as crucial in explaining inequality. I also defined voice (following Hymes 1996) in general as the ways in which people manage to make themselves understood or fail to do so. This capacity to make oneself understood, I argued, is a capacity to generate an uptake of one's words as close as possible to one's desired contextualisation. It is, in other words, the capacity to accomplish desired *functions* through language. More accurately, it is the capacity to create favourable conditions for a desired uptake: if I want to formulate a polite request, I shall attempt to make my words come across as a polite request and not as a rude command; if I want to declare my love to someone, I shall try to make sure that the object of my love understands it that way. In each case I shall mobilise what I believe are the most (denotationally) adequate, contextually appropriate, semiotic means to do so, hoping that the interlocutor will follow my directions of contextualisation.

But such a capacity is not self-evident, I stressed in chapter 3, for this capacity – while essentially creative – is subject to several conditions and constraints. Hence, we need to find an analytic way to see voice at work and relate it to larger patterns of inequality. This will be the topic of this chapter. Chapter 5 will dwell at length on the tension between creativity and constraints.

Let me outline the case I shall try to make in this chapter. The issue of voice is an eminently social issue, and a linguistic description of what goes on in the interaction will not suffice to produce an analysis of voice. It is about function, and function is affected by the social 'values' – in a politico-economic sense – attributed to particular linguistic resources (hence Bakhtin's emphasis on the *evaluative* aspect of understanding, see chapter 3). In general we can say that every difference in language can be turned into difference in social value – difference and inequality are two sides of a coin, a point often overlooked or minimised in analysis. As John Gumperz puts it (1982: 6–7):

> Language differences play an important, positive role in signalling information as well as in creating and maintaining the subtle boundaries of power, status, role and occupational specialization that make up the fabric of our social life. Assumptions about value differences associated with these boundaries in fact form the very basis for the indirect communicative strategies employed in key gatekeeping encounters . . .

Such values are nested in particular *orders of indexicality*, a concept I shall explain below. These orders of indexicality are unevenly distributed throughout societies; not everyone has access to them. They operate unequally within units often conceived as 'one society' or 'community', and they operate *a fortiori across* such units. Consequently, when people move through physical and social space (both are usually intertwined), they move through orders of indexicality affecting their ability to deploy communicative resources, and what functions well in one such unit may suddenly cease to function or lose parts of its functions in another such unit. Consequently, voice in the era of globalisation becomes a matter of the capacity to *accomplish functions of linguistic resources translocally*, across different physical and social spaces. Voice, in other words, is *the capacity for semiotic mobility* – a capacity very often associated with the most prestigious linguistic resources ('world languages' such as English, literacy, and more recently multimodal internet communication) and very often denied to resources ranking lower on the scales of value that characterise orders of indexicality (minority languages, 'unwritten' languages, dialects, and so forth).

I shall first have to work my way through a theoretical exposé clarifying the notions of functional relativity and mobility, orders of indexicality, and pretextuality. After that, I shall offer two substantial case analyses illustrating my points. The first case will discuss inequality in the field of globalised literacy; the second one will be about narrative inequality.

## 4.2 TOWARDS A THEORY OF VOICE

Functional relativity and mobility

Dell Hymes' voluminous œuvre is well known and recognised as foun-
dational to sociolinguistics and linguistic anthropology. Yet, some of
the theoretical wealth of his work remains largely untapped. A central concern in his work is with *function*, and it is in this respect that
he developed his notion of 'second linguistic relativity'. The argument
(originally presented in Hymes 1966 but recapitulated in Hymes 1980
and 1996) is, of course, cast in a performance-view of language (as
opposed to a competence-view), emphasising contextual embedded-
ness and variability, and thus paying tribute to Whorf's 'first relativity'. While indispensable to Hymes' view of language, Whorf's relativity of structure assumed stability in function. This is problematic,
for

> the role of language may differ from community to community; . . .
> in general the functions of language in society are a problem for
> investigation, not postulation . . . If this is so, then the cognitive
> significance of a language depends not only on structure, but also on
> patterns of use. (1966: 116)

And consequently:

> the type [of relativity] associated with Sapir and Whorf in any case is
> underlain by a more fundamental kind. The consequences of the
> relativity of the structure of language depend on the relativity of the
> function of language. Take, for example, the common case of
> multilingualism. Inferences as to the shaping effect of some one
> language on thought and the world must be qualified immediately
> in terms of the place of the speaker's languages in his biography and
> mode of life. Moreover, communities differ in the role they assign to
> language itself in socialization, acquisition of cultural knowledge
> and performance. . . . This second type of linguistic relativity,
> concerned with the functions of languages, has more than a critical,
> cautionary import. As a sociolinguistic approach, it calls attention to
> the organisation of linguistic features in social interaction. Work has
> begun to show that description of fashions of speaking can reveal
> basic cultural values and orientations. The worlds so revealed are not
> the ontological and epistemological worlds of physical relationships,
> of concern to Whorf, but worlds of social relationships. What are
> disclosed are not orientations toward space, time, vibratory
> phenomena, and the like, but orientations towards persons, roles,
> statuses, rights and duties, deference and demeanor . . . (Hymes 1996:
> 44–45; also Hymes 1980: 38)

Hymes' emphasis on the *problematic* nature of language functions needs to be underscored: according to Hymes in 1966, such functions have been taken for granted by linguists while, in fact, they should be one of the foci of empirical investigation. Even if language forms are similar or identical, the way in which they get inserted in social actions may differ significantly and, consequently, there may be huge differences in what these (similar or identical) forms *do* in real societies. Hymes thus shifts the focus of attention away from 'linguistic systems' to 'sociolinguistic systems': systems that are based on 'fashions/ways of speaking' (a classic concept pre-War American linguistic anthropology). What we need to investigate is the way in which language actually *works* in societies, and function is the key to this. This means, paradoxically at first sight, that we shall need more *ethnography* the more we intend to investigate phenomena of globalisation (see Englund 2002; and the essays in Burawoy 2001).

The impact of this relativity of function on our research agenda is considerable, and so is its critical dimension. Part of linguistic inequality in any society – and consequently, part of much social inequality– depends on the inability of speakers accurately to perform certain discourse functions on the basis of available and accessible resources. Language functions and the ways in which they are performed by people are constantly assessed and evaluated: function and value are impossible to separate. Consequently, as said before, *differences* in the use of language are quickly, and quite systematically, translated into *inequalities* between speakers. This observation holds for what language does in stratified societies and it is central to, for example, Bernstein's and Bourdieu's arguments on language; it accounts for almost any dynamics of prestige and stigma in language, and sociolinguistics has built a remarkable track record of descriptions of such processes in single and synchronically viewed societies or speech communities. But there is more as soon as we start looking at globalisation.

Globalisation results in intensified forms of flow – movements of objects, people, and images – causing forms of contact and difference perhaps not new in substance but perhaps new in scale and perception. Consequently, key sociolinguistic concepts such as speech community (always carrying problematic suggestions of closure, synchronicity, or achronicity and homogeneity) become more and more difficult to handle empirically (for an early critique, see Hymes 1968; Silverstein 1998; see Rampton 1998 for an excellent survey and discussion). But even more disconcerting is the fact that the *presupposability of functions* for linguistic resources becomes increasingly problematic, because the linguistic resources travel across time, space, and different orders of indexicality. The functions which particular ways of speaking will perform, and the functions of the particular linguistic resources by means of which they are accomplished, become less and less a matter of surface inspection in terms of commonsense linguistic categories (e.g. 'is this English?'), and some of the biggest errors (and injustices) may be committed by simply projecting locally valid functions onto the ways of speaking of people who are involved in transnational flows. In our work on asylum seekers' narratives, for example, we found that the particular kind of anecdotal sub-narratives performed by asylum seekers and which we called 'home narratives' (we saw an example in chapter 3) were easily dismissed by Belgian officials as anecdotes that did not matter, whereas for asylum seekers such home narratives contained crucial contextualising information without which their story could be easily misunderstood. Whenever discourses travel across the globe, what is carried with them is their shape, but their value, meaning, or function do not often travel along. Value, meaning, and function are a matter of uptake, they have to be *granted* by others on the basis of the prevailing orders of indexicality, and increasingly also on the basis of their real or potential 'market value' as a cultural commodity.

The fact is that functions performed by particular resources in one place can be altered in another place, and that in such instances the 'value' of these linguistic tools or skills is changed, often in unpredictable ways. The English acquired by urban Africans may offer them considerable prestige and access to middle-class identities in African towns. It may be an 'expensive', extremely valuable resource to them. But the same English, when spoken in London by the same Africans, may become an object of stigmatisation and may qualify them as members of the lower strata of society. What is very 'expensive' in Lusaka or Nairobi may be very 'cheap' in London or New York. What people can actually accomplish with these resources is likewise affected. 'Good' and status-carrying English in the periphery may be 'bad' and stigma-carrying English in the core of the world system. The opposite may, of course, also occur: otherwise minorised varieties can acquire considerable prestige and value in specific contexts (Heller 2003). Rampton's work on the delicate reshuffling of linguistic and stylistic repertoires in contemporary multi-ethnic peer groups has brought us a long way in understanding the relativity (and the renegotiability) of associated 'values' to linguistic modes of conduct caused by diaspora or globalisation flows in general (Rampton 1995, 1999, 2001; Harris, Leung, and Rampton 2001). What we have to learn from this, I believe, is that the more we investigate mobility of discourses, linguistic resources, or messages, the more we shall have to foreground problems of form–function mapping. Mobility – often seen as the defining feature of globalisation – is a communication problem for many people.

## Difference and value: orders of indexicality and pretextuality

We have seen how problems of mobility generate problems of function in language. Mobility, we have to understand, is not mobility across empty spaces, but mobility across spaces filled with codes, customs, rules, expectations, and so forth. Mobility is an itinerary across normative spaces, and these spaces are always somebody's space. Now, how can we understand this inherent normativity projected onto language use? Bakhtin (1986) offers us some useful suggestions. As seen in the previous chapter, Bakhtin stressed the fact that 'the speaker himself is oriented . . . toward such an actively responsive understanding' (1986: 69), i.e. an immediate dialogical uptake of his/her utterances. But, at the same time, the speaker orients towards what Bakhtin calls a 'superaddressee', 'whose absolutely just responsive understanding is presumed'. Bakhtin provides some examples of such a 'superaddressee': 'God, absolute truth, the court of dispassionate human conscience, the people, the court of history, science, and so forth' (1986: 126).

Let us now reformulate this. While performing language use, speakers display orientations both towards the immediate result of their actions (Bakhtin's immediate responsive understanding) as well as to higher-level, non-immediate complexes of perceived meaningfulness (the superaddressee). We would say: they display orientations towards *orders of indexicality* – systemically reproduced, stratified meanings often called 'norms' or 'rules' of language, and always typically associated with particular shapes of language (e.g. the 'standard', the prestige variety, the 'usual' way of having a conversation with my friends, etc.) (Silverstein 1998, 2003a).[1] Stratification is crucial here: we are dealing with systems that organise inequality via the attribution of different indexical meanings to language forms (e.g. by allocating 'inferior' value to the use of dialect varieties and 'superior' value to standard varieties in public speech).

The notion of 'orders of indexicality' will be central in much of the argument in this book, so perhaps some clarification may be in order. In introducing this notion I try to combine two things:

a the fact that the indexical meanings discussed earlier – connections between linguistic signs and contexts – are 'ordered', i.e. they are not matters of random attribution but closely related to other social and cultural features of social groups. This aspect of indexicality has been captured by Silverstein's (2003a) notion of 'indexical order';

b the fact that such ordered indexicalities themselves occur in the form of stratified complexes, in which some kinds of indexicalities are ranked higher than others: they suggest prestige versus stigma; rationality versus emotion; membership of a particular group versus non-membership, and so forth. Much in the sense of Foucault's (1982) 'orders of discourse', we have to conceive of indexicalities as organised in 'regimes' which invoke matters of ownership and control and allow and enable judgements, inclusion and exclusion, positive or negative sanctioning, and so forth.

Taken together, 'orders of indexicality' allow us to focus on the level of the concrete, empirically observable, deployment of semiotic means, while at the same time seeing such micro-processes and semiotic features as immediately connected to a wider sociocultural, political, and historical space. By orienting to orders of indexicality, language users (systemically) reproduce these norms, and situate them in relation to other norms. Thus, orders of indexicality endow the semiotic process with *indexical order* in the sense of Silverstein (2003a): we get conventionalised patterns of indexicality that come to 'mean' certain things. And these, in turn, feed into orders of indexicality, thus creating a dialectics of context and indexicality often captured under 'micro' and 'macro'.

There is always identity work involved, and the orientations towards orders of indexicality are the grassroots displays of 'groupness'. To give an example: young people communicate through orientations to peer group norms; in that way they reproduce the peer group and situate it *vis-à-vis* other peer groups and society at large, thus making the group recognisable both from the inside and from the outside – the particular peer group norms have a specific place in the orders of indexicality to which members orient. This, then, accounts for the differences between 'groups' (i.e. inhabitable identities, identities one claims and performs for oneself) and 'categories' (i.e. ascriptive identities, identities attributed by others). The difference lies in differences in *indexability*. Using a particular slang variety – say, Hip Hop jargon – in a sophisticated way may signal group membership, even leadership, and status to members of, for example, young urban groups celebrating American Hip Hop culture. At the same time, it may signal non-membership of 'the majority', marginality and dissent, and even suggest a culture of violence and aggression to older bourgeois groups. The same semiotic signs index different things that are ranked differently in different orders of indexicality (that of the Hip Hop community versus that of the older bourgeois community), and they lead to different identities, one inhabitable and another one ascriptive.

The systemically reproduced indexicalities are often tied to specific, authoritative actors which we call *centring institutions* (Silverstein 1998: 404), and which are often also 'central' institutions imposing the 'doxa' in a particular group (i.e. the stratification of value in the indexical system). The centring function is *attributive*: it generates indexicalities to which others have to orient in order to be 'social', i.e. to produce meanings that 'belong' somewhere. These attributions are emblematic: they centre on the potential to articulate (hierarchically ordered) 'central values' of a group or system (the 'good' group member, the 'ideal' father/mother/child, 'God', 'the country/nation', the 'law', the 'economy', the 'good' student, the 'ideal' intellectual, the 'real man/woman' . . .).[2] And this centring almost always involves either perceptions or real processes of homogenisation and uniformisation: orienting towards such a centre involves the (real or perceived) reduction of difference and the creation of recognisably 'normative' meaning.

Centring institutions occur at all levels of social life, ranging from the family over small peer groups, more or less stable communities (e.g. university students, factory workers, members of a church), the state and transnational communities, all the way through to the world system. They are a central feature of what Benedict Anderson (1983) called 'imagined communities': though imagined, they trigger specific behaviours and generate groups. But it is worth underscoring that the social environment of almost any individual would by definition be *polycentric*, with a wide range of criss-crossing centres to which orientations need to be made, and evidently with multiple 'belongings' for individuals (often understood as 'mixed' or 'hybrid' identities). To paraphrase Sapir (in Darnell 2001: 127): there are more groups of significance than members participating in them. Furthermore, such environments would be polycentric *and stratified*, in the sense that not every centre has equal range, scope, and depth. Small peer groups are not equal to a church community or to the state, and while some centres are what they are because of consent (e.g. peer groups), others generate normativity primarily through coercion (e.g. the labour environment or the state in various respects). Consequently, orders of indexicality are stratified and not all ways of speaking have equal value.[3]

Let us return now to some of what has been said above. When using language, we map form onto function. Function, as said, is tied to social evaluation of meaningfulness, and this relates to orders of indexicality emanating from centring institutions – the inherent normativity of language use. Function is thus clearly not an 'essence', but a relational, relative phenomenon which depends on the structure and scope of the repertoires of speakers and their value in relation to orders of indexicality (Hymes 1966; Silverstein 1998, 2003a). The process of mapping presupposes and requires the existence of contextualising spaces in which particular forms can be attributed meaning. Two problems can, and do, frequently occur – they are to some extent the core problems of sociolinguistics:

(i) *differential access to forms*, to linguistic/communicative resources, resulting in differential capacities to accomplish certain functions. Think of absence of access to literacy or to particular *types of* literacy; absence of access to particular language varieties, codes, jargons, styles, genres, resulting in small or truncated repertoires;

(ii) *differential access to contextual spaces*, i.e. spaces of meaning-ratification where specific forms conventionally receive specific functions, resulting in differential capacity to map forms onto functions, in other words, in differential capacity to *interpret*.

Regulating both kinds of access is, in general, one of the functions of centring institutions (in the form of 'gatekeeping', see Gumperz 1982), and notably of the state – an institution which is, and remains, a major centring institution regulating access to linguistic form and contextualising spaces, even in the era of globalisation. We shall return to the question of the state as a regulator of access in chapter 8.

As we have seen, one of the features of communication in contemporary societies is the fact that it is often the object of intricate text trajectories: texts, discourses, images get shipped around in a process in which they are repeatedly decontextualised and recontextualised. In such processes, all kinds of mappings are performed, often deeply different from the ones performed in the initial act of communication. Consequently, categories or other features that did not occur as salient in the initial act were added to it in later phases. For instance, talk can be 'gendered', 'raced', 'classed' afterwards, by someone who was not involved in the initial act of communication (not only a fact of bureaucratic or other institutional practice but also a common feature of our own professional practices). Depending on the way in which access to contextual spaces is structured, lots of acts of communication are 'replaced' and given other functions – a process in which the initial functions often get removed (Mehan 1996).

Given the two dynamics of access, to forms and to contextual spaces, we have defined an axis of inequality. Inequality will occur whenever *pretextual gaps* occur: differences between capacity to produce function and expected or normative function (Maryns and Blommaert 2002; see also Hinnenkamp 1992). People enter communication events with pretextually marked resources and capabilities: resources and capabilities that have a particular 'load', a value in terms of the orders of indexicality in which they move into. Such pretextualities will condition what they can accomplish. Whenever the resources people possess do not match the functions they are supposed to accomplish, they risk being attributed *other* functions than the ones projected, intended, or necessary. Their resources fail to fulfil the required functions; speakers lose voice. Sometimes, this can amount to a simple and repairable misunderstanding, at other times however, it can be highly consequential. And, in the meantime, it may be wise to keep in mind that many misunderstandings, innocent or not, have their origin in inequality, not just in difference.

With pretextuality, we find ourselves clearly in the realm of 'invisible' contexts, contexts that influence language long before it is produced in the form of utterances and that define the conditions under which utterances can be produced, or fail to be produced – as we have seen, the absence of particular forms of discourse is also a relevant topic for a critical analysis of discourse. Pretextuality thus emphasises the evaluative aspect of Bakhtin's intertextuality, and it highlights the fact that every instance of language is both historically – *inter*textually – and politico-economically – *pre*textually – charged.

I shall argue in chapter 5 that this view does not preclude creativity. In fact, every semiotic act is intrinsically creative. At this point, however, it is important to underscore that every semiotic act is also oriented towards one or several centring institutions, the work of which may result in all kinds of remarkable social facts occurring simultaneously. An act of communication may break the rules of one order of indexicality by following the rules of another one. Thus, using Hip Hop jargon, or ironically adopting someone else's speech style, may be a transgression in the eyes of some, while it may be an accurate display of membership competence in the eyes of others. Such phenomena, often assuming the shape of a Bakhtinian carnival in which established roles and relationships are inverted, have often been seen as a form of revolt *against* norms. This is true, but only partially so. It is true to the extent that one assumes a social world dominated by only one set of rules; adopting a polycentric image of society shows a more complex and more nuanced picture in which a reaction *against* something is also a marker of *adherence* to something else. This has important effects on how we should perceive ideology and identities, and to this we shall devote more attention later.

To summarise my argument: if we want to understand voice, we have to look into mapping of form onto function, for mobility of resources is lodged precisely in the capacity to realise intended or conventional functions with resources across different contexts, to keep control over entextualisation processes. Such processes develop in reference to orders of indexicality that emanate from centring institutions, in a polycentric and stratified system that regulates access to resources as well as to contextualising spaces. Shifts across orders of indexicality as well as changes in such orders may cause rather drastic problems of understanding, of 'hearability' or 'readability'. Even if linguistically and pragmatically correct in terms of one particular order of indexicality, utterances may simply be not understandable in terms of another, or their perceived meaning may be quite different from the ones intended.

I shall now try to illustrate these phenomena. First, I shall examine some samples of discourse that got transferred from one geographical place in the world to another, and consequently from one set of orders of indexicality to another. Next, I shall investigate a case in which orders of indexicality dramatically changed due to historical circumstances, thus creating opportunities for voice but simultaneously causing problems of voice for those who did not 'move along' with the change, those who still spoke in the 'old' regime. Both types of data are characterised by displacement: in the first case, we are dealing with geographic displacement causing a shift in orders of indexicality; in the second case, we are dealing with historical displacement causing a similar shift. In both cases we shall see pretextual problems.

## 4.3 TEXTS THAT DO NOT TRAVEL WELL: INEQUALITY, LITERACY, AND GLOBALISATION

The first set of cases I shall discuss is that of written documents that are moved from one place to another across the world system. The places matter: the documents travel from the periphery of the world system, Sub-Saharan Africa, to one of its core regions, Western Europe. In this process of transfer, they move into a place with very different orders of indexicality, very different values attached to linguistic signs and messages. The documents travel from one set of 'placed' orders of indexicality to another; from one locally operational economy of signs to another.

The first text I shall examine is a handwritten letter addressed to me by a 16-year-old girl from Dar es Salaam, Tanzania. The girl, whom I shall call Victoria, is the daughter of a family I stayed with during field trips to Tanzania, and I first met her when she was 2. Her father is an academic, and she was in secondary school when she wrote the letter. Secondary education in Tanzania is done through the medium of English, while the majority of the pupils (and teachers) have either Kiswahili or other African languages as their mother tongue(s). In primary school, Kiswahili is the medium of instruction and pupils get English as a subject. Consequently, at the age of 16, Victoria would have had several years of 'deep' exposure to English. The girl is definitely a member of the local middle class, a class which uses proficiency in English as an emblem of class belonging (Blommaert 1999b). It is, in other words, an 'expensive' resource in Dar es Salaam.

Let us now take a look at her letter. What follows is a transliteration of the handwritten version, in which line breaks and graphic organisation are rendered as precisely as possible. All names except my own are pseudonyms.

**Example 1**

> 20/9/1999
> Dear!
> Uncle Jan
> How are you? I hope you
> The main aim of this letter is to tell
> you that, here in Tanzania, we have
> remember you so much. Dady, Mum, Uzuri
> Patrick, Furaha, and Victoria and other members
> like Kazili, Helena, Bahati, Fatima and
> and others. Other people forget to write for you
> a letter, geat all your family I don't
> have much to say. Sorry if you will
> came Tanzania we will go to beach
> BYe BYe From VICTORIA MTANGULA

A few comments are in order. When using a punitive and normative reading, the first thing that strikes the observer is the frequency of rather severe errors in the text at the level of grammar ('we have remember you so much', 'to write for you', 'if you will came Tanzania') as well as at the level of punctuation (absence of periods), orthography ('geat all your family', the alteration of upper and lower case symbols in the concluding line), and narrative style and control over literary-stylistic conventions (the awkward list of names dominating the letter, the separation of 'Dear!' and 'Uncle Jan', the unfinished sentence 'I hope you'). Victoria struggles with general literacy conventions in English; her control over the medium is incomplete. At the same time, her act of writing can best be seen as 'language display' (Eastman and Stein 1993): the mobilisation of the best possible resources for a specific act of communication. Given the particular relationship I had with Victoria (and given the references to the other family members *not* writing to me), the act of writing itself is loaded with indexicalities, constructing a relational identity of a 'good girl', someone who behaves and performs well, is probably among the best pupils in her age-group, and is worthy of compliments from her European Uncle. Victoria mobilises the maximum status resources within her reach: the best possible (school) English, the code of status and upward social mobility in Tanzania. And it is in that respect that the errors become important. Transplanted to an equivalent situation in Europe, and applying the orders of indexicality valid there, the code used by Victoria fails to index elite status and prestige. The value of this variety of written English in Europe is deeply different from the value it has in Dar es Salaam. The indexicalities of 'good girl' only work within a local economy of signs, one in which even a little bit of English could pass as good English.

The second example is in French but belongs to the same sphere. It is a school essay written by a pupil in the third year of secondary education from a school in Kinshasa, Congo, probably in 1997.[4] The pupil must have been approximately 13 years old, and s/he must have had exposure to French for a number of years. The medium of instruction in Kinshasa schools is French, and, while nobody should overestimate the intensity of educational involvement of children in Congo, the pupil clearly has had some years of schooling. French was the official language of Mobutu's Zaire (now Congo) and it was the language of colonial government. It was, and is, the prestige language, and access to French equals access to status and social mobility.

Judging from the texts of the essays, the teacher must have given the pupils the assignment to elaborate on whether the fall of Mobutu and the installation of the Kabila regime in May 1997 had had any effect on their lives. This is what the pupil wrote (again I use a transliteration in which the graphic features of the text are mirrored).

## Example 2

> commé moi je vu Rien a changé
> pour toute notre maison
> paR-ce que ju cas présent Il n'apas
> acomné a rengé la pays

The text is hardly understandable as a written document, and it is replete with orthographic and grammatical/lexical inconsistencies. Again we note the alteration of upper and lower case in writing and the absence of punctuation. But when the text is read aloud, it starts making sense. This is what I believe the pupil wrote, first converted into standard French and afterwards translated into English:

> Comme moi je l'ai vu, rien n'a changé
> pour nous tous,
> parce-que jusqu'à présent il n'a pas
> [?commencé] à arranger le pays

> The way I saw it nothing has changed
> for all of us
> because until now he hasn't
> started to organise ('arranger') the country

A striking feature of this text is the way in which writing proceeds on the basis of a spoken, vernacular variety of French. The pupil appears to have fundamental problems with conventional spelling for French terms which s/he probably uses in vernacular speech. Consequently, homophones from spoken French are written in symbols that carry crucial grammatical or lexical differences: 'arranger' is written as 'a rengé', for instance, or 'jusqu'à présent' is written as 'ju cas présent'. This pupil not only struggles with the practice of writing, s/he has very little access to the normative written codes of French. On top of that, s/he seems to be at pains to construct a narrative in the literate code: what we get is four lines of text on an event which, no doubt, must have left some impression with the pupil. But, again, we have to keep in mind that we are facing a literacy product produced by someone who has had access to French-medium education, and we have to take into account that this particular code could qualify as 'French' – 'bad French' perhaps – in a particular, 'placed' economy of signs. The text identifies a 13-year-old pupil demonstrating his/her control over the elite language, someone who should already have accumulated literacy experiences and who may even be a member-to-be of the literate urban lower middle class. Lifted out of that economy and transferred into another one, the text highlights the deficiencies and the other aspects that would qualify it as a 'non-text'.

This brings us to our final example, which is a written statement by a Congolese woman in her thirties, produced on a Belgian police form after being arrested for shoplifting. In Belgium, the accused have the right to produce their account of the events in writing and in a language of their choice. This form is then used both by the prosecution and by the defendant's lawyer, and it is a rather important document. In the procedure, it counts as 'the story of the accused', and if the defendant changes his/her account afterwards this may be seen as highly problematic and may jeopardise the defendant's case. It is therefore important to get the facts right in this written account. The Congolese woman chose to write in Lingala, and this is her text. Graphic features have been rendered here as in the previous two examples.

Example 3  ▰▰▰▰▰▰▰▰▰▰▰▰▰▰▰▰▰▰▰▰▰▰▰▰▰▰▰▰▰▰▰

> BaKANGI NGAI NAYIBI, eZALI YALOKUTA
> baKANGI NGAI na bilamba minei
> 4 Pantalon na yebi [nb]atu te moSuSu
> oyo baZALAKI na MAGASIN te

The Congolese woman produces four lines of Lingala written in a highly unstable orthography (note the frequent alteration between upper and lower case) and with corrections indicating insecurity about grammar and orthography. The text is also written in a colloquial variety of Lingala, with code-switching into French in two places ('pantalons' – pair of trousers, and 'magasin' – shop). Translated into English, this is what she writes (the French terms are left in italics):

> They caught me (because) I had stolen, that is a lie
> They caught me with four pieces of clothing
> 4 *pantalons* I don't know the other people
> who were with me in the *magasin*

This is hardly an account of events, and it is hard to imagine how a lawyer would build a solid defence on the basis of this written (official) version. The fact is that this woman has very little command of literacy conventions. She can write, in the sense of performing the activity of writing, but she has no access to a standardised orthography, a standard literate variety of the language, or the literate narrative skills that would allow her to construct a detailed, linear account of the events. The kind of literacy she deploys is probably enough for her to self-qualify as someone 'who can write', and most probably, the police officer would have asked her whether she could write, affirmation of which would have led to an invitation to write her account of the events on the police form. But it is clear that this degree of literacy falls short of what is expected from her in this particular context. The literacy that may be enough to get around in Kinshasa is dramatically insufficient in Belgium. The text has as its referent 'the story of the accused'; but moved into the kind of economy of signs characterising Belgian bureaucratic procedures it loses function and value. In fact, it is pretty worthless in that economy.

In each of these three examples, we have seen huge discrepancies between what linguistic resources and ways of using them mean in local environments – that of grassroots literacy in Africa – and what they mean in other, transnational environments in which they get inserted. The kind of literacy shown here is, I believe, widespread in Africa, and it characterises much of what exists in the way of literacy in the sub-elite strata of many African societies. In these societies, it may be quite sufficient to communicate adequately; in fact, it may even be an object of status and prestige. In the peripheries of the world, such literacy may be 'expensive' and exclusive. But once lifted out of these margins and placed into the value attribution system of the core of the world system, these forms of literacy lose their functions and get attributed new ones. From a rather high rank in their own hierarchies of signs and communication practices, they tumble down to the lowest ranks of others' hierarchies.

We are facing '*placed resources*' here: resources that are functional in one particular place but become dysfunctional as soon as they are moved into other places. This process of globalised flow creates difference in value, for the resources are being reallocated different functions. The indexical links between signs and modes of communication, on the one hand, and, on the other hand, social value scales allowing, for example, identity construction, status attribution, and so forth – these indexical links are severed and new ones are projected onto the signs and practices. Meanings disappear in the pretextual gap thus created. I would claim that such reallocation processes are central to the kind of flows that characterise globalisation. Consequently, a critical approach to discourse in the era of globalisation should look carefully into such processes of reallocation, the remapping of forms onto function, for it may be central to the various forms of inequality that also characterise globalisation processes.

## 4.4 INEQUALITY AND THE NARRATIVE ORDER

There is a long tradition of research on narrative in sociolinguistics and anthropology, and authors in that field have tended to emphasise that narrative is a privileged window on human experience: it is experience-as-told and as made social (Ochs and Capps 1996 provide an overview). Narrative, Hymes insists, is a universal function of language (1996: 115; cf. also Hymes 1975). But it has been overlooked as a format of knowledge production and reproduction because of its deep context-embeddedness, its often 'irrational' or emotive key, and its connection to non-generalisable individual experience. Despite this neglect of narrative, it continues to be one of the most common and widespread modes of human communication. In fact, to the extent that such distinctions make sense, it would not be unreasonable to see narrative as the 'basic', most 'essential', mode of human communication. People may have – but this remains to be explored – a 'narrative view of the world' (Hymes 1996: 112).

Narratives are never 'flat' but always structured into units, segments, episodes. Relations within and between such units are patterned and structured, and such forms of patterning reflect cultural ways of organising knowledge, orientations to knowledge and affect into discourse. Formal patterns, consequently, are part of 'content', and one of the key features of narrative is its performance-related character, i.e. the fact that it is brought about in aesthetic, formally elaborate kinds of activity often captured under the label of 'poetics' (Jakobson 1960; Hymes 1981, 1998; Johnstone 1990; Bauman and Briggs 1990; Briggs and Bauman 1992; Haviland 1996). Narrative, consequently, is usually replete with indexical elements – connections between linguistic-narrative form and context, situation, and social order. And, because of that, it is, of course, subject to various kinds of judgements and assessments by others, it is subject to norms, codes, and standards, and 'one form of inequality of opportunity in our society has to do with rights to use narrative, with whose narratives are admitted to have cognitive function' (Hymes 1996: 109).

I shall explore this theme by means of an analysis of a narrative produced as testimony during the hearings of the Truth and Reconciliation Commission in South Africa. After the collapse of the Apartheid regime and the election of Nelson Mandela as president of South Africa, the new government decided that it had to come to terms with its Apartheid past. It opted for a formula of pacification rather than revenge, and a central instrument in the symbolic pacification of the country was the construction of the Truth and Reconciliation Commission (TRC) chaired by Archbishop Desmond Tutu. The TRC started in 1996 by inviting testimonies from victims of human rights violation under the Apartheid regime. People were interviewed all over the country and a formidable body of evidence was collected. As a next step, public hearings were organised in a number of places in the country, where selected cases would be heard. These hearings were recorded by the South African Broadcasting Corporation and broadcast nationwide. There were two types of hearings: Amnesty hearings, during which perpetrators of human rights violations were offered the opportunity to tell their full and detailed story in return for amnesty; and Human Rights Violations hearings (HRV hearings) during which victims told their stories (Buur 2000; VanZanten Gallagher 2002; Ross 2003).

The TRC occasioned a historic shift in conditions for voice in South Africa. Stories of suffering and cruelty that were – necessarily – unspoken and unspeakable during the Apartheid era suddenly became central stories of the nation. The invisible was made visible; the marginal was given prominence: a set of completely new conditions for 'allowable' stories was introduced and caused a monumental series of dramatic, formative narrations. Yet not all stories that were told during the TRC hearings were produced under similar conditions, and the historic shift in conditions for narration did not mean that every narrator could accomplish narrations according to the new – implicit and evolving – narrative criteria.

Whenever we communicate we have expectations of iconicity: expectations about mappings of style and content; correspondences between ways of speaking and topics or domains. We are expected to adopt a 'serious' style when talking about serious topics; a funny one when talking about funny things. Failure or refusal to meet these expectations may be a source of, for example, humour, irony, or sarcasm; often it generates misunderstandings and wrong-footing. In a context such as the TRC where nuances and details were crucial for the reconstruction of a historical record of the past, failure to meet expectations of iconicity resulted in parts of the story not being 'memorable' or hearable, hence not becoming a resource for interpreting the experiences of the people who provided testimony.

In the HRV hearings, the overarching topic of the narratives produced by the witnesses was *suffering*. People told heartbreaking stories of violence, abuse, and loss of life and dignity. Along with a number of other themes (reconciliation, restoration of the community) suffering was explicitly thematised by the TRC officials, and witnesses were often directly invited to produce discourse that would orient to these themes. Typically, a witness would be called to the stand by the chairperson of the hearing (a TRC commissioner). The chairperson would briefly introduce the case, and would ask another commissioner – the 'facilitator' – to start questioning the witness. The structure of questioning (as well as the whole sequential structure of the hearings) was highly standardised. The witness would be invited

to tell a story; after that, the commissioner would ask a number of
follow-up questions and other TRC members would also be invited to
interrogate the witness. After that, the chairperson would conclude
the interview with a brief closing (often expressing sympathy for the
suffering and articulating ideals of peace and reconciliation).

One story that was particularly striking was that of Colin de Souza,
a young man from the Cape Town area. De Souza was not asked to
testify about one or some particular events: his testimony was about
a whole life of suffering and violence. De Souza got involved in the
armed struggle at the age of 15 when he became a member of the
Armed Wing of the ANC, and had been a victim of harassment, arrest,
violence, imprisonment, and torture ever since. His life had been all
but destroyed by the Apartheid conflict, and he still bore deep traces
of his past at the time of his testimony before the TRC, having severe
medical problems, difficulties in finding a job, and difficulties in his
personal life.

De Souza produced a long narrative. He did most of the talking,
often in long stretches triggered by questions from the facilitator,
Wendy Orr, and commissioner, Denzil Potgieter. His mother sat next
to him, and at one point she was asked to tell how Colin's tragedy had
affected the whole family. The framing of de Souza's story as a narrative
of suffering is also made explicit in the introduction by Wendy Orr:

> 'Colin you're a young man, but in your life, I think you've gone
> through experiences which people much-much older than you
> probably never ever dream of.'

Wendy Orr also elicits descriptions of suffering in other places, as does
Denzil Potgieter. We shall come back to this in greater detail below.
So the topic is clearly stated, and expectations of iconicity can be activated. The main problem, however, is that Colin de Souza doesn't meet
these expectations: he does not produce his narrative of suffering in
a style that flags the topic. There are few, if any, explicit expressions
of emotion. Colin de Souza doesn't cry, but tells his story in a composed, rather flat, and factual way, emphasising more the 'adventur-
ous' side of his experience than the devastating effects it had on his
life. At least, that is the first reaction the story triggers, based on commonsense interpretations of the contextualisation cues provided by de
Souza. On the basis of such readings of the story, de Souza's story is not
so much a story of deep suffering, but one of danger, excitement, fear,
kicks. Work is needed in order to interpret this story as a testimony
of how someone's life could be destroyed by the struggle. In rather
unexpected ways, suffering is a hidden narrative in Colin de Souza's

story. We need to uncover this hidden narrative and delve deeper into the structure of the story.

## Where is the suffering?

Colin de Souza is a skilled narrator who can produce elaborate event narratives in an even, balanced style, using a rather narrow and very stable range of intonation, pitch, and loudness features. His main key is factual, and even when he is asked explicitly to tell about suffering, he opts for a factual event-narrative style. He uses only very small features of style to mark certain parts of his story as more involved or more affect-laden. In three places of the hearing, Colin is explicitly asked to comment on forms of suffering. After an initial question on the conditions surrounding his first arrest, Colin embarks on a long, detailed and vivid event narrative. Wendy Orr (WO) interrupts him with the question:

> WO: 'Colin I am sorry to interrupt, did they assault you or torture you while they were questioning you?'

The answer produced by Colin consists first of a comment on violence, after which he shifts again into an excited event narrative on how he outwitted the police people. Similarly, after one of the most vivid and engaging parts of the story, Wendy Orr attempts to elicit comments on suffering:

> WO: 'I know you've only told us a small part of what you experienced in those five years and I am sorry that there is not time for us to hear more. But it's very obvious that a large part of your life was spent being harassed, detained, tortured, intimidated, threatened, imprisoned, how has that affected your life?'

Colin responds by providing an account of his life after the struggle: the impossibility of finding a job and the fact that he is physically and psychologically damaged. After his response, Wendy Orr invites Colin's mother to tell about the way in which Colin's problems have affected the lives of their families. A third explicit opportunity for Colin to talk about suffering is provided by Denzil Potgieter (DP) in a question following the main narrative:

> DP: 'Thank you, then just finally, briefly in your statement you made a statement to the effect that they hurt your father and your girlfriend.'

So efforts are being made to keep Colin de Souza on the track of 'suffering', from which he apparently deviates by using a vivid and excited event-narrative style.

The relation between epistemic and affective modes is a complex one. Biber and Finegan (1989: 93) coined the term 'stance' for complexes of lexical and grammatical expressions of attitudes, feelings, judgements, or commitment concerning the propositional content of a message, and demonstrated that different 'stances' could be distinguished ranging from 'emphatic expression of affect' to a 'faceless stance'. Labov (1984: 43–44) defined 'intensity' as 'the emotional expression of social orientation toward the linguistic proposition: the commitment of the self to the proposition'. And Haviland emphasised the symbiotic relationship between epistemic and affective modes: 'contending (or hedging or denying) the truth may be inherently argumentative and hence, by its very nature, *affective*' (1989: 59). So what we are looking for is mixtures of expression, in which *knowledge* is produced as well as *orientations to* knowledge expressed by means of affective, emotional stances. And we have to do this, as said above, within a narrow range of textual-stylistic markers characteristic of Colin de Souza's narrating style, using small contrasts between parts of the narrative as inroads into different orientations towards knowledge.

A close look at Colin de Souza's narrative reveals two small, hardly noticeable, features that may be used as such inroads into differing orientations. One the one hand, there are *pitch rises*, places where de Souza shifts into a louder, higher, and more agitated voice; on the other hand, there are clusters of *you know* hedges. Both occur in nonrandom ways. Other stylistic features of performance are rare, though they occur in places: repetitions, refrains, etc. Let us take a closer look at their distribution. Given the importance of small but observable detail here, I shall have to provide rather long extracts from the story. I shall use a so-called 'ethnopoetic' transcript aimed at rendering performance features of the oral narration. Such performance features are indicated by means of indentation (specifying relations between superordinate and subordinate narrative parts), italics (specifying reported speech), slashes (indicating pauses), and underlining (specifying pitch rises and/or 'you know' clusters) (Hymes 1981, 1996, 1998).

Case 1: de Souza gives an account of an interrogation, in which a policeman identifies himself as 'the Wit Wolf of the Western Cape'. The policeman acknowledges that he murdered a friend of Colin's ('Ashley' – Ashley Kriel) and threatens to kill Colin as well.

After they were finished with that two weeks with me eh that
interrogation at Elsies River police station,

they took me this <u>one</u> morning to a field in Bonteheuwel
where I had to show out where this arms cache were
      as they would call it a DLB that time,
          dead letter box eh
we <u>went</u> at five o'clock at that morning on the <u>fifteenth</u> of
   October 1987
we went to this field opposite the (?Machete).
The Security Police they were digging up that <u>whole</u> field,
apparently they found nothing
and eh there was this one boer
   all that I know about him,
   he said he was the wit wolf of the Eastern Cape/
He said to me
   *yes Porky eh*
   *I will necklace you=I will necklace you*
   *just the way I necklaced all the other comrades*
      *in=mainly in the Eastern Cape*
   *and/ you mustn't play jokes with us,*
   *this were=this is the spade that I hit Ashley with/*

<u>Case 2</u>: Colin tells a story of torture, in which at one point he is hung
upside down, causing extreme sensatory confusion.

so when they came in,
they saw that I was still conscious,
   they were expecting somebody after a half an hour to be
   unconscious,
so what they did is eh/
they undress me
and eh they chained me up,
     <u>you know</u> my feet,
     my hands to my feet
and they had a special chains <u>you know</u>,
     that they would use with the prisoners that is on
     awaiting trial <u>you know</u>,
     that chains <u>you know</u>
and they would chain me up on my feet and my hand
and put me up against this metal gate <u>you know</u>,
     this metal eh
and chained me up to that gate,
then start beating me with the batons over my head/
Van Brakel would pull my hair and/ <u>you know</u>
and eh/ they was <u>beating me till I was out.</u>
I don't know if it was the next day or if it was that night,

but I regained consciousness
    while I was laying hanging on that door,
        metal door and eh/
when I was regaining conscious
I=I=I thought to myself
    why=why am I seeing this people you know eh/ not the right
    side up,
        but you know eh/ the other way around you know
        I was// I don't know how to explain it now
but I was actually half way upside down you know

**Case 3:** Again Colin provides an account of torture involving repeated beatings and choking.

And then Du Plessis would just every time hit me with his fist
and say
    *jong go to hell with that,*
    *still giving you time to think over and plan*
and he would hit me so badly you know
    I would just lay on the ground
and then they put a chair against the door you know,
open the door
and they put the chair in the door
and they said to me
    *look here we want you stand on top of this chair*
    *because we want to take your height*
and eh without I knowing that Captain Du Plessis was standing
    on top of a table or a chair at the back side of this open door
and then he grabbed me around my neck
and choked me with his arm you know.
    Choked me all/
    till I was like out you know
and after that ten twenty minutes of beating up there,
they left me, you know
took me to a cell
and throw me=threw me in the cell there.

**Case 4:** Here a story is told of how comrades of Colin's chased him and attempted to kill him, believing that he had become a police informer.

and apparently at that time Jacques draw out a gun
    to force his way into the house
    like to shoot me/
and eh my father grabbed him
and there was a whole twist outside
and my brother-in-law/ eh he hit Jacques you know
and the gun fall=fall over the balcony right down you know
and they chased the group,

it was a group of youths
it was about <u>sixteen</u> of them <u>you know</u>.
    Some of them were with me in this/ in this trials of the
       BMW
and eh/ the chase went right around the street
and eh my father and my brother-in-law they arrived.
At that time I <u>had</u> a firearm/
    but it was for my own purpose.
I took out the firearm,
I put it underneath my jersey/
I went outside
    because I check
        now it's too dangerous to be inside the house.
      And I want to <u>move</u> now,
          out of the area.
As we were still standing outside to move eh
this group of comrades
and there was some gangsters also with,
they came <u>shooting</u> around the corner,
   <u>before</u> even they take the bend the shots was firing
and they were <u>shooting</u> and <u>throwing bricks</u>
and my mother and eh/ my father they ran into this/
and with my baby brother ran into this people downstairs
   house,
    that the=the=their surname were Brooks,
they ran into this house
and these people locked the door,
and <u>I</u> and my brother-in law Kevin Arendse was still outside/
   locked outside.
The people inside didn't want to open the door
and here these people were preparing to shoot/
   and/ eh/ there was like a <u>BIG</u> fight <u>you know</u>
and one guy he was still trying to=to cock the gun
but the gun <u>jammed</u> <u>you know</u>
and at that time as I was shouting open the door,
the people inside opened the door
and as my brother-in-law Kevin Arendse and I <u>ran</u> into the
   house,
and the door <u>closed</u>
the shots just went down
and the bullets ran through the doors and through the
   windows and all that.

<u>Case 5:</u> A very agitated part of a chase story, in which Colin again gets
shot at by security personnel.

   we drive through Mandalay
   and then they catch up against us,

Constable Kahn drove <u>right</u> in front of us
and as we passed through them into Mitchell's Plain,
   <u>without</u> knowing that they were having a helicopter
     monitoring us from the air <u>you know</u>.
Then they were chasing us right down (?Baden Powell) Drive
   as you take the=to turn into Swartklip.
As we took that road into Swartklip
   we were actually driving very fast <u>you know</u>,
    they couldn't catch up with <u>their</u> cars eh
I immediately see at the back of us
there was like this maroon eh metallic eh blue Alfa Romeo
came <u>right</u> from the back
   <u>very</u> fast
and this guy he was hanging out with a machine gun
and he was shotting at=shooting at our wheels.
And at that time they shot our wheels flat/
   <u>both</u> our back wheels were flat
and they shot through the windows eh
   the back windows were in,
   the front windows,
   all the windows of the car was in,
   the car started to burn,
and at that time
Van Brakel and his other Security cops had the time/ eh
   to=to=to come near us
and they were shooting just –
<u>you know</u> they were driving next to us <u>you know</u>
and shooting with the sixteen-shooters/ <u>you know</u>
but/ most of the koeëls=most of the bullets missed us by
   seconds.
I can remember I was sitting <u>low</u> in my seat
and the head cover of the seat <u>you know</u>
it was full of=full of bullets <u>you know</u>
   because the sponge <u>you know</u>, it grabbed some of the bullets
    there <u>you know</u>

<u>Case 6:</u> Colin tells about his medical condition as described to him by
an army doctor.

   and eh he said/
     I was tortured so severely <u>you know</u>
     that the stress built up on my eh=eh small brain <u>you know</u>
     because of keeping secrets and that stuff all in <u>you know</u>
     and it formed almost like a cancer in my brain,
     that's why all my hair,
     I lost all my hair <u>you know</u>
     during that time when I was in prison for that two years <u>you</u>
     <u>know</u>.

<u>Case 7:</u> Colin tells how, when he intended to file a complaint against a police officer, a senior officer confronted him with his own death certificate. Note that apart from pitch rises in 'shocked', Colin also uses repetitive patterns to stress the feeling of shock.

> And he showed to me eh a paper
> that was actually a death certificate
>> that was stamped and was being signed by the State Security branch,
>> the head of the State Security police branch.
>> I read the name
>> with the name of Viljoen/ on the signature/
> He showed it to my mother
> we all were <u>shocked</u>,
> he said
>> *here I am having all the other comrades' names,*
>> he named the names Ashley Kriel, Anton Fransch, Andrew November and Colin de Souza/
> And I was like <u>shocked</u> <u>shocked</u> for what this guy showed me
>> there at that office/
>> So eh/ during that <u>you know</u> the harassing us

## Discussion

Colin de Souza's event narratives are stylistically dense in the sense that he uses sequences of clauses introduced by 'and' or 'so' to mark rapid sequences of events. But they contain relatively few of the well-known markers of performance and affect: ethnopoetic patterns such as repetitions, pitch alterations, exclamations, or ideophones (see Hymes 1998 for a survey). So the places where he deviates stylistically from his main line of narration are salient and need to be looked at in greater detail. We singled out two features: pitch rises seen against a general pattern of flat pitch contours, and clusters of the hedge 'you know'. Both features, I would suggest, are features of performance and should be seen as markers of different 'intensity' in Labov's terms, different orientations towards what he tells.

These features occur in rather expected places: they occur whenever Colin de Souza narrates extremely disturbing events – torture scenes, being shot at, being assaulted by his friends, being diagnosed as very sick, being shown his own death certificate. The fact that they are salient is best understood when contrasted with places where they are absent. These features do not occur in most of the stories of arrest, interrogation, or escape, and they do not occur in the account of the terrible damage inflicted on his father and his girlfriend (the latter

underwent a forced abortion), an event which he tells in a composed style, marked with just one single repetitive pattern (indicated by ←):
Case 8:

> And eh my girlfriend she was pregnant=pregnant at that time
> and what they actually did is
> they sent her to this Dr Siroky at Bellville South
> and eh/ he actually gave her this abortion pills in/
>   they forced it into her ←
> and she knew/
>   because they forced in ←
> and after having her two days in detention,
>   she would start bleeding
>   and everything would come down
>   and they sent her home//

Ochs and Schieffelin (1989) drew our attention to the fact that affect markers are not a stable and closed category, but that any feature of talk can potentially serve affect-marking functions when it is stylistically contrastive with other features. Colin's story is a story of suffering disguised as an event narrative. The problem in detecting this suffering aspect of his story is that he does not use 'common' conventional markers of affect – the usual ethnopoetic patterns – but that he uses less visible stylistic markers to set out 'a moral universe' (Haviland 1989: 61) in his story. The question is why, and I can only offer a few conjectures in this respect.

## Suffering as a way of life

'Hidden transcripts' is a term introduced by James Scott (1990) to identify processes of resistance against hegemony. Classical treatments of hegemony often assume that hegemony proceeds by the incorporation of elite values, assumptions, and arguments into the consciousness of the oppressed – the adoption of 'orthodoxy' (see chapter 7 for detailed discussion). Against this view, Scott argues that, more often than not, what we meet are 'hegemonic appearances' or 'orthopraxy' (1990: 85). In fact, it is precisely the existence of a public transcript based on hegemonic appearances that makes hidden transcripts (containing very different and often opposing positions) invisible, obliterates resistance, and shapes an image of ideological incorporation. Upon closer inspection, we can see these 'hidden transcripts', the very different versions rooted in very different traditions of talking and thinking about topics and very often leading us into a more 'subcultural' view of particular representations of reality.

Colin de Souza displays emotion, but does so by means of unpredictable, rather unexpected, features of talk, small stylistic contrasts between parts of the story he tells. He aligns his story with the stylistic tradition of his Military Wing subculture: that of factual event narratives from which explicit emotion or accounts of suffering are all but elided. His narrative displays traces of the subcultural illegitimacy of suffering: the absence of explicit suffering markers defines Colin de Souza as a historical subject, setting him in the larger picture of Apartheid and indexing his role (and identity) of a member of the Military Wing in this larger picture. He was not a victim but a warrior. The history of unspeakability of suffering was a theme in many of the hearings, victims often referring to the silencing of stories of suffering performed by the Apartheid system. And, as seen above, the TRC hearings often used this motif as a crucial ingredient of the performances: for the first time, victims could tell their stories and receive legitimacy for their expressions of pain and anger. Colin de Souza, however, did not 'open up', he stuck to the codes of the hidden transcript, to the orders of indexicality of his subculture, a community of people in the Military Wing in which sacrifice was a central virtue, and for whom having beaten the system was the most important claim to glory. In his hearing, a hidden transcript is brought to the surface, full of codes of expression that do not match the new public transcript, and therefore easily misunderstood as a narrative *without* pain and suffering. It requires an effort to uncover his narrative as one in which pain and suffering are indeed expressed: they are expressed *subculturally*, not *culturally* in terms of the new post-Apartheid culture of recognition of suffering. Colin de Souza did not 'travel along' with the momentous shift in pretextuality conditions precipitated by the end of Apartheid.

## 4.5 CONCLUSIONS

The case studies demonstrate how particular resources can fail to perform certain functions when they are moved from one environment marked by particular orders of indexicalities into another such environment. These resources, consequently, appear to have restricted mobility: they may be adequate in one environment but not in another. Those who possess such resources fail to produce voice across contexts; pretextually, they are structurally disenfranchised. I say structurally, for what we encounter in such cases is not a matter of choice but of capacity. These people don't seek to be misunderstood, the misunderstanding is an effect of what they actually are capable of accomplishing, given their pretextual backgrounds. The next chapter will elaborate on this theme.

The phenomena discussed here account for what Jupp, Roberts, and Cook-Gumperz (1982) called the 'hidden process' of disadvantage through language. We are facing invisible contexts – pretexts – that will not show up in transcripts or recordings of interactions. They condition such interactions; they enable (or disable) speakers and predefine to some extent what *can* happen in such interactions. In conjunction with the comments made on contextualisation in the previous chapter, I thus hope to demonstrate that there is analytic virtue in addressing *sociolinguistic* issues in discourse analysis. The resources deployed by people are 'loaded' ones, they are not neutral, not perfect, not infinitely creative, flexible, and negotiable. Very often, they are clumsy, endangering, useless. Resources that are perceived to function in one way actually function in the opposite way because of different pretextualities. The request to the Congolese lady in example 3 above to write her account of the events leading to her arrest is based on excellent intentions grounded in a firm culturally encoded belief that writing is empowering and that it provides people with the opportunity to produce a lasting, consequential, thoughtful discourse artefact. In the case we discussed, writing was actually disempowering. It exposed the Congolese woman to various kinds of attributions relating to herself and her account of the events – attributions that definitely created a negative impression with the police.

A critical analysis of discourse needs to start where the conditions for discourse are being formed: in sociolinguistic systems marked by authority and indexically attributing functions to linguistic forms. If we overlook this stage of analysis, we shall either fail to spot crucial phenomena of inequality, or mistakenly locate them in the detailed analysis of single instances of communication. If we take it on board, we may be able also to address the absence of particular discourse events or the fact that some discourse events *systematically* take the same course, regardless of speakers' intentions or creativity. In sum, we may be able to see language as a *systemic* phenomenon, a phenomenon that is part of a general system, a regime we usually call society.

## SUGGESTIONS FOR FURTHER READING

I am strongly influenced by Hymes (1996) in my views on linguistic inequality, and by Michael Silverstein's work (e.g. 1977, 1979, 1998, 2003a) on indexicality. On that topic, see also Hanks (2000) and

Mertz and Yovel (2000). Readers with some ambition and stamina will read Hanks (1990). Schieffelin, Woolard, and Kroskrity (1998), Kroskrity (2000), and Gal and Woolard (2001) are landmark collections on language ideologies. The last book discusses the connections between language ideologies and social patterns of power, authority, and inequality, and this topic is also wonderfully elaborated in Bauman and Briggs (2003). Obviously, Bourdieu (1991) is always a good choice as well in respect to this topic. On narrative, Ochs and Capps (1996) provide a useful starting-point. Hymes (1981, 1996, 1998) are the basic sources for ethnopoetic analysis.

# 5   Choice and determination

## 5.1  INTRODUCTION: CHOICE OR VOICE?

Many traditions in the study of language in society take the creative, negotiable features of human interaction and meaning-production as their points of departure, often in the form of unspoken assumptions, which becomes apparent in the use of a terminology emphasising (rational) choice, strategic moves, preferences in interactional organisation, and so forth. When communicating, people 'choose' from a range of options, they 'select' discourse forms deemed appropriate in the particular context, and they consciously 'plan' the sequential moves, either by 'choosing' to 'follow rules' or by 'flouting' these rules. We have already mentioned H. Paul Grice's influential discussions on 'conversational maxims' (Grice 1975) as a case in point. A lot of conversation-analytic terminology betrays similar assumptions (e.g. 'preference organisation' leading to 'preferred' or 'dispreferred' moves in a conversation; see, for example, Levinson 1983: chapter 6); theories of speech comprehension such as Relevance Theory (Sperber and Wilson 1986) see understanding as a selection of context/meaning out of a range of possible alternatives; and more specific sociolinguistic theories also emphasise choice, selection, and even rational calculation as basic to human communication. This is notably the case in some models of code-selection and code-switching, where speakers are supposed to calculate the relative advantages and disadvantages of shifts into particular codes (e.g. Myers-Scotton 1993).

I am sure that some of this terminological effort to emphasise the (relative) freedom of communicating people is a matter of widely accepted conventions for social-scientific writing about people in societies. Many people who use such terminology would readily accept that their terms do not accurately or comprehensively describe social reality. But the point is that we are probably meeting an ideology of scholarly perception here – a 'professional vision' in Charles Goodwin's (1994) terms, a way of seeing and decoding reality-as-we-know-it. It is also a boundary of critical analysis beyond which we just accept a particular state of affairs as given. This chapter starts from the understanding that we need to bring this issue to the level of conscious theorising, for it may be fundamental to understanding what people do with language and what language does to them. The issue is, I believe, central to an understanding of language and inequality, hence indispensable for an attempt to arrive at a critical analysis of discourse. We need to be more precise in our descriptive expressions of the dynamics of communication in social life.

This chapter extends the argument developed in the previous chapter. The main point will be that a lot of what we observe in human communication is not a matter of freedom, choice, or creativity, but that it is constrained by normativities, *determined* by the general patterns of inequality discussed in the previous chapter. This, I shall argue, does not eliminate creativity, choice, or freedom from an analysis of discourse; it situates individual agency in a wider frame of constraints and thus, paradoxically, brings it analytically sharper in focus. People do indeed creatively select forms of discourse, but *there is a limit to choice and freedom*. It is the interplay between creativity and determination that accounts for the social, the cultural, the political, the historical in communicative events – the connection between agency and structure, or micro-events and macro-relations and patterns in society.

I shall start by discussing a number of key concepts that can help us decode, imagine, and understand the phenomena discussed here. I shall explore the analytical purchase of Michel Foucault's notion of 'archive' and Raymond Williams' view of creative practice, connecting both concepts to some of the elements gathered in the previous chapters. Next, I shall offer a case analysis illustrating the interplay between creativity and determination; and finally I shall come back to questions of the world system.

## 5.2 THE ARCHIVE

Michel Foucault's work has been influential in CDA, mainly through the incorporation of some of his views on discourse in the theoretical framework developed by Norman Fairclough (esp. Fairclough 1992a).[1] Rightly so: Foucault's œuvre indeed offers a wealth of theoretical suggestions, both for conceptualising discourse and for analysing it in conjunction with knowledge, power, and the historical rise of institutions (Dreyfus and Rabinow 1982; Deleuze 1989; Martín-Rojo and Gabilondo-Pujol 2000). The conjunction between the various (usually

separated) elements is important. Discourse cannot be isolated from
the rest of Foucault's arguments on knowledge, power, and institutions, nor from the complex ways in which he situates his arguments
on an axis of synchronicity and history. It is often forgotten: Foucault
was very much a public intellectual deeply concerned with ongoing
debates in French society. His work was an example of 'critique' in
the sense outlined in the introduction to this book: the analyses were
critical materials for a debate about the present, about contemporary
French society, an understanding of which in Foucault's eyes required
an analysis of the way in which it came into being. The 'diagnostic'
about contemporary French society needed to be based on an 'analytic' of the past (Deleuze 1989). The relevance of his work for the
study of discourse needs to be seen in this light. Foucault presses us
to see actually occurring discourse as firmly and inextricably embedded in dimensions of social being and social organisation that are
often separated from it, and he forces us to see occurrences of discourse as intrinsically historical, as events that are *occasioned* and
*enabled* by histories of becoming. More on this will be said in the next
chapter.

It is at this point that I wish to turn to a concept which is rarely mentioned in discourse-related studies: *the archive*. The concept is pivotal
in Foucault's *Archaeology of Knowledge* (1969, 2002), a book in which he
thematised discontinuities in the history of ideas: 'the problem is no
longer one of tradition, of tracing a line, but one of division, of limits;
it is no longer one of lasting foundations, but one of transformations
that serve as new foundations, the rebuilding of foundations' (2002: 6).
Observing that such discontinuities were rife and that, consequently,
historical analysis needed to assume discontinuity as a core feature of
analysis, a number of theoretical issues arise with regard to how such
discontinuities can be identified and analysed. What is needed first,
according to Foucault, is to 'unthink' existing continuities in the history of ideas and reduce such a history to its raw material: statements.
Thus, '[o]ne is led . . . to the project of a *pure description of discursive
events* as the horizon for the search for the unities that form within it'
(2002: 29–30, italics in original; cf. also 2001a: 724–759). This, Foucault
insists, is not a linguistic approach:

> The question posed by language analysis of some discursive fact or
> other is always: according to what rules has a particular statement
> been made, and consequently according to what rules could other
> similar statements be made? The description of the events of
> discourse poses a quite different question: how is it that one
> particular statement appeared rather than another? (2002: 30)

In other words, what is it that occasioned particular statements? The answer lies in the *relations between discursive events*, the way in which such events can be seen as belonging together in 'discursive groups that are not arbitrary, and yet remain invisible' (2002: 32). This investigation leads him through several chapters that can be easily misread as elements of a formal theory of (linguistic-textual) discourse, until he introduces his highest-level concept: the archive.

Foucault first rounds up his arguments from previous chapters by saying that the 'positivity' (i.e. the real existence) of a discourse (e.g. medical discourse) characterises its historical unity and explains why it works the way it does. Dispersed statements, individual books, and œuvres

> communicate by the form of positivity of their discourse, or more exactly, this form of positivity (and the conditions of operation of the enunciative function) defines a field in which formal identities, thematic continuities, translations of concepts, and polemical interchanges may be deployed. This positivity plays the role of what might be called a *historical a priori* (2002: 143, italics in original)

Thus, historically, such discourses exist, and they exist in a particular configuration which is regulative and organises its functions:

> we have in the density of discursive practices, systems that establish statements as events (with their own conditions and domain of appearance) and things (with their own possibility and field of use). They are all these systems of statements (whether events or things) that I propose to call *archive*. (2002: 145, italics in original)

What follows next is a long series of elements of a definition of the archive (a well-known stylistic feature for those familiar with Foucault's work). I shall give the full list, for all of them matter. One should keep in mind that Foucault is trying to establish a *historical* object here, not a linguistic one. Historical analysis has hitherto focused either on 'meaning' (i.e. what a text says) or on people (i.e. who said something). Foucault suggests that the reason for discursive events and the occurrence of particular discursive 'things' (we would say, text-artefacts) resides in

> the system of discursivity, in the enunciative possibilities and impossibilities it lays down. The archive is first the law of what can be said, the system that governs the appearance of statements as unique events. But the archive is also that which determines that all these things said do not accumulate endlessly in an amorphous mass, nor are they inscribed in an unbroken linearity, nor do they disappear at the mercy of chance external accidents; but they are

> grouped together in distinct figures, composed together in
> accordance with multiple relations, maintained or blurred in
> accordance with specific regularities . . . It is that which, at the very
> root of the statement-event, and in that which embodies it, defines
> at the outset *the system of its enunciability*. . . . [I]t is that which defines
> the mode of occurrence of the statement-thing; it is *the system of its
> functioning*. . . . [I]t is that which differentiates discourses in their
> multiple existence and specifies them in their own duration. (2002:
> 145–146, italics in original)

And finally:

> between tradition and oblivion, [the archive] reveals the rules of a
> practice that enables statements both to survive and to undergo
> regular modification. It is *the general system of the formation and
> transformation of statements*. (2002: 146)

Therefore, the archive is the key to describing the discontinuities in the history of ideas, for 'its threshold of existence is established by the discontinuity that separates us from what we can no longer say, and from that which falls outside our discursive practice' (2002: 147). The archive allows Foucault to describe the 'local' discourses that can enter into a history of struggle for power/knowledge.[2]

Foucault offers a historical argument, not a linguistic one. But he expresses concerns that are central to what I see as critical analysis of discourse, and his concerns remind us of some of the concepts and arguments discussed earlier and in a literature more familiar to scholars in the field of language in society. Let me try to summarise and convert his argument in terms of the discussions in the previous chapters.

Foucault addresses the issue of macro-sociological forces and formations that define and determine what can be said, expressed, heard, and understood in particular societies, particular milieux, particular historical periods. These largely invisible contexts of discourse operate both at the level of discursive events – communicative behaviour – and at the level of the discursive product – the text-artefact, the document. And the effect of their operation is to create and impose boundaries of what can be meaningfully (functionally) expressed within the scope of the archive.[3] Whenever we speak, we speak from within a particular *regime of language* (the title of Kroskrity 2000). The effect of this is hardly a matter of individual awareness. In a formulation reminiscent of some of Pierre Bourdieu's statements on 'habitus', Foucault says: 'it is not possible for us to describe our own archive, since it is from within these rules that we speak' (2002: 146). This general idea

of invisible or only partially visible (macro) discursive systems imposing constraints on what people can do with language has been central
to the discussions in the previous chapters, and it can be connected
to concepts such as orders of indexicality, intertextuality, entextualisation, voice, and pretextuality in such a way as to provide a better
historical grounding for these concepts.

The orders of indexicality discussed in chapter 4 appear to operate
*within an archive*, a historical 'system of the formation and transformation of statements' in Foucault's terms, and they should be seen as
the empirical side of such a system. The system operates at the lowest level by imposing 'conventional', normative indexical meanings to
utterances and communicative events, a task usually fulfilled by centring institutions such as the state, schools, role models, peer groups,
cultural icons. The historical discontinuities Foucault emphasised create new archives, new rules for the formation and transformation of
statements, but they need not eliminate older existing orders of indexicality, as we saw in the example of Colin de Souza's TRC hearing in
chapter 4. One can speak within a (new) archive but do so while orienting to obsolete orders of indexicality, and so be *partially* understandable. Thus, orders of indexicality and archives must be seen as
layered but not necessarily coterminous, the former pertaining to the
immediate and meso-level operation of discourse, the latter to the
macro-historical level. We shall come back to this in the next chapter.

As for intertextuality and entextualisation, we see similar effects.
The notion of archive allows us to assume that intertextuality and
entextualisation are not unbounded, infinite processes of creative
insertion, but historically situated processes of insertion into a particular regime of language, a particular archive. Thus, we now have a
better view of how intertextuality and entextualisation processes are
historical processes. They represent moves of text across historically
delineated spaces of 'formation and transformation of statements'. The
same applies to voice and pretextuality: the capacity to produce 'understandable' utterances is a capacity to speak from 'within' an archive
and in reference to a particular order of indexicality related to that
archive. It is, at the highest historical level, the capacity to produce
meanings that fit a particular archive. Voice and pretextuality involve
historical positioning.

The main advantage of the concept of an archive, however, is that
it reminds us of the limits within which discourse operates, of the
constraints on choice and creativity in discourse. These limits are historical but, following Foucault, this immediately entails that they are
political, social, and cultural.

## 5.3 CREATIVE PRACTICE AND DETERMINATION

Given these limits and constraints, how do we conceive of creativity? What is the scope and range of creativity? The message offered by Foucault may sound somewhat gloomy: we are not all that free and operate within boundaries of the sayable and the hearable. But that does not, of course, eliminate creative practice from analysis; on the contrary, it brings it sharper in focus.

We shall have to distinguish between various kinds of creativity. On the one hand, there is the observation that every discourse event is absolutely unique and *creates* meanings never before created, though entailed from, conventionalised meaning-potential (Silverstein 1977). These processes we have seen at work in our discussion of contextualisation: people 'brought along' various capabilities for making sense, but sense still needed to be made, to be 'brought about' in the interaction itself (Hinnenkamp 1992). So discursive practices are inherently creative, for the meanings that are (dialogically) constructed cannot be explained by reference to the latent potential of the speakers alone. I consider this a given, and the discussion here should not be read as a denial of this kind of creativity. But apart from this 'local' creativity, there is the question of 'translocal' creativity, of which we now know that it is severely constrained by several higher-than-local factors. The first kind of (local) creativity has to be set against, and within, the second (translocal) one, which is perhaps better called 'innovation'. In order to elucidate this, I shall turn to Raymond Williams (1965, 1973, 1977).

Like Foucault, Williams develops a primarily historical problematic. Williams' views on creative practice have to be set against a wider questioning of matters of consciousness in the emergence of capitalist societies. These questions he shared with other 'New Left' scholars such as Perry Anderson, Terry Eagleton, Rodney Hilton, and Edward P. Thompson, and they were focused on the relationship between the so-called 'base' and the 'superstructure' in Marxist theory as well as on the possibility of a Marxist, Gramscian theory of ideology and culture (Williams 1973; Anderson 1977; Kaye 1984).[4] Reacting against then-dominant interpretations of Marxism centred on economic determinism they offered a more 'humanist' reading of the old question of 'social being and social consciousness', the way in which superstructural phenomena such as ideas, belief systems, ideologies, and culture related to economic and political-historical processes. E. P. Thompson (1968; see also 1978, 1991) developed the famous thesis that the English working class was, on the one hand, generated by the objective conditions of emergent capitalism, but, on the other hand, 'made itself' into a class because of the fact that capitalism produced particular experiences among workers, which translated into class consciousness and a self-imagination by 'objectively determined' workers as a 'subjectively determined' working class. It was the emergence of such consciousness and self-imagination that allowed workers to define themselves as a community, a working *class*, and to engage in class struggle.

This meant that the supposedly linear connection between 'objective' relations of production and political-historical dynamics of class and class struggle needed to be seen in a new light, as mediated by symbolic, semiotic, community-forming practices (for which one could use terms such as 'culture' or 'ideology'). It also meant that such practices were now a crucial object of study, of considerable theoretical relevance to the development of a new Marxism. Williams played a major role in this development as a scholar of literature and cultural history. His work addressed the 'cultural forms' of class, class stratification, and class struggle, as sedimented in writing and 'creative practice' in general.

Creative practice was a central topic in his œuvre. Expanding and revisiting a discussion started in *The Long Revolution* (1965), he summarises the issue as follows in *Marxism and Literature* (1977: 212):

> Creative practice is thus of many kinds. It is already, and actively, our practical consciousness. When it becomes struggle – the active struggle for new consciousness through new relationships that is the ineradicable emphasis of the Marxist sense of self-creation – it can take many forms. It can be the long and difficult remaking of an inherited (determined) practical consciousness: a process often described as development but in practice a struggle at the roots of the mind – not casting off an ideology but confronting a hegemony in the fibres of the self and in the hard practical substance of effective and continuing relationships. It can be more evident practice: the reproduction and illustration of hitherto excluded and subordinated models; the embodiment and performance of known but excluded and subordinated experiences and relationships; the articulation and formation of latent, momentary, and newly possible consciousness.

Williams offers us a view of creativity here which is *determined*. Creativity develops in relation to – often as a struggle against – 'inherited practical consciousness', i.e. a hegemony sustained by 'objective' social relationships. But this notion of determination is not static but *elastic*, so to speak. Determination generates both 'push' and 'pull' forces, forces that pull someone into the existing hegemonies, and forces that push someone out of these hegemonies (cf. Williams 1973). Creative practice, then, is something that has to be situated *in the borderline zone of existing hegemonies*. It develops within hegemonies while it attempts to alter them, and so may eventually effectively alter them by shifting the borders and by creating new (contrasting) forms of consciousness; it produces 'supplements' to what is already in the 'archive', so to speak. The centre of this process is the individual agent, a subject often living with idiosyncratic ideas and concepts, fantasies and nightmares, who out of his/her own personal experience in society starts to feel that dominant understandings do no longer work.

For the analysis of literature, this has considerable consequences; for one thing, the traditional question 'what did this author do to this form' can be 'reversed, becoming what did this form do to this author?' (Williams 1977: 192). We have already translated this question here as that of the tension between what people do with language and what language does to them. The point we need to understand here is that the first kind of creativity mentioned above – local, entailing creativity – is very often not innovative, not creative in the second sense, but something that develops within boundaries of hegemonies, the boundaries of Foucault's archive. We could go even further: we often seem to consider 'creative' (in the first sense) that which is *not* 'creative' in the second sense of the term. It becomes creative because it is measurable against normative hegemonic standards, because it creates *understandable* contrasts with such standards.

There is a very practical import to this in the field of globalisation as well, for we may be facing new issues of creativity and determination here. The transfer of texts from one environment to another also causes shifts in judgements of creativity, as outlined above, and thus also in the capacity to be perceived as creative. This phenomenon may explain why forms of discourse that are eminently creative in the first sense of the term – think of the letter by Victoria discussed in the previous chapter – may not be recognised as such when lifted out of their original regime and placed into another one. As I argued in chapter 4, this process causes a pretextual gap between orders of indexicality valid in the locus of text production and other orders of indexicality valid in the locus of reception and uptake. We can now see that it also falls outside of the borders of our hegemonies, or rather, that our hegemonies force it into patterns of similarity and contrast that do not apply to the text. And seen from within these hegemonies, the text is not creative but 'wrong'.

In what follows, I shall illustrate the complex interplay of creativity and determination with an analysis of documents typologically similar to that of Victoria. Again, we shall have a look at grassroots literacy from sub-Saharan Africa produced in the context of globalisation processes. We shall see how an act of literacy, that may from one perspective be seen as creative and meaningful, is turned into a failure to communicate by a refusal to consider it as non-hegemonic, as 'innovative' in the sense outlined above.

## 5.4 CREATIVITY WITHIN CONSTRAINTS: HETERO-GRAPHY

The data I shall discuss here came to me by 'structured accident': a coincidence conditioned by my social position. In my capacity of professor of African linguistics and sociolinguistics, I am summoned rather frequently by official services – the police, the Prosecutor's office, the immigration and asylum services – to provide linguistic expertise on African languages. Over the last number of years, asylum applications have become a major domain in which African text material is being produced in the form of statements, testimonies, and so forth. Thus, in 2001 I received the set of seven documents given below.

The request added to the documents was to 'translate these documents into Dutch' – a request in itself speaking to the pervasiveness of textualist ideologies. The request came from the Prosecutor's office and, though I was not (and never am) informed about the specifics of the case (apart from the cursory mentioning of a *male* subject), I immediately noticed that this was a rather typical document from an asylum application. The applicant had claimed to be from Burundi. Being from a country suffering from war or civil war is an advantage in the Belgian asylum procedure (which is highly selective and has the highest rejection rate in the EU: approximately 96 per cent). As so often, the applicant had no official documents substantiating his claim to Burundese citizenship, and the authorities, almost automatically, refused to accept this claim and demanded proof. The assignment, in this case, was to produce 'as much information about his country as he possibly could'. The product of this exercise would then be subject to an examination as to its 'credibility' (a common practice in asylum applications: see Blommaert 2001b). As seen in earlier examples, this examination relies heavily on textualist criteria of coherence, transparency, correctness – in short, those discourse features which we tend to associate with 'truth'.

As for formal features: we are confronting a heterogeneous collection of documents here, with different authors (or, at least, *scriptores*). The first five pages of the text are on official police case stationery, recognisable from the case register number and page number at the top right corner of the paper. The two remaining pages are not numbered, less structured, and probably a set of 'notes' separate from the more structured text. Furthermore, the first four pages are in one handwriting – Author A – and highly structured; the notes on document 6 are clearly written by someone else – Author B – and are more messy. The map (document 5) and the notes scribbled above the address on document 7 are authored by yet another 'scriptor' – Author C. Fragments of Author B's handwriting also appear in the first four documents (see, for example, the bottom of document 1) as well as at the top of the map, document 5. We are witnessing traces of different stages of collaborative text-production, with Author B as the 'desk editor' filling in and correcting here and there. Yet the whole set of seven pages was sent to me as one document.

I shall now embark on two series of reflections: the first one on how we must appraise the function of these documents; the second one (deriving from the first) on how to comprehend such documents against the background of general, different, regimes of literacy on a worldwide scale.

## Documents made for reading?

In a society saturated by literacy, the typical set of activities connected to written language is 'reading': a complex of physical and cognitive actions organised so as to extract 'meaning' from a written text. The purpose of writing is to be read. The relation between writing and reading is assumedly direct and unmediated: one 'reads what is written'. If things are not written, they are not made for reading: few people would qualify the perceptual activity organised around a photograph, a building or a painting as 'reading'. We *read* written text; we *look at* photographs, buildings and paintings.[5]

This unmediated one-to-one view has been challenged by several scholars (see, in particular, the collection of essays in Boyarin 1992). What is understood by 'reading' can differ across communities and contexts, and across genres: we read an academic paper differently from a poem or a newspaper. Some documents are designed for particular kinds of reading – in fact, what we understand by 'genre' in writing may reflect in *genres of reading* as well. Looking at the documents under scrutiny here, we already sense that the question whether

Bijlage aan P.V. nr. BG. 55.26.100561/91

## <u>Rais</u>

<u>Rais</u> wa kwanza alietawala alikua MIChombero 1966 (3)
wa pili Ndaye Melkior alitawala kwa mezi mitu
baadae aliuuawa na wanajeshi wa Tutsi ndihi ya
Julu Ndadae alikua (Mohutu).
Baada ya hapo akaja Cypria ntanyamira nae aliu-
ma kwa ajali ya ndege pamoja na rais aliekua rais
wa rwanda habyarimana walipokuo walirejea mkutanani
Arusha T.Z, baada ya hapo akachukua "Sylvester
Ntibantunganya na akapinduliwa na Meje "Pierre
Buyoya" Lakini hakuuuwa.

Chuo kikuu kipo Mutanga (SUD)
Kinaitwa "Kampis Mutanga"
(Bujodaya)

## <u>majibu au mitaa mengine</u>

Nyagabiga ni Sehemu ya watutsi Sehemu hujo yamefany
ka navaji mengi ya wahutu wakaoishi hapo
Chini ya nyagabiga ni Bwiza Chini ya Burito ni Buyenzi
Bwiza Sehemu hiyo yamesanyika mavaji mengi ya watutu
wahutu wakaoishi wengi hapo ni tutsi
Buyenzi Buyenzi ni mtaa wa washuahili, hapo
ni weshuahili wengi utawapata hapo na wengine
hata kifansa na kirundi hawajui
Mbele ya hotel "Novotel" kuna bara
mbili zimepita hadi Chuo kikuu "Kampis Mutanga"

## <u>Sehemu muhimu</u>

Ikulu ya Rais ipo karibu na kiwanja Cho mpira F.F.B
ziwa Tanganyika lipo Avenii de Plage.
Unarija na F.F.B, Ufa Avenii de State

## <u>Timu za mpira</u>

Timu ya Taifa inaitwa "INTAMBA"
time nyengine ni "Vitalo" Inter star

## <u>Museu</u> (makumbusho)

Museu vivant ipo Avenii du 13 october
<u>Independece</u> (Uhuru)
Imepata Uhuru tarehe 1.7.1962 Kutoka kwa belgium

Ntanyamira died - 6/4/94

**Document 1**

Bijlage aan P.V. nr BG.55.26.1.0056.1/01    B(2.3/6

**1** Mikoa 16

① Bujumbura, ② Gitega
③ Ngozi ④ Kirundo
⑤ Makamba ⑥ Kayanza
⑦ Muramvya ⑧ Bururi
⑨ Cibitoke (Khibitw) (10) Remonge
(11) Rutana (12) Bubanza
(13) Ruvubu

**Miji 11**

(sw 1) Buyenzi ③ Bwiza †
3) Ngagara (4 Jabe T
5) rohero ⑥ Kinama
T 7) Kamenge ⑧ Kanyosi
9) Mutanga (N) 10 Mutanga (
T 11 Nyagabiga

**2** Milima

Teza, Heha, Twinyoni
{Nyambuye, Bohanga}
milima ya bujumbura

Mito

Ruvubo ndahanguwa
Kanyosha rusizi
uliopita buyenzi

**3** Magazeti za Serikali

Ubumwe kwa maandishi ya Kirundi
Gazeti lenigine la Serikali limeandikwa kwa Kifaransa

Kitambulisho

Kinaitwa Karanga mundu ratigi ya Kijani kwa K
2 cha Simba

**4** Pesa  Zimeitwa Burundi franc

1000 picha ya ngombe watatu
100 " " prince Lois Rwagasore
50 picha ya mto anapiga ngoma tatu
20 picha ya mtu yoko noso uchi kavaz robega (red)
Coens (10) na (tano)(5) simba
10 - Ramani (green) Hotel

**5** Novotel ⟶ zipo karibu na kiwanja cha mpira cha P.P
MERIDIAN
Albatros — karibu na Busee primary school

**6** Sehemu Muhimu

Mtambo wa redio upo Kabondo
Ikulu ya rais ipo karibu na kiwanja cha mpira
cha Prince Lois Rwagasore

Pesa

**7** 5000 ina picha ya benki kuu na bandari (green + white)
500 Cikumbuki Rwagasore

**Document 2**

BLZ 4/6

Bijlage aan P.V. nr BG.55.26.100561/02

Mbuga za wanyama
Ruvubu na Kibira
Pleti namba za magari ~~ya binafsi~~
1 magari ya binafsi,
pleti nyeupe namba nyekundu
pleti namba za magari ya serikali
pleti namba nyekundu mzandishi meusi
Namba zinzenzia BR.B.N BD B.U BA
Mabasi
Kamponi ya mabasi inaitwa OTRACO
Vituo vya mabasi vipi Prince Lois Rwagasore
Wimbo wa taifa
(nzujoa Kidogo) Borondi buacho Borundi buhire

HOSPITA
1 Rua Khalid ipo Kamenge } 6.9
2 Rejee. Charles ipo Buyenzi
Clinic Prince Lois Rwagasore ipo mjini

Masoko
Soko mjinga bara bara ya 19 Buyenzi
Soko mjinga lipo bara bara 8 "
Soko Kuu lipo Shosii Prince Lois Rwagasore Buyenzi
Posta
Posta ipo Kwenye Kona ya Avenci du Comerce na Boulevard Lumumba
Viwanda
Kiwanda Cha Sigara Kinaitwa Supa match
Kiwanda Cha ngdo " Kotebu
Kiwanda Cha Chai " CK BUKIPO
Kiwanda Cha bia
bia zenyewe Primus Amstel

CNDD, (PP, RPB) Tutsi
/
Hutu

**Document 3**

Bijlage aan P.V. nr BG.55.26.10056/61

*Vyama*

FRODEBU                          UPRONA

Kwa na Hutu                      Kwa watusi

NYEUPE →                    NYEUPE →

← KIJANI

↑ NYEKUNDI

<u>Makabila</u>

Makabila yapo matatu (3)
Hutu 85%    TUTSI 14%    TWA 1%

<u>POLISI</u>

Wanavaa nguo Khaki blou bahari
Vituo vyao vinaitwa Sebokuve
Askari wa Kuzuia fujo wanaitwa Jandarma

<u>TAXI</u>

rangi yake blou Chini juu nyeupe
daba dala zinaitwa Bisi hazina rangi maalum

<u>Mitaa</u>

1. Prince Luis Ruagasore
2. Avenii de la Dierre ngenda ndumwe
3. Avenii de la Univasity
4. Avenii du Opital
5. Shosii du People Burundi
6. Boulevard de la Uprona
7. Boulevard Lumumba
8. Avenii du 13 October
9. Avenii du 28 November

<u>School</u>

1. Jumuiya ipo bara bara ya 8
2. Stela ipo Karibu na Kanisa la regine Mundi
3. Atene ipo Karibu na duka le Viatu
4. BASEE ipo Buyenzi, Karibu na hotel Albatros

<u>SEKONDARY</u>

SAINT ESPIRIT ipo karibu na Seleum ya Kuaiujia Ngonbe

<u>MSKITI</u>

Ups miza we rve Tanganyika na rve Pachaus
Umejengwa na Peritali ya Libita

**Document 4**

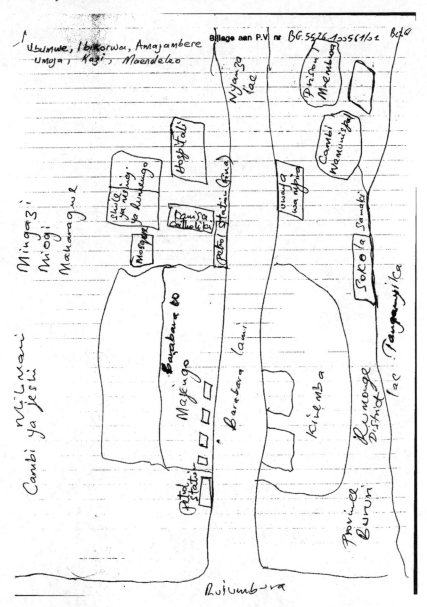

**Document 5**

1. Prince Louis Rwagasore ✠ 1963 Died
2. Michombero. Michael        1976
3. Bagaza  Jean Baptist  1986 — 1987
4. Buyoya  Pierre
5. Ndadaye  Melkio   1976 (3 months)
6. Ntaryamira  Cyprian s
7. Ntsibantunganya  Silvester (overthrown 1996)
8. Buyoya

**Document 6**

Independence ⎱ Tutsi   Balance ⎱ Hutu
Umoja   ⎰          Nyabusorongo ⎰

To GEORGE MICHAEL
         LONDON
         U.K

**Document 7**

these documents are designed for reading will not receive a simple answer.

Kress and van Leeuwen (1996) discuss the complex, multimodal design of contemporary documents such as advertisements, textbooks, and clips. New forms of literacy have emerged, in which both the visual and the textual combine in one sign. This forces text consumers to combine different activities: 'reading' as well as 'looking at', and synthetic (the whole sign) as well as analytic decodings (different constituent parts of the sign). Furthermore, they emphasise the primarily *visual* character of written text, and advocate the visual as the point of entrance into any text: 'Writing is only one way of visualizing meaning, a very exceptional one' (1996: 18). In fact, what we call alphabetical writing may be a residue of original, more complex, multimodal ways of visualising meaning, the result of a gradual restriction of the scope of visualising meaning to writing. In the same move, writing became less and less an object of visual inspection – it became devisualised – and it became the object of a new, exclusive activity-type, reading. Kress (1996) expands the argument by looking at the development of early writing skills in children, arguing that children move from highly multimodal representations of meanings (drawings with some written texts and often accompanied by oral narrative) to devisualised 'text only' representations. Learning how to write is unlearning how to produce multimodal, visual meaning representations. This, it should be underscored, is an *ideological* process. Every written document is a visual document, and when we write we continuously deploy a wide range of meaningful visual tactics (differences in font and size, lines, arrows, indentation . . .). Reading, similarly, involves the visual decoding of the document. Thus, visuality is not lost in *practice*, but it is lost in *ideological conception* of the writing and reading process.

It is hard to avoid seeing the documents produced by the Burundese man as primarily and overwhelmingly *visual* signs. The documents are distinctly multimodal. Textual features combine with drawings: the map (document 5), the national flag (document 3), and the banners of the political parties Frodebu and Uprona (document 4). But these are only the most striking visual items. In document 4 we also see how the part headed by 'mitaa' (roads) has drawings of two roads (or lanes of a highway) next to it, with the note 'bara bara kub[wa]' (main road, highway). Furthermore, the texts are replete with solidly visual structuring features: chapter headings completely or partially in capitals, with single or double horizontal lines marking them; double vertical lines separating columns (document 2); a play with different sizes of symbols, highlighting specific words or parts (see, for example, the 'INTAMBA' in document 1, or OTRACO in document 3), and, of course, the enormous numbers in the left margin, marking 'chapters' or 'sections' in the document. Note also the careful spatial alignment of parallel series, such as, for example, at the bottom of document 3:

| Kiwanda | cha | sigara |
| Kiwanda | cha | nguo |
| Kiwanda | cha | chai |
| Kiwanda | cha | bia |

In sum, we see how the author deploys several outspokenly visual graphic techniques to provide clear, transparent structure and meaning in the documents.[6] The differences with any other document produced within this genre are not differences of substance, but of degree: there is *more* visuality in this document, and the visual elements seem more important.

The tight, visually organised structure of the documents gives us one clue as to what kind of text is being produced here. But, in order to get the full picture, we need to turn to *what* the author is trying to express. The texts are written in a vernacular variety of Swahili, with traces of vernacular French and English in the parts authored by Author A, and English in the parts authored by Author B. Author A, for instance, uses loans from French reflecting local phonetics of spoken vernacular French. The same goes for a couple of English loans in Author A's text. Examples are:

'Kampis' (French 'campus') document 1
'Avenii de Plage' (French 'Avenue de la Plage') document 1
'Avenii de State (French 'Avenue du Stade') document 1
'Museu vivant' (French 'musée vivant') document 1
'Independece' (French 'independence') document 1
'Coens' (English 'coins') document 2
'Supa machi' (French 'Super Marché') document 3
'Jandarma' (French 'gendarmes') document 4
'Shosii' (French 'chaussée') document 4
'bisi' (French 'bus') document 4
'Avenii de la Univasity' (French 'Avenue de l'Université', English 'University') document 4
'Avenii du Opital' (French 'Avenue de l'Hôpital') document 4

Note that the French loans 'Museu' and 'Independece' are accompanied by Standard Swahili glosses, 'makumbusho' and 'uhuru', respectively, indicating the fact that, most probably, the author would use the French loans in everyday, mixed-language speech (see Blommaert

1999a; similar 'reverse glosses' occur in Fabian 1990b). The French loans produced by Author A are almost all vernacular, i.e. a graphic replica of spoken forms, marked by, for example, unrounding of vowels, as in 'avenue' > 'avenii', 'campus' > 'kampis', (French) 'bus' > 'bisi' (English 'bus' would most likely result in 'basi').

Author B uses English terms such as 'died' (document 1), 'green + white' (document 2), and 'overthrown' (document 6), all of them are correctly spelled. Author C uses colloquial Swahili with embedded, unglossed French loans such as 'cambi wamunisipal' ('le camp municipal') and 'prison', as well as the English loans 'mosque' and 'petrol station'. We are confronted with probably three different levels of literacy competence here, three different individuals with differential control over writing skills. Authors A and C use vernacular spoken language varieties as the basis for writing, which is a clear indicator of sub-elite literacy. This is most striking in the case of place names ('avenii', 'shosii', 'cambi wamunisipal' . . .): the point of reference in writing here is not how these names are spelled, but how these names are pronounced.

This is important, for the collective effort of these three *scriptores* is one of *remembering*. It is a painstaking effort, the clearest sign of which is the fact that the whole set of documents – the four 'structured', numbered pages as well as the map and the notes – were submitted to the authorities as the answer to the initial assignment. Throughout the documents, we see a struggle with 'getting things right'. Witness, for example, how Author B makes a list of street names on top of document 5, to be added to the map drawn by Author C. Similarly, document 6 is a list of the presidents of Burundi in chronological order, but with dates lacking for several of them. Incomplete lists are rather frequent: in document 2, Author A announces '16 districts' but only provides a list of 13; the name of the 'beer factory' in document 3 is not provided; in document 2, the section numbered 4, on money, is complemented by another one at the bottom of the page (marked by Author B with '4 – look'); and Author B appears to have added elements of remembering in several places (see, for example, document 2, the location of the Albatros Hotel). Author C has made notes on Hutu-Tutsi divisions on document 7, but they have not found their way into the text. Everything taken together, the text is a series of thirteen rather loosely ordered sections of 'factual' remembering, strongly organised around naming practices and geographical location. Three people have collaborated in this reconstruction of a school-atlas kind of inventory of 'facts' about Burundi and its capital Bujumbura. The writing process itself structures remembering – numerous traces of this process of writing-as-remembering can be found in the form of notes, corrections, or additions in the text; remembering has to be done on the basis of highly fragmentary material, textually – visually – organised in a particular format (cf. Fabian 1996; Blommaert 2001c, 2003b, 2003c).

This brings us to another aspect. Apart from an effort at remembering, the texts are also an effort at *generically regimented text production* – a text that satisfies both the purpose of structured remembering and the generic requirements (real or perceived) of 'official', literate, 'on record' discourse. The authors are not constructing just any text, they are trying to craft an ordered text full of tables, lists, and separate, neatly marked, topical divisions in sections and chapters: an *encyclopaedic text*. I am avoiding the verb 'writing' here, for what they do is more than writing, it is 'document design': textual, visual, spatial architecture, generic differentiation – it is all there. Every available linguistic and communicative skill (including the skills of others) is mobilised in order to make sense.[7] Consequently, the kinds of actions we have to deploy in order to make sense of the text are wider and more varied than 'reading'. If we reduce the text to its propositional content, what would stand out would be the gaps, incomplete lists, corrections, and errors. We have to add 'reading' to the visual inspection mentioned earlier, and accept the fact that a lot of what the text tells us is lodged in its visual makeup, for the visual aspects of the text inform us about its history and modes of production. To quote Fabian (1990b: 164): '[m]uch of *what* the document tells us . . . is inscribed in *how* it was conceived, composed, presented and diffused'. These visual-material features tell us a lot, consequently, about who the author is – he is more than one individual – as well as how remembering comes into being. We have not a product here, but a generically structured *process* of knowledge-construction.

What we have to learn from this, I believe, is that the function of a set of documents such as these is not primarily or exclusively *reading*. The documents are crafted in such a way that they have to be *looked at*, read, decoded, reconstructed. The activities we need to deploy in order to make sense of them are as varied as the modes of activity that went into their production. In terms of an ideology in which writing is made for reading, such writing often confronts us with *hetero-graphy*: the deployment of writing skills for functions *we* don't usually allocate to them, and which we consequently cannot understand as *ortho-graphic*. Thus, in order to make sense of such documents, we have to shift our own ideological frames; we have to locate the texts in the borderline zones of our archive. This, alas, does not happen often.

## The non-exchangeability of literacy values

Fabian (1990b) provides a groundbreaking analysis of a document from Katanga (Congo), the *Vocabulaire d'Elisabethville*. The *Vocabulaire* is a grass-roots historiography of the city of Elisabethville (now Lubumbashi) and it displays graphic, narrative, and genre features very similar to the ones I encountered in the documents shown here. In a retrospective paper on the analysis of such forms of literacy, Fabian insists that we should see such forms of literacy practice not as 'deficient' writing, but as 'liberating', creative practice. What is meant by this is seen in the following quote:

> it is a literacy which works despite an amazingly high degree of indeterminacy and freedom (visible in erratic orthography, a great disdain for word and sentence boundaries, and many other instances of seemingly unmotivated variation). (Fabian 2001: 65)

I would certainly not want to challenge the creative dimensions of writing practices such as the ones discussed here. But, in light of the discussion in this chapter, I want to qualify the general association of writing with opportunity and freedom. My argument will be that whether or not writing offers opportunities for its practition-ers is a fact to be established by ethnographic and sociolinguistic analysis.

Let us return to the issue of functions and recapitulate what has been said on the topic so far. Functions are a matter of dialogical uptake, of reception. Furthermore, there is no way in which we can detach 'function' from 'value': discourse modes are made meaning-ful because of their insertion in stratified indexical scales of social value-attribution. And like second-hand cars, a chunk of discourse is worth precisely as much as other people are willing to give for it. The problematic point, however, is that such value-scales are pri-marily *local*, though they connect, obviously, with scales and hierar-chies at all kinds of other levels. As a consequence – and here we encounter the issue of relativity of function – what works well in one context may not work at all in other contexts. To put it simply: prestigious ways of using language in one community may be stigma-tised in other communities, and discourse forms may 'lose function' – stop making sense, or be interpreted in terms of completely differ-ent frames of reference – as soon as they are moved into different environments.

Let us now consider our own example. The text was produced in a transnational context: a Burundese subject producing text in Belgium, addressed to Belgian officials. The Burundese subject clearly mobilises the resources he could mobilise: his own literacy skills, his own memory, as well as the skills and memories of two of his friends. But, as said above, this complex of resources betrays an economy of literacy – or to put it in Foucault's more general terms, a system of the formation and transformation of statements – which is different from the one that applies in societies with fully saturated literacy environments: both the writing itself and the remembering were 'incomplete' when measured against the textualist norms used by the addressees. So what we have here is a clash of two different economies of literacy: one guiding the production of the documents; another one guiding its uptake. The bridge between both is formed by the documents themselves: texts that are moving from one place into another, from Africa into Belgium, or, to be more precise, from a sub-elite stratum of society in Burundi through a diasporic community of Africans in Europe (where the two other *scriptores* come in) to the core of the bureaucratic system in Belgium.

Let us assume for the moment that the form of writing displayed by the Burundese subject would qualify as acceptable writing skills in his place of origin and his current place in the diasporic community of which he is part – let us assume, in other words, that it is locally *ortho-graphic* in the etymological sense, and that it fits well into existing local orders of indexicality. This may be good, useful, and functionally adequate literacy in the sub-elite stratum of society in Burundi and in the African diaspora. It may also be the 'best possible' document in terms of the subject's available skills and competence (e.g. with respect to remembering place names, presidents, schools, etc. in Bujumbura). But the fact is: it is not good, useful, and functionally adequate literacy in the Belgian bureaucratic world. When transferred from one place to another, the documents get re-placed in a different economy of literacy, and subjected to assessments that derive from that. They lose function at a rather dramatic pace: they become *hetero-graphic*. In the Belgian bureaucratic world, features such as incomplete lists, vernacular writing of street names, and different orthographies of the same name (e.g. 'Ndaye' and 'Ndadae', document 1) are sufficient to cast doubts as to the truthfulness of the account produced by the Burundese subject. From the perspective of a literacy-saturated society, the name of the president, street names, and the list of provinces of one's country are things one is supposed to 'know', i.e. to remember exhaustively and reproduce 'correctly'. Failing to do so becomes a sign either of individual deficiencies (e.g. low intelligence – a current and widespread association of communicative skills with personality features) or of the lack of truthfulness of the act of communication.[8]

Consequently, the suggestion of 'freedom' with regard to these literacy practices sounds literally out of place. The inconsistencies and different forms of coherence observed by Fabian in the *Vocabulaire* may be a feature of freedom and offer immense semiotic opportunities to their producers *in Katanga*. As soon as these people and resources start to travel across the world, however, all these features become objects not of distinction or distinctness, but of *inequality*. The opportunities offered by particular, creative forms of literacy in the peripheries of the world system may turn into foci of discrimination, disenfranchisement, and injustice elsewhere. Opportunities, just like function and value, do not travel along with the texts, they are left behind. In the global system, values of semiotic forms are not always exchangeable and, consequently, whereas writing may be a tremendously rich instrument for social mobility in the peripheries, it may be just another problem in the centre – a problem of 'fixing', of tying subjects to their place of origin with its own economies of literacy. In sum: it may become a problem of denying mobility to communicative resources.

## 5.5 CONCLUSIONS

In the present world, we encounter more and more instances of texts moving from the peripheries of the world systems to its centres, and this move in space is also a move across different 'archives' (Foucault) or 'hegemonies' (Williams) – across different systems of value-and-function allocation to particular discourse forms. This is the semiotic face of globalisation. In the case of the written documents discussed here, this transfer involves a transition from ortho-graphy to hetero-graphy, from 'readable' to 'unreadable' in terms of the orders of indexicality in which we place written texts. The inferior value of texts from the peripheries – e.g. from Africa – is *systemic* and even to some extent *predictable*. Given its peripheral position in the world system, resources that have exceptional value in Africa do not necessarily have this value in Europe. The transfer of linguistic signs does not entail the transfer of their functions and values, for the latter are determined by the general structure of the world system, that is, by global patterns of inequality. This systemic character of inequality is the reason why, typically, the bureaucrats in the Belgian asylum procedure or the police show little inclination to consider documents such as these as instances of *semiotic innovation*, as texts that challenge existing normative codes and call for the construction of new ones. They refuse to see the texts as 'poetically' constructed, as graphic visual compositions and organised along hetero-graphic lines; instead they draw the texts firmly into their archive, subject them to the scrutiny applied to typical instances of literacy within that genre, and then judge them as inadequate. As observed by Foucault, they usually have no idea of the structure of their own archive (hence, of the fundamental injustice generated by this procedure), because they are working 'from within these rules'.

It is important to realise that constraints on choice, or indeed the absence of choice, are features of monumental proportions in the study of discourse in the era of globalisation. As said earlier, people do not choose to be misunderstood. Inquiries into this connect ethnography and history, for no analysis of specific instances of discourse can afford to look at the discourse materials only. We have to look into the wider social and historical patterns that direct the hands, gaze, mouths, ears of those who communicate. Realising that there are important constraints on what people can do with language, not because of free will but because of conditions beyond their control, may be the insight that bridges the gap between micro-analyses and macro-explanations, between discourse and society.

The next chapter will delve a little bit deeper into the same problematic. The historicity of discourse has repeatedly been emphasised here and, indeed, we drew our inspiration from formulations of questions and theoretical positions from historical work. But there is more to be said about history.

## SUGGESTIONS FOR FURTHER READING

Foucault should be read, not only read about. The effort invested in reading his *Archaeology of Knowledge* (1969, 2002) certainly pays when it is combined with the reading of some of his other works. A classic appraisal can be found in Dreyfus and Rabinow (1982). Fairclough extensively discusses Foucault in his *Discourse and Social Change* (1992a). Equally seminal is Raymond Williams' work. His *Marxism and Literature* (1977) is highly readable. It is worthwhile, though, to combine it with a thorough reading of some of E. P. Thompson's work (e.g. 1978), so as to understand the broader intellectual landscape in which Williams operated. The study of literacy has been revolutionised by works such as Street (1995) and Gee (1990). Collins and Blot (2003) represent the most recent synthesis of work done in the New Literacy Studies. Kress and van Leeuwen (1996) are a landmark study on multimodal forms of literacy. It is also worthwhile reading Bourdieu on 'habitus' (e.g. 1990) in relation to the issues discussed in this chapter.

# 6   History and process

## 6.1 INTRODUCTION

So far, we have followed an itinerary that has taken us from observations on the inadequacies of notions of 'context' in the study of textual detail, over a view of discourse as conditioned by general patterns of inequality related to systemic differences in the way in which discourse is given functions (an effect of orders of indexicality), to a view in which we have to see discourse as both creative at a micro-level and constrained (determined) at higher levels. This itinerary has gradually taken us away from the micro-level analysis of the text – the text as single text – to higher levels influencing, conditioning, and occasioning texts – the text as part of a textual tradition, as a social, cultural, historical phenomenon. This chapter will partly dwell at this higher level of analysis, but it will also mark the beginning of a move back into the direction of the single text.

I am emphasising the importance of higher level conditions on text for two main reasons. First, such considerations have not been central to mainstream discourse analysis, and, as we have seen in several places in the previous chapters (and will see below), this absence of concern for higher level 'context' has led to analytical difficulties. These can be summarised as the inflation of context: several layers of context, operating at various levels, had to be squeezed into the single text or communicative event, often in an analysis that presupposed creativity, intentionality, and awareness from the participants. I shall be commenting on this problem in this chapter as well as in the next chapters. A second reason for my insistence on higher level contexts is the importance of the world system as a perspective on communication. If we wish adequately to investigate discourse that bears marks of globalisation processes, we need to contextualise such discourses in such a way that the deep and systemic differences in the world system are accepted as meaningful conditions for the emergence, production,

125

and exchange of such discourses. In other words, if a critical analysis of discourse wishes to come to terms with discourse in globalisation, it will have to talk more about the world system as a system which, apart from other things, also affects language in society.

We are not yet through, though. We need to follow up on some points raised in the previous chapter, notably issues that have to do with the way in which history forces us to recognise 'layered simultaneity' in texts: meanings simultaneously produced, but not all of them consciously nor similarly accessible to agency. This, I believe, is a consequence of the view on creativity and determination outlined in the previous chapter. We shall also have to address, in conjunction with the previous point, issues of continuity and discontinuity – that which creates or defeats impressions of coherent, sharable discourse. And, finally, we shall have to specify what history means when it enters in one text or one communicative event. It is not sufficient to say that texts are intrinsically historical. The question for discourse analysis is: how? I shall advocate a view which is based on positioning, on stance: people speak *from* a particular point in history, and they always speak *on* history.

## 6.2 TIMES AND CONSCIOUSNESS: LAYERED SIMULTANEITY

Simultaneity is a rule in discourse, not an exception (Woolard 1998a). Going back to our discussions of contextualisation, what we now see is that every utterance displays a wide variety of meaningful features which, each in isolation, are pretty meaningless but become meaningful precisely through their simultaneous occurrence in the utterance. The best example is poetry: when we read a line of verse we perceive the rhythm, the meter, the phonetics, the word-meanings, and so forth, and we perceive all of these simultaneously in relation to the whole of the poem (see Jakobson 1960). Furthermore, recent linguistic-anthropological work has shown how linguistic/communicative form and social stratification collapse into one 'meaning' through processes of *iconisation* (Irvine and Gal 2000). Historically older linguistic forms, for example, are often seen as 'archaic' as well as 'upper class' (cf. Silverstein 2003a). All of this is simultaneity, and meaning emerges as the result of creating semiotic simultaneity, but we shall have to qualify such processes.

Let us first specify some of the statements on history made in the previous chapter. Both Foucault and Williams insisted on limits of awareness due to what they called, respectively, the archive or inherited consciousness, hegemonies. The same motif, that of distinctions between meaningful practices that are open to conscious elaboration and practices that are not but are rather routinised, normalised, performed without conscious planning, is shared by several other scholars. Pierre Bourdieu's concept of 'habitus' (Bourdieu 1977, 1990) is designed to cover the same set of phenomena: 'principles which generate and organise practices and representations that can be objectively adapted to their outcomes without presupposing a conscious aiming at ends or an express mastery of the operations necessary in order to attain them' (Bourdieu 1990: 53). Undoubtedly, we shall find identical attempts at description in many accounts of ideology in which Gramsci's concept of hegemony is being invoked as something which thoroughly saturates consciousness in such a way as to reduce ideology to the 'normal state of affairs'. Thus, Fairclough (1989) strongly emphasises the 'common-sense' aspect of ideologies, and John B. Thompson (1990) would equally stress the 'naturalising' tactics involved in ideological circulation (see the discussion in chapter 7). All of these authors identify ways in which unique, situated activities become repositories of historical precedents; they all admit that such condensation processes – long history condensed in single human activities – involve restrictions on the scope of what participants can 'control' so to speak. Part of what people do is conscious production; and part of it is unconscious *re*production. History does strange things to our consciousness and knowledge.[1] How can we start deciphering such processes of production-and-reproduction, operating at different levels of consciousness? Let us start by looking for adequate metaphors, and again I shall look for inspiration with historians.

Fernand Braudel's work is well known. As the author of the monumental *The Mediterranean* (Braudel 1949), editor of the famous journal *Annales*, and mentor of a whole generation of creative social scientists at the *Maison des Sciences de l'Homme* and what is now the *École des Hautes Etudes en Sciences Sociales*, Braudel had an enormous influence on the development of the social sciences in the post-Second World War era in Europe, and his work was seminal to the development of world systems analysis (Wallerstein 1983, 2001).[2] His historical œuvre focused on the so-called *longue durée* (the long term): the slow, invisible transformations of systems and societies which accounted for the 'limits of the possible' in human life (Braudel 1981: 27). But the 'longue durée' could only be distinguished by reference to other timescales. Braudel distinguished between three such layered time-scales: slow time or structural time (the 'longue durée'); intermediate time, or conjunctural time (the time of long cyclical patterns, e.g. the time of particular political regimes or the cycle of growth and crisis in cap-italism); and the *événement*, event-time. The latter was defined as 'the short time, measured on individuals, everyday life, our illusions, our understandings and awareness' (Braudel 1969: 45–46). Single events, such as the Battle of Waterloo or the French Revolution, evolved in 'event' time, but also needed to be explained with reference to both the conjuncture (deep economic and political transformations – or the kind of transformations of regimes of power/knowledge described by Foucault) and the structure (the slow unfolding of the system) in which they occurred.

According to Braudel, the slow patterns of history are beyond the grasp of subjects-in-history: 'there is a limit, a ceiling which restricts all human life, containing it within a frontier of varying outline, one which is hard to reach and harder still to cross' (Braudel 1981: 27). For instance, the range of possible ways to organise one's life between the fifteenth and eighteenth centuries was restricted by 'inadequate food supplies, a population that was too big or too small for its resources, low productivity of labour, and the as yet slow progress in control-ling nature' (*ibid.*). Participants in social events, consequently, had a restricted horizon of awareness of the deeper structural causes of such events, and they could only exert agency on the immediate, event-related time-frame. The higher level developments were usually beyond individual control and consciousness, and they could only be observed in hindsight, through historical reflection and analysis.

These limits of agency and awareness are important, for the layered temporal developments do not always develop coherently – not syn-chronically, so to speak. The different time-scales need to be seen as 'multiple and contradictory temporalities' resulting in 'this vivid, inti-mate and infinitely repeated opposition between the single moment and the slow unfolding time' (Braudel 1969: 43). Different aspects of reality, consequently, could develop at different speeds. As an example, Braudel suggests that we imagine being transported to the era of Voltaire. We would be able to have long and congenial conversations with Voltaire, because '[i]n the world of ideas, the men of the eigh-teenth century are our contemporaries'; at the same time, however, 'the details of his everyday life, even the way he looked after himself, would greatly shock us' (1981: 27–28). Thus we have differential devel-opments of various aspects of social life, all of them simultaneously operating in the unfolding of single events, and often perceived as unified, equivalent features of the single event. We have a tendency to perceive only what manifests itself synchronically, but this synchronic-ity hides the fact that features operate on different levels and scales, have different origins, offer different opportunities, and generate different effects. Synchronicity, in other words, combines elements that are *of a different order*, but tends to obscure these fundamental differences.

This, I believe, is an important qualification of intertextuality. Not everything which is mobilised in processes of intertextuality is of the same order; we also have different levels and scales of intertextuality. There is, it seems to me, a rather fundamental difference between intertextualities depending on whether or not such intertextualities invoke historically 'charged' categories of meanings, such as gender, race, ethnic, or political-ideological categories such as 'bandit', 'freedom fighter', 'terrorist', 'conservative', 'progressive', or 'radical' – categories with a long history of politicised use.[3] And, consequently, it is important to bear in mind that such sensitive categories may change in role and value over time due to *durée* developments. Let us turn to an example.

Carlo Ginzburg's *The Judge and the Historian* (1999) discusses the difference between judicial and historical interpretation in a widely publicised terrorism trial held in 1990 in Italy. The trial involved Adriano Sofri, a friend of Ginzburg's. Sofri was arrested in 1988 and charged with the murder of a police officer in 1972, which was a time of intense political unrest in Italy and other places in Europe. It was the time of the *Brigato Rosso* and the *Rote Armee Fraktion*, of the assassination of Italy's former prime minister Aldo Moro and German captains of industry such as Schleicher. The groups perpetrating these acts were radical political organisations waging a war against capitalism and the system of bourgeois democracy controlled by large industrial complexes, as in Italy and Germany. By the time of Sofri's arrest in 1988, however, such forms of political terrorism had disappeared and Italy was locked in a war between the state and organised crime. Police officers, judges, and public prosecutors had been assassinated by members of the Camorra and the Sicilian mafia, and the state had launched an all-out offensive against such criminal organisations. Some members of the organisations had come forward – the *pentiti* – and a number of leaders of important crime syndicates had been brought to justice. Consequently, by the time Sofri stood trial, the assassination of the police officer in 1972 was not placed against the *historical* background, that of political terrorism, but against the *synchronic* background of terrorism by crime syndicates. The nature of the perpetrator and the victim had been modified accordingly as well as the act itself, its motives and effects. Sofri was sentenced to twenty-two years in prison.

Ginzburg argues that judges and historians apply different categories of 'facts' and 'truth' to events and actions. The former reduce complex historical developments to strict synchronicity, that of the legal-here-and-now; the latter attempt to restore the different historical frames in which events occurred. Consequently, whereas categories may appear straightforward from the perspective of the judge – guilty or innocent – they may look rather more contradictory and complicated to the historian, who also has to keep track of the various recategorisations that occur through history.

I would say that they also look rather more contradictory and complicated to the discourse analyst, for we are involved in a business very similar to that of the historian. A lot of discourses that arrive on our desks bear traces of such recategorisations over time. Applying the categories of today to discourses that display categorisations belonging to another regime – another archive, in Foucault's terms – results in an anachronism, an operation structurally similar to the refusal to grant transcontextual mobility to discourse organised on the basis of different orders of indexicality, of which we saw several examples in the previous chapters. If we return to the example of the TRC hearing of Colin de Souza discussed in chapter 4, we can now see how the TRC commissioners, who try to construct a post-Apartheid archive, recategorise Colin de Souza as a 'victim', while his own self-construction hinges on a refusal of that category. In terms of the *synchronicity* invoked by the TRC – the hearing set in the post-Apartheid universe – Colin de Souza was a victim; but *historically*, from within Colin de Souza's narrative frame, he was a victorious freedom fighter. Colin spoke from within the struggle; the TRC commissioners spoke from a post-struggle position. This difference involved all kinds of complex reversals of roles, categories, and attributions of actions and resulted in deeply hidden and hardly recognisable expressions of suffering in Colin de Souza's narrative. The participants in this event spoke from positions on different scales of historicity and, as Braudel noted, this may result in paradoxical relations between the different scales of time. Concretely, Colin de Souza was placed in the new post-Apartheid archive, but he oriented towards orders of indexicality that belonged to another timescale, that of the struggle against Apartheid.

To summarise the argument made so far: we have to conceive of discourse as subject to *layered simultaneity*. It occurs in a real-time, synchronic event, but it is simultaneously encapsulated in several layers of historicity, some of which are within the grasp of the participants while others remain invisible but are nevertheless present. It is overdetermined, so to speak, by sometimes conflicting influences from different levels of historical context. The different layers are important: not everything in this form of overdetermination is of the same order; there are important differences between the different levels and degrees of historicity. As we have seen and shall see in more detail further on, people can speak from various positions on these scales. The synchronicity of discourse is an illusion that masks the densely layered historicity of discourse. It is therefore easy, but fallacious, to adopt synchronicity as the level of analysis in discourse analysis, because we run the risk of squeezing the analytically crucial differences between the layers of historicity in a homogenised and synchronised event, thus having to make 'either–or' decisions on aspects of meaning that occur simultaneously, yet are of a different order.

## 6.3  CONTINUITIES, DISCONTINUITIES, AND SYNCHRONISATION

An awareness of layered simultaneity in texts turns discourse into a complex, historically layered, and overdetermined object. The different layers of historicity to which people can orient, and from which they can speak, create enormous amounts of tension between continuity and discontinuity in meanings, between coherence and incoherence in discourses. I have tried to capture these tensions in an imagery of different speeds between archives and orders of indexicality, the former being wider in scope and higher in scale than the latter, and both developing asymmetrically in such a way that there will be degrees of overlap while they need not be coterminous at any time. Such tensions are often 'synchronised', seen as differences within one single scale, and in this process of synchronisation they may be often translated in political positions articulated in language use.

To give a rather straightforward example: in some universities or faculties, institutional conventions would insist that senior faculty be addressed with the term 'professor', while in other universities or faculties it would be perfectly acceptable to address such faculty with 'Mrs' or 'Mr' followed by the family name, or even by their first name. All of this occurs within one synchronic system, that of universities; it may even occur in the space of one single university. In terms of institutional history, the persistence of the usage of 'professor' would be an orientation to an old order of indexicality, one that characterises a now largely defunct archive of discourses in universities; the usage of 'Mrs' or 'Mr' would be an orientation to a new, post-May 1968 set of norms, operating within a new archive of discourses in universities in which equality, democracy, meritocracy would be more central.[4] From the perspective of this new archive, remnants of the older one such as the persistent use of 'professor' would be converted into a political position of 'conservatism'. The anachronism is thus converted into a difference within one scale of historicity; it is synchronised.

We can see through the window of this example how different aspects of a system change at different speeds, and we see how those aspects of reality that are closest to us (the *événement*) are seen telescopically as standing for a change in the whole system. Let us try to identify some of the layers in this process.

1. The highest layer is that of the general structure of the university itself. Whether one calls a senior faculty member 'Professor Smith' or 'Mrs Smith', that senior faculty member will be the one who designs and offers the course, who will do most of the talking during the class hours, who will give assignments to students, and who will grade their exams. The difference in terms of address does not affect the general role-patterns in universities. This general pattern of authority goes back centuries, it is a *durée* phenomenon with a very slow pace of change. It provides enormous continuity at a very large scale: almost every university will be characterised by this basic relationship of authority between senior faculty and students.

2. Another layer is that of the general sociological makeup of universities: who participates in the system? On this scale, we would see more gradual change and differentiation between universities. Whereas until quite recently the 'professor' was a male individual belonging to the dominant groups in society (usually the white, 'autochthonous' upper middle class), we would now see a growing (though still exceedingly small) cohort of female professors in universities, and we would now also meet more professors who are not of upper middle class background or who did not graduate from prestigious schools, as well as some (very few) professors who belong to ethnic or other minorities. The same gradual transformation could be witnessed in the structure and composition of the student population, though this is often a matter controlled by the state. Nevertheless, the difference between state-sponsored universities and private universities is often also a class difference. So, in this layer, we perceive more or less visible changes in universities (visible, at least, for members of a generation who witnessed the transition), and we would probably see differences between universities as to the degree of change in their sociological makeup.

3. Another layer would be that of the organisation of university discursive practices: the 'who, what, and how' of university discourse. At this level, we would probably see rather drastic changes in the patterns of communication over particular spans of time. Stand-up professorial lecturing in front of large student audiences has been complemented during my lifetime by small-group interactions with considerable space for interventions and initiatives from students; the written course book that covered most of the course materials, has been gradually replaced or complemented by flexible sets of course materials – books, articles, internet materials, and so on. Students would be encouraged to collect their own libraries, and books would be offered to them at affordable prices. My ways of organising discourse regimes with my students is rather fundamentally different from those of my immediate predecessors. Part of this development is enabled by technological and economic changes such as the emergence of electronic communication modalities and the mass circulation of printed materials. But at this level we would see enormous synchronic differences. There are still universities in the world where faculty and students have hardly any access to printed or electronic course materials and where the typical model of interaction is the stand-up professorial lecture with students taking notes; there are universities where students are tutored on-line, can independently complement what was provided in the lectures with reading material drawn from excellent libraries or bought at bargain prices. And universities nowadays market themselves with arguments pertaining to such patterns of communication – intensive tutoring, excellent, abundant, and affordable course materials, opportunities for independent research, and so on. This is therefore a very visible aspect of change, and people would probably observe this layer when they choose to enrol in a particular university.

4. Finally, we would have the layer of everyday interactional practices in which senior staff can be addressed as 'Professor Smith' or 'Mrs Smith'. This would be the most palpable, experiential level, the level at which the university becomes a real everyday environment for faculty and students. Differences here would be visible at very low levels: there would be differences between various faculties, programmes, even individuals.

The different layers operate at different scales. The highest, slowest layer would most probably cover the totality of the university system.

As we descend towards everyday experiential reality, the scope of the changes becomes gradually narrower – from universities in one part of the world versus another, to particular groups or 'types' of universities (e.g. private versus public, Ivy League, vocational schools, etc.), all the way down to faculties, programmes, and individuals. As we move through the world of universities, we would use observations pertaining to the visible layers of the system – informal, congenial contacts between faculty and students, availability of good course materials, intense discussions during and in between classes – as the basis for assessments of relative quality, politics, 'university culture', and so on. In making such assessments, we squeeze all the layers into one: that of observable, experiential reality, that of the *événement*. We *synchronise* and thus create continuity and coherence in the patterns we observe and in the way in which we talk about them. We are able synchronically to compare universities in the poorest countries in Africa with Yale, Cambridge, and the Sorbonne, and to construct coherent comparative discourses, of quality, competitiveness, and 'culture' within the here-and-now. The real work of comparison, obviously, would need to take into account the histories of origin and development, the different speeds of change, and so on.[5]

Synchronisation creates a particular point from which one speaks, a point in history often crystallised in particular epistemic stances or ways of speaking. Every instance of synchronisation will be particular and specific to local conditions: the synchrony of an upper middle-class American or European is arguably different from that of his or her equivalent in Togo, Tanzania, or Bangladesh – the point from which they speak is the product of different conditions of emergence, of different histories. And people would have different capabilities to incorporate chunks of history in their discourses. Depending on one's place in the world, history has a different meaning; the world is a different place depending on the point from which you look at it.[6] In discourse analysis all of this is usually gathered under the label of 'context' – *the* context, a singular point but a nexus of layered simultaneity, for in every context we shall find features of different orders operating at different speeds and scales. As we have seen in chapter 3, such differences have often been uneasily debated in terms of 'micro' and 'macro' contexts; I would suggest that we see such perceptions of context in themselves as (professional) acts of synchronisation.

Perhaps synchronisation explains a lot about the way power works in societies. It may be a tactic that suggests clarity, coherence, and transparency, even quality, by eliminating attention to the nature of differences and contradictions. It is powerful, for it connects to everyday rationality: we do not observe the deeper layers of our system, we see and experience its surface. Thus, someone who can make us feel that our own experiential reality is the only relevant one and our historical position the only 'normal' one, stands a good chance of convincing us that we are right after all, and that intellectuals' analyses are just abstract, elitist (i.e. class hostile) hullabaloo. He or she may win our hearts and our votes, for chances are that we shall consider him or her a truly democratic person, who 'listens to us' and 'says what we think' or 'is like us'.[7]

Some contemporary politicians are masters of the game. Perhaps remarkably, George W. Bush is a case in point. Michael Silverstein (2003b) compares the brilliant and aestheticised rhetoric of Abraham Lincoln's *Gettysburg Address* to the stammering rhetoric of Bush, characterised by 'presidentiary misspeakingfulness' (Silverstein 2003b: 84). Bush produced statements replete with misnomers, grammatical errors, hypercorrections, and register misfits. Consider the following breathtaking examples from Silverstein's collection:

> Natural gas is hemispheric. I like to call it hemispheric in nature because it is a product that we can find in our neighbourhoods (3)

> The vast majority of our imports come from outside the country (68)

> The Holocaust was an obscene period in our nation's history – I mean in this century's history. But we all live in this century. I didn't live in this century (68)

> I believe we are on an irreversible trend toward more freedom and democracy – but that could change (69)

Whereas such disasters in public speaking would be sufficient to disqualify anyone for appointments to regular jobs involving some demands on communicative skills, Silverstein explains how Bush is 'on message', how his rhetoric fits the peculiar cultural semantics of a present-day American president, in very much the way as Lincoln's rhetoric fitted the cultural semantics of his time. In a society pervaded by commercially circulating catch-phrases and images of 'power language' such as 'corporate standard register' (qualified by Silverstein as 'indexical Viagra for the yupwardly mobile', p. 119), single terms can become 'a shortcut for understanding the world', because they are 'particularly precise in suggestively communicating the identity "who" and the contextual "why" of their use' (Silverstein 2003b: 119). In other words, as long as Bush produces enough terms such as 'freedom', 'democracy', 'freedom-loving nations', his rhetoric is fully adequate. To the segment of the American polity that would vote for Bush, such rhetoric embodies both 'our way of speaking' and that of those we admire: business CEOs. No Lincolnian poetics is needed: Bush is in line with the discourses of the dominant. He does not need to be knowledgeable about the issues at hand – he is the CEO, and expertise is something the middle management has to ensure. According to Silverstein, Bush iconicises his regime: a government run by top business executives and supported by an affluent middle class. His act of synchronisation consisted of the fact that he managed to depict previous presidents or contemporary contenders (such as Al Gore) as middle-management executives rather than as CEOs, and as members of an intellectual middle-class elite out of tune with 'ordinary people', who, like Bush speaking in public, just 'try hard' and do their best.

Synchronisation in discourse is a tactic of power. The denial of the layered nature of simultaneity in discourse, or, to put it differently, the reduction of overdetermination to just one single (clear, transparent) meaning, results in images of continuity, logical outcomes, and textual coherence. It is a denial of the complexity of the particular position from which one speaks, and of the differences between that position and that of others. Instead we get a flat comparison within one time-frame, the present, *our* experiential present, denying the rather fundamental differences between such time-scales and the various positions people assume on such scales. Analytically, such flat comparisons generate anachronistic results. A flat comparison between Lincoln's *Gettysburg Address* and George W. Bush's jargon would undoubtedly lead to a conclusion that Lincoln's rhetoric was far 'better' than that of Bush. But that does not explain why Bush's rhetoric works *now*. A historical analysis of both forms of rhetoric, on the contrary, leads to the surprising result that, despite phenomenal differences, Lincoln's and Bush's rhetoric are *functionally equivalent within the particular archives of the time*. From within these different positions in time, both produced adequate, 'coherent' discourses.

If we take layered simultaneity and synchronisation together, two things seem crucial to me. First, we need to recognise that every discourse is a discourse *on* history; a discourse in which we shall see references and pointers to a variety of historical time-frames; a discourse which combines heterogeneous historical materials in one seemingly coherent act. Second, every discourse will simultaneously be a discourse *from* history, one that articulates a particular position – or various, shifting positions – in history. Disentangling both dimensions is a task that locates discourse analysis squarely in history, and vice versa.

It forces discourse analysts to address historical dynamics as part and parcel of their scholarly practices, and it forces historians to consider discursive dynamics as part and parcel of theirs.

I shall now provide two illustrations of this mixture of discourse on-and-from history. The first illustration is a piece of public discourse produced during the build-up towards the Iraq invasion of early 2003. It will show how history occasions or sediments in voice, in a particular set of conditions that generate specific statements on and from history. The second illustration is a case of synchronisation in professional vision. I shall discuss the analytic procedures used during a discourse-analytic workshop explicitly devoted to the analysis of historical discourses. It will show some of the lasting problems in our field – problems encountered in earlier chapters as well – but it will show that they are obvious and not hard to overcome.

## 6.4 SPEAKING FROM AND ON HISTORY 1: 'THEY DON'T LIKE US-*us*'

The position from which one speaks is historically determined and it changes over time; it is historically contingent. Statements incorporate views of history while speaking from a particular point which organises, groups, and categorises the views. Moments of crisis may create conditions for greater explicitness – 'hidden transcripts' rising to the surface of public discourse, as James Scott (1990) puts it. During such moments, we may see the (otherwise implicit) historical position and viewpoint on historical events in full glory.

The build-up to the Iraq invasion of 2003 was such a moment of crisis. Political and military escalation was confronted by large-scale anti-war protests, and, as in every crisis since the early 1990s, the Internet quickly became a forum for exchange of views, networking and heated polarised debate. In February 2003, I received the following message on my email account at the University of Chicago. It was not an exceptional message: during that period, several long 'historical accounts' circulated over the Internet, and historical discourse apparently became one genre of popular political debate.

> If you aren't interested in the ramblings of an old man, please delete now. If you're still there, pull up a chair and listen.
> Is there anyone else out there who's sick and tired of all the polls being taken in foreign countries as to whether or not they 'like' us?

The last time I looked, the word 'like' had nothing to do with foreign policy. I prefer 'respect' or 'fear.' They worked for Rome, which civilized and kept the peace in the known world a hell of a lot longer than our puny two centuries-plus.

I see a left-wing German got elected to office recently by campaigning against the foreign policy of the United States. Yeah, that's what I want, to be lectured about war and being a 'good neighbor' by a German.

Their head honcho said they wouldn't take part in a war against Iraq. Kind of nice to see them taking a pass on a war once in while. Perhaps we needed to have the word 'World' in front of War. I think it's time to bring our boys home from Germany. Outside of the money we'd save, we'd make the Germans 'like' us a lot more, after they started paying the bills for their own defense.

Last time I checked, France isn't too fond of us either. They sort of liked us back on June 6th, 1944, though, didn't they? If you don't think so, see how nicely they take care of the enormous American cemeteries up above the Normandy beaches. For those of you who've studied history, we also have a few cemeteries in places like Belleau Woods and Chateau Thierry also.

For those of you who haven't studied it, that was from World War One the first time Europe screwed up, and we bailed out the French. That's where the US Marines got the title 'Devil Dogs' or, if you still care about what the Germans think, Teufelhunde. I hope I spelled that right; sure wouldn't want to offend anyone, least of all a German. Come to think of it, when Europe couldn't take care of their Bosnian problem recently, guess who had to help out there also. Last time I checked, our kids are still there. I sort of remember they said they would be out in a year. Gee, how time flies when you're having fun.

Now we hear that the South Koreans aren't too happy with us either. They 'liked' us a lot better, of course, in June 1950. It took more than 50,000 Americans killed in Korea to help give them the lifestyle they currently enjoy, but then who's counting? I think it's also time to bring the boys home from there. There are about 37,000 young Americans on the DMZ separating the South Koreans from their 'brothers' up north. Maybe if we leave, they can begin to participate in the 'good life' that North Korea currently enjoys. Uh huh. Sure.

I also understand that a good portion of the Arab/Moslem world now doesn't 'like' us either. Did anyone ever sit down and determine what we would have to do to get them to like us? Ask them what they would like us to do. Die? Commit ritual suicide? Bend over? Maybe we should follow the advice of our dimwitted, dullest knife in the drawer, Senator Patty Murray, and build more roads, hospitals, day care centers, and orphanages like Osama bin Laden does. What with all the orphans Osama has created, the least he can do is build some places to put them. Senator Stupid says if we would only 'emulate' Osama, the Arab world would love us.

Sorry Patty, in addition to the fact that we already do all of those things around the world and have been doing them for over sixty years, I don't take public transportation, and I certainly wouldn't take it with a bomb strapped to the guy next to me. Don't get me wrong: I'm not in favor of going to war. Been there, done that. Several times, in fact. But I think we ought to have some polls in this country about other countries, and see if we 'like' THEM. Problem is, if you listed the countries, not only wouldn't the average American know if he liked them or not, he wouldn't be able to find them. If we're supposed to worry about them, how about them worrying about us?

We were nice to the North Koreans in 1994, as we followed the policies of Neville Clinton. And it seemed to work; they didn't restart nuclear weapons program for a whole year or so. In the meantime, we fed them when they were starving, and put oil in their stoves when they were freezing.

In a recent visit to Norway, I engaged in a really fun debate with my cousin's son, a student at a Norwegian University. I was lectured to by this thankless squirt about the American 'Empire', and scolded about dropping the atomic bomb on the Japanese. I reminded him that empires usually keep the stuff they take; we don't, and back in 1945 most Norwegians thought dropping ANY kind of bomb on Germany or Japan was a good idea. I also reminded him that my uncle, his grandfather, and others in our family spent a significant time in Sachsenhausen concentration camp, courtesy of the Germans, and they didn't all survive. I further reminded him that if it weren't for the 'American Empire' he would probably be speaking German or Russian.

Sorry about the rambling, but I just took an unofficial poll here at our house, and we don't seem to like anyone.

Happy New Year.

Provided by Joe Galloway, author of *We Were Soldiers*.

With such data, analysis is easy. We see in this message an abundance of orientations to history, and, consequently, comments on historical events, formulated from a particular point in history. This point in history is also a point in the structure of the synchronic event: here speaks someone who embodies a doctrinaire American, contemporary point of view in the build-up towards the Iraq invasion. The position of the US generates the position of the 'us' in this text: the man refers to an 'us' as the synchronic (or panchronic) United States; he assumes an evaluative speaking position which is determined by his association with the particular, contingent position of his country in the crisis. This position was that of a a country striving for recognition of leadership ('peace keeping') in world affairs;

b and experiencing severe difficulties in convincing other countries (notably France and Germany) of their leading role;

c a country heavily bent on military force as a preferred means for enforcing world leadership;

d a country which converts a predilection for military enforcement of leadership into 'national' features of Americanness: America is a nation of competent, proud, courageous, and determined soldiers, and it has demonstrated these characteristics throughout history;

e consequently, a country which is entitled to recognition of its leading role as well as to gratitude from other countries for the historical military assistance from the US to these countries.

The US state deployed these ingredients of their position in thousands of discursive events, internationally as well as nationally, regionally and locally, with actors ranging from President Bush over all sorts of civil and military officials, over the dominant press, all the way through to the level of ordinary citizens proselytising over the Internet, as in this example.[8] The author of this text also poses as an individual who embodies all of these features: this is an old man who can look back on history; he is a veteran who has been involved in several military operations overseas; he is a taxpayer part of whose tax money flows to places like Germany and Korea, where considerable American military presence is seen as defending these countries from their enemies; he is therefore someone who has reasons to be hurt by the fact that citizens of those countries do not 'like us', has reasons not to 'like them', and believes that they should 'fear or respect us'. Arguments deriving from this position are deployed against foreign culprits as well as against American dissenting views.

This point in history – a moment where the US-us articulates bitter disappointment about having done so much and getting so little in return, now that it asks for assistance – is the viewpoint from which the author starts assembling bits of history. This assemblage is evidently a reduction of enormously complex processes and events to a very simple scheme organised around oppositions between the US ('us') on the one hand, and 'Europe', 'Korea', the 'Arab/Muslim world', and dissenting US politicians, on the other hand. The other countries are put in a particular relation to the US, which can be summarised as follows:

- Germany: they are in no position to lecture us on war, because they are warmongers; we should stop protecting them;
- France: we saved them in 1944 as well as in the First World War; many Americans were killed in France;
- Europe: we solved 'their' Bosnian crisis, and we are still there;
- South Korea: we saved them during the Korean War; many Americans got killed;
- the Arab/Muslim world: they expect us to respect them, a US senator also says that we should do more for them, but we would be better off if they feared us;
- North Korea: the Clinton strategy of accommodation has backfired; they should not forget that we helped them; and
- Europe: American strategy is not imperialist but has liberated Europeans from German/Soviet imperial oppression.

Again, here is the voice of an old war veteran, someone who has firsthand experience with international affairs, in particular with their military aspects. Here is also 'vox populism', the anti-intellectual voice of everyday rationality (iconicised also by the use of colloquial expressions such as 'head honcho', 'gee', and 'uh huh'). There are two oblique references to intellectuals: one when the author appears to remind 'those who've studied history' that US military involvement in France goes back to the First World War; and one when he talks about his cousin's son, a 'student at a Norwegian university', who is 'a thankless squirt' and believes he has to 'lecture' the author on history. So, interestingly, we see a 'rational' discourse on historical facts blended with a rejection of a particular, disciplined, form of rationality and an affirmation of experiential, subjective, everyday rationality. But, just as in the rhetoric of George W. Bush, such experiential everyday rationality has become a legitimate analytical stance for talking about politics and history. It is within the archive. It displays an enormous degree of absorption of viewpoints from the 'centre' – the US government – and translated into the experiential, everyday rational voice of an individual American it becomes a display of hegemony, suggesting that the government's point of view should be that of every right-minded and historically conscious American citizen.[9]

The author of this text manages to collapse layered simultaneity into synchronicity. The synchronic point is that of the here-and-now, of the US government drumming up support to launch an attack on Iraq and being disappointed about the response it receives. The layered simultaneity consists in the act of bringing together in one message elements of history that are of fundamentally different orders. There is *long history*, that of world relations since the beginning of the twentieth century, a history of conjunctures, shifting alignments within Europe and between Europe, the US and other parts of the world, the gradual emergence of the US as a superpower. There is *episodic history*, reflected in the condensed stories of wars and crises, all of which are in turn nested in longer developments: the First World War is a crisis couched in different world relations from the Korean War and the military presence in Germany, which were Cold War crises. There is a *history of segmented episodes*: D-Day, June 1950, the references to (recent) Arab/Muslim terrorism, and the Clinton administration. There is *momentary history*, in references to statements made by the German minister of foreign affairs, Senator Murray, and by the Norwegian university student. And all of it is cross-cut by the author's own *autobiography* (having been involved in several military conflicts, being an American taxpayer, being an old man).

This autobiography is the telescopic lens through which the author looks at world history. And with a government celebrating such everyday rationality, the author's autobiography nicely coincides with the viewpoint of the government – a coincidence that becomes easily convertible into 'everyone's viewpoint', another bit of evidence that the US is a democratic system. The viewpoint is that of 'vox populism' and it allows for synchronic political distinctions. Democracy is presented as fundamentally monological, a perfect mapping of government rhetoric on people's rhetoric. Therefore dissenting views (such as those of Senator Murray, President Clinton, and the Norwegian student) are quickly turned into undemocratic ones, elitist, or inspired by specific interests.

In sum, we see how this author talks about history from within a historical viewpoint, one that reflects the systemic as well as momentary qualities of the US government. The particular assemblage of references to history is enabled by the specific position assumed by the author of the text. This position is not just chronological (which is obvious), but historical, in the sense that it displays political alliances and viewpoints, relationships between the individual and features of the system that characterise the historical moment from which the author writes. History is synchronised into this position, and this synchronisation is an act of power.

## 6.5  SPEAKING FROM AND ON HISTORY 2: 'LET'S ANALYSE'

Synchronisation also occurs in our own academic practices. It is of the same nature and has the same effects as the kind of synchronisation discussed in the example above. I shall illustrate this by means of an account of a discourse analytic workshop I attended some years ago. The workshop was entitled 'Frame and Perspective in Discourse' and was held in the Netherlands in November 1996 (Ensink and Sauer 2003). The organisers had selected a well-defined target of analysis: the speeches held in Warsaw at the occasion of the 50th anniversary of the 1944 Warsaw Uprising. The corpus was a collection of ten speeches from leading international politicians (representing the countries directly involved in the war operations during the Warsaw Uprising) and one letter by Pope John Paul II.

Prior to the workshop, all the participants had received a rather substantial amount of documentation, including various versions of the speeches (written, audiotape, videotape) and some 'historical information'. This historical information was judged necessary for us to get an idea of the importance of the Warsaw Uprising in light of the post-war international relations and of its significance to the Polish collective historical memory. The research question offered to the participants was to see how historical roles and relationships were being shaped and oriented to in the various speeches – in other words, how history was being re-enacted in a political-discursive event developing in a totally different context and, hence, allowing for far-reaching reinterpretations of historical events. This technique of providing us with historical 'background' meant that, in the minds of the organisers, historical context was not contained in the texts themselves. The texts were seen as *momentary texts*, accompanied by *historical contexts*. History was background, situated outside the texts, the texts themselves offering reflexes, reflections, representations, or comments on history. Conditions were created for synchronisation.

## Separating text and history

We shall first take a closer look at a number of practices that have to do with constructing the object (the data) and with what could be called 'pre-formatting' the workshop. The latter is done by inscribing a number of assumptions and theoretical decisions onto the data, so that a sense of uniformity (both in terms of data and in terms of analytical preferences) can emerge. In both instances, the analytical work done by the workshop participants has been 'framed' by the organisers – it has been made coherent by means of a number of meta-qualifications of data and analytical approaches. The procedure of distributing a uniform set of materials to all the prospective participants already contains a number of significant methodological assumptions, and thus to some extent frames the workshop. The undifferentiating distribution of material neutralises different preferences and approaches of the various participants, by grouping them into one shared activity-type: this particular workshop. Despite potentially great differences in approach or method, all the participants' contributions are defined as part of one big discourse event, the discussion of *one text/event*. In the letter referred to as document (1) below, this uniformity is further emphasised by announcing that 'we [the organisers] will offer all participants and visitors the texts of the addresses in the same format as you now receive them. Hence, you may refer to line numbers as indicated.'

After an initial email message, inviting me to participate in this seminar, I received a package of information, containing four documents:

1. a two-page letter from the organisers;
2. a brochure containing the English translations of the 'addresses spoken on the occasion of the Warsaw Uprising 50th anniversary commemoration';
3. an audiotape containing recordings of the spoken versions of these addresses;
4. a six-page text, 'Some historical notes on the Warsaw Uprising' (an extract from a book called *Poland in the Twentieth Century*, written by M. K. Dziewanowski and published in 1977).

Somewhat later, I received a fifth and, still later, a sixth document:

1. some copies of an official conference announcement and registration form;
2. a videotape of the commemoration event.

The intended function of these six documents is clear: together, these documents should provide the participants with sufficient instructions and 'background' information for preparing their interventions in such a way as to fit into the programme.

But let us take a closer look at the various documents. Document (1) is a letter of invitation for those participating in this particular sub-event of the conference. It first informs us of the other materials sent to us. Then, it says:

> As you know, the conference is about discourse analysis. We have asked you to present a discourse analysis of one of the addresses, focusing on problems of framing and/or of perspectivizing the events talked about. Maybe it is useful to you if we formulate some questions which are relevant to such an analysis.

This paragraph is followed by two paragraphs containing historical information (to be discussed below), and then by a series of questions qualified as a list 'not . . . either complete or mandatory', but 'of use to you in order to give some direction to your analysis:

- how do speakers formulate their role in the ceremony, as a person, and as a representative?;
- how is reference made to events of the Uprising itself, to particular actions within the Uprising, and to the participants and their respective roles?;
- which symbolic and other meanings are attributed to the events of the Uprising?;
- how is the Uprising related to a larger context – especially in relation to earlier and later events in history?;
- how is the act of commemorating conceived?;
- how does the time-distance of fifty years appear in the addresses?;
- how are present-day relationships conceived, and related to historical relationships?;
- are audiences other than the immediately present one explicitly or implicitly addressed?'

In these few paragraphs, an amazing amount of directions is given with regard to the types of practices we should engage in. We are reminded of the fact that our discourse analysis should be focused on some of the questions suggested by the organisers. The mentioning of 'line numbers' (which can be referred to in analysis) further explicitises the type of practice captured under discourse analysis: referring to specific, uniformised parts of the texts could (should?) be part of the discourse-analytical dialogue we shall have with the audience.

This problematisation of the texts themselves (i.e. of text structure and text content, and of the relation between these two elements and elements of contexts) is further specified in document (5). There, frame and perspective are both defined as features of communicative practice, resulting in characteristic linguistic phenomena *in* certain forms of texts (as, for example, 'framing *in* press releases'). Our seminar is announced in this document as

> a discourse analytic reconstruction of the Warsaw Memorial Ceremony . . . focusing on the different frames and perspectives *as manifested in the different speeches*. (emphasis added)

What, then, is the status of the other materials included in the information package? Adopting commonsense categories, I would suggest that documents (2), (3), and (6) are the *data*, the texts, in written (and translated), spoken, and performed versions. Document (4) contains some '*background facts*', necessary for a situated understanding of some of the things that are in the texts. Document (5) is an organisational document, the relevance of which for our purpose lies in its *doctrinaire* character. It summarises in a few lines the subject-matter of the conference, and it sketches the types of practices that participants will engage in. We now know that the texts are separate from the 'historical background'. They are the object, and the 'background' is effectively backgrounded, only relevant to the extent that elements from it can be directly fed into the texts. The texts will become the point of synchronisation.

## The making of history: whose background?

Let us now take a closer look at the 'background' materials that were provided to us in view of preparing this seminar. The central document here is document (4); but related elements are also found in document (1) and in a very minimal way in document (5).

### The historical account

Document (4) provides us with an authoritative historical account of the Warsaw Uprising. It is taken from the kind of historical book that would be perceived by many among us as a standard reference work: a book on Polish history in the twentieth century (i.e. written with a wider scope of topics, including the Warsaw Uprising), published by a Polish scholar (i.e. involving assumptions about access to Polish-language sources and eye-witnesses' accounts, as well as a degree of general credibility), and published by a prominent Western academic publisher, undoubtedly after detailed refereeing by other acknowledged specialists. The work is also rather old (it was published in 1977). The use of this text now, almost twenty years after its appearance, would suggest that it is still a standard account of Polish history, unmatched by other, more recent, works. This is how I, at first, received and perceived this document. I read the colophon, decided that it was 'good', then read the whole text and found it instructive and balanced. The story sketched by Dziewanowski is focused on four issues:

   a the optimistic perception of the Soviet offensive among the Polish underground (the Soviets were irresistibly moving towards Warsaw, while the German defence was becoming weak);
   b the political dimension of the decision to unleash the Uprising (the struggle for supremacy by the London émigré government against the communists);

    c the unexpected halt of the Soviet offensive, jeopardising the suc-
      cess of the Uprising, combined with the refusal of help to the
      insurgents by the Soviets suggesting a deliberate move to let the
      pro-London forces bleed to death; and
    d the altogether cynical attitude of Stalin towards the Uprising,
      and the fact that the Soviet inactivity was inspired by political
      rather than by military motives.

Upon a second and more inquisitive reading of the text, I noticed two things. First, it looks as if all the moves and messages of the Soviets were ambiguous and allowed interpretations of encouragements to organise the Uprising – and, in hindsight, as encouragements to commit suicide. There is a wealth of modal and mitigating qualifications when the information about Soviet actions and intentions prior to the Uprising is discussed. The Red Army's offensive '*appeared* irresistible', the Germans '*showed signs of* exhaustion and demoralization', To the insurgents, '*it seemed that* the Wehrmacht would be unable to offer resistance along the Vistula line', a Soviet radio appeal to the Polish people '*apparently indicated* that the Soviet command was about to launch an assault on Warsaw', hence the leader of the underground '*judged the situation ripe* for the Uprising to begin'. The Polish resistance make a string of inferences about, and interpretations of, Soviet actions, and use them as the basis for planning the precise date of an offensive in Warsaw. This complex calculation would involve estimates of the speed and scale of the Soviet ground offensive and undoubtedly a few other technical issues – a series of impressions and appearances that would hardly vindicate the decision, it seems in hindsight. All the perceptions of the Soviet moves are clearly marked as conjectural in the historical account: these *may* have been the meanings of Soviet moves and messages, but they might just as well have been different. Nevertheless, these conjectures are plausible for the historian. Dziewanowski interprets the Soviet communiqué saying that Marshal Rokossovsky's armies 'were advancing on Warsaw' as an unambiguous announcement that the troops 'had been about to capture Poland's capital', thus sanctioning the Home Army's estimate of the timing for the Uprising as realistic and legitimate, and so blaming the Soviets for not keeping their pace.

    The second point that struck me was that the author was very selective when it comes to quoting people. Dziewanowski quotes the comments of (i) Arthur Bliss-Lane, US ambassador to Poland; (ii) Eisenhower (quoted by Bliss-Lane); (iii) General Bor-Komorowski; (iv) an unidentified 'Communist member of the new Polish government' mediated through

Bliss-Lane's words; (v) George F. Kennan; and (vi) Jan Ciechanowski, 'a Western-oriented Polish historian' who revised the standard account of the Uprising. The statement made by the communist member of the new government (narrated by Bliss-Lane) corroborates the thesis that political rather than military considerations guided the Soviet actions during the Uprising. They corroborated, in other words, the post-war anti-communist version of the story. Similarly, Ciechanowski's amendment to the dominant historical account in which both Nazis and Soviets were held responsible for the débâcle of the Uprising is accepted, but serves as the starting-point for a new line of argument in which the Soviet actions are seen as foreshadowing an inevitable geopolitical reshuffling of post-war Europe. The failure of the Uprising was a consequence of the Polish government's overestimation of international support, the Soviets having bargained beforehand that Poland would become part of their sphere of influence. Still, the Allied agreements concluded in Yalta had to be implemented, and so the Soviets decided to let the Polish Home Army be slaughtered by the Nazis. The 'middle position', taken by the Polish historian, does not take away the burden of guilt from the Soviets in the eyes of Dziewanowski; it merely reformulates the nature of the guilty behaviour.

Dziewanowski mentions the fact that the Warsaw Uprising led to bitter controversies in which communist historians were pitted against non-communist historians. The communist account, however, is not mentioned. Dziewanowski refers to the works of a Polish historian, Zenon Kliszko, who is qualified as 'Gomulka's friend'. This is an interesting point, for it indicates how Dziewanowski perceives communist history as biased (the historians are friends of the communist leaders), while people such as Bor-Komorowski, Bliss-Lane, Eisenhower, or Kennan are treated as historical sources with some authority. He calls their camp of historiography the *non*-communist camp rather than the *anti*-communist camp. We know that they are not communists, but what *are* they? Surely, Eisenhower, Kennan, and Brzezinski, let alone Bor-Komorowski or Bliss-Lane, cannot be treated as ideologically neutral actors in the story and its narrative history? Is the non-/anti-communist version of a controversial historical issue *the* undisputed version? Then why is it controversial?

The point we have to take on board before we move any further is that the historical background offered in document (4) is *a particular* historical account, in itself begging for critical analysis. Dziewanowski's account of the Uprising is perfectly in line with the memory of the Uprising articulated in the various speeches, because it is the anti-communist account and, hence, implicates the Soviets as well as the Nazis in the guilt for the crimes.

Let us now briefly return to document (1). At the bottom of the first page, one brief paragraph instructs us how to insert this 'historical background' into discourse analysis. I shall quote it in full, adding emphasis where I believe it is needed:

> In the event four major roles are *relevant*: The Polish role of the occupied country/people who started the revolt, the German role of the occupant who suppressed the revolt, *the Russian role of Ally who did not help, thus becoming a betrayer*, the Allies (the USA, the UK, France, Canada, South Africa, New Zealand, Australia) who did help but were at a too great distance. The Warsaw Uprising is *also important* because of post-war history in which the nations involved here took new relationships along the lines of Yalta, leading to new alliances, *covert occupation*, and hostility. These relationships underwent again revolutionary changes in 1989 and 1990.

Document (5) further emphasises these roles: 'The different nations played different roles in the Uprising: either they were victim, perpetrator, ally or betrayer.'

I take it that the organisers, by writing this, intended to set the record straight for as far as background facts go. They must have assumed that these points are indeed 'facts', and need not be disputed in themselves. The Soviets' role as betrayers is an accepted fact, just as the post-war relationship between the USSR and Poland is suggested to have been one of 'covert occupation'. I do not wish to suggest that any of these assumptions is wrong or unfounded, and even less that the organisers consciously tried to defend an anti-communist agenda by summarising and distributing one particular version of the historical record. The point is, however, that this provides us with a preferred metadiscourse on the various speeches we are supposed to analyse: the roles and responsibilities sketched in the historical background serve as a glossary for reading the texts. It is, in itself, an unintended but quite common case of framing discourse analysis, a case of suggesting an obvious, unquestioned, and unquestionable bottom-line reading of the texts.

*Soviets are Russians*

We have to delve somewhat deeper into the issue of background facts. I hope to have argued clearly in the previous paragraphs that the entextualisation suggested in the background facts represents – broadly speaking – an anti-communist account of the Warsaw Uprising. The mainstream, reliable source selected by the organisers to provide us with some knowledge of what happened in 1944, takes sides in the historical controversy. Its sympathy lies clearly with the Polish Home Army. The author is, furthermore, adamant with respect to the Soviets' role as betrayer guided by political strategies rather than by military ones.

When we look at the speeches of the Commemoration, we see that the roles sketched by the historian as well as by the organisers of this seminar are all, to various degrees, accepted by the speakers, including the Russians and, with some ambivalence, the Germans. The Russian representative, Sergey Filatov, is somewhat circumspect with regard to the issue, and calls for more historical research on the events of 1944. At the same time, however, he refers to 'old-time mistakes' and 'ignominious blunders' in a way which is hard to detach from the particular occasion and topic of the speech. Does this mean that the *Soviets* are acknowledging their unfortunate role of betrayer? This seems to be accepted by the organisers of the workshop, who speak of 'the Russians' rather than 'the Soviets' when discussing the roles played by the various actors in the event.

It has become common practice to equate (post-1990) 'Russians' with (pre-1990) 'Soviets', especially when historical periods such as the Second World War are concerned. A simple political-historical observation that imposes itself, however, is that today's Russians are not yesterday's Soviets, just like today's Germans are not yesterday's Nazis. And the problem with Commemorations such as this one is that a time-span of half a century – a period full of momentous historical events and changes – has to be neutralised or denied by means of a series of simple equations and projections, or synchronisations in the terms defined earlier. In fact, of all the parties involved in the Warsaw Uprising, two are not represented during the Commemoration simply because they have disappeared: the Nazis (the 'perpetrators'); and the Soviets (the 'betrayers'). In the case of the Nazis, the original Nazi perpetrators are still presented as perpetrators (and so, some distance can be kept by Herzog, the president of the 'Germans' and not of the 'Nazis'). In the case of the Soviets, however, a political-historical role-reversal is performed, and from 'ally' they have become 'betrayers'. All this is made explicit in the preparatory materials as well as in the texts of various speeches. Furthermore (but related to this role reversal), whereas the German president only has to acknowledge guilt for one crime – the crushing of the Uprising in 1944 – the Russians have to acknowledge guilt both for their betrayal during the Uprising and for the post-war imperialist oppression of Poland between 1944 and 1990.

The link between both historical events, the Uprising and the post-war communist rule, is constantly made during the Commemoration, and speakers celebrate the heroism of 1944 alongside the collapse of communism in 1989–1990. This is what I meant by synchronisation: a central trope in the Commemoration is the (almost seamless) continuity between events of 1944 and events of recent years, a case which hinges on an equation of 'Soviets' to 'Russians' and which can only be performed from a post-1990 point in history.

This trope obviously begs all kinds of questions. Equating 'Russians' with 'Soviets' across a historical space of half a century involving far-reaching transformations of the socioeconomic and political system entails a number of conceptual and factual problems. In light of the ethno-national terminology in vigour for referring to the post-Soviet states, the equation across time and system reduces a multi-ethnic complex system to one ethnicity. One effect of this reduction is the historical perception of the Soviet Union as dominated by ethnic Russians. This historical perception connects nicely to a (now popular) explanation for the collapse of the Soviet empire as a result of the revolt of the 'hidden nations' after seventy years of systematic oppression of ethnic groups or nations by the (Russian-dominated) Soviet state, and it represents a step in the reinterpretation of the history of the Soviet Union.

Applied to the Commemoration event, the projection of contemporary sociopolitical situations and relations onto historical ones is far from simple. Apart from the Poles, the Germans, and the Soviets/Russians, a number of other countries were represented: the USA, Great Britain, France, South Africa, Canada, New Zealand, and Australia. Together they formed what could be called the 'Western' allies. But in historical and military terms, troops from South Africa, New Zealand, and Australia were all incorporated into the British forces and did not participate in the war as separate national armies. Their pilots flew RAF planes over Warsaw. Still, representatives of all these contemporary states participated in the Commemoration event, and thus for the Western allies the contemporary political situation (the post-empire one) is taken as the point of reference for interpreting past events. Let us now return to the Soviets. Stalin, to my recollection, was a Georgian and not a Russian. It is also rather certain that the Soviet armies in the Warsaw theatre, seen in terms of their contemporary post-Soviet national equivalents, contained not only Russians but also Byelorussians, Lithuanians, Kazakhs, Georgians, Ukrainians, Armenians, and so on. Where are they in the Commemoration event? They are all represented by *one* representative, that of the Russian

Federation. To the contemporary Byelorussians, Lithuanians, Kazakhs, and so on this means that they are represented by their former oppressor, by the former 'empire'. The point of reference in their case is not the contemporary political situation, but the historical one. Whereas the British empire has disappeared from the stage of the Commemoration event, the Soviet empire is still there.

Why? We are probably witnessing the rewriting of history in action, articulated in a complex, but politically correct, synchronised role play. The Russian representative, Filatov, acts simultaneously as the spokesman of the old superpower responsible for so much misery in the past, and as the spokesman of the new superpower inspired by better intentions than its predecessor. He simultaneously speaks on behalf of Stalin, Krushchev, Brezhnev, and Yeltsin. Hence the close associative link between 1944 and 1989–1990: the Warsaw Uprising becomes such a big historical event, precisely because it can be inserted as a trope or an exemplum in a contemporary discourse of post-communism (and legitimised anti-communism). Adopting for a moment the dominant voice of the Commemoration event, we see that the *Russian* representative can afford to dismiss responsibility for the *Soviet* actions, because he (as a spokesman of Boris Yeltsin) embodies post-communism more than any other representative. It was Yeltsin who tolled the bell for the Soviet Union; it was Yeltsin who ascertained a peaceful transition from one superpower to another, turning it from an aggressive and threatening enemy into an altogether meek and co-operative partner in international affairs. In that sense, Filatov's reference to the need for historiography would not be so much an attempt to dodge difficult questions, but rather an expression of the *new* post-communist relations between his country, Poland, and the former Allies, guided by the spirit of rationality, objectivity, and honesty (here all seen in contrast to – Soviet – 'ideology').

*The absent voice*

Synchronisation elides all kinds of possible voices. With regard to the military and political events of 1944, the absence of a Soviet voice is striking, the more since the issue of guilt and responsibility with regard to the Uprising is consistently referred to as controversial and unclear. The reason for this absence cannot be the lack of available sources. I myself have bought quite a few books published by Soviet publishers, and at least two of them contain accounts of the Warsaw Uprising. Needless to say, they provide a quite different view on the events. I shall discuss these two sources at some length. But, before that, I want to stipulate that it would be all too easy to dismiss these sources as fake or forgery. They are significant as *Soviet voices* (regardless of whether the authors have actually written their own autobiographies or 'were autobiographised'), reflecting with all due caveats the way in which Soviet historiography saw the events of 1944. In that sense they are equivalent to Dziewanowski, Bliss-Lane, Eisenhower, or any other source of historical accounts.

The first Soviet account I found in the memoirs of Marshal Georgi Zhukov (1974), the commander of the Red Army in charge of the operations in that area and hence directly responsible for the military aspects of the Soviets' involvement. Let us briefly recall the thesis articulated in Dziewanowski's book as well as in the documents distributed by the organisers of the workshop. It was said that the Soviet army stopped in front of Warsaw and watched the Warsaw people being slaughtered by the German troops. It was also said (and at this point the issue of guilt emerges) that they did this because of *political* reasons, whereas in military terms, nothing would have prevented them from giving (militarily decisive) assistance to the Home Army.

Throughout Zhukov's amazingly informative memoirs, great emphasis is put on the frailty of the Soviet offensives. Nowhere do we meet the image (so widespread elsewhere, and also present in Dziewanowski's account) of the Red Army as an irresistible steamroller crushing all German opposition once it got moving. On the contrary, Zhukov consistently emphasises the precariousness of the operations, the difficulties encountered in preparing for the mammoth offensives of the Eastern Front, the immense losses, and, above all, the fierce opposition of German troops (Zhukov repeatedly mentions the fact that German crack SS divisions were transferred to the Eastern front after D-Day). In Zhukov's account, whenever the Red Army stops, it is because of military-technical reasons. Let us now take a look at the passage in his memoirs in which he discusses the operations in the Warsaw theatre in 1944 (Zhukov 1974: 301ff.). Zhukov is very brief with regard to the Uprising itself. He emphasises Bor-Komorowski's unwillingness to accept co-ordinated actions, the military efforts that were made by the Red Army (including airborne supplies of food, ammunition, and medicines for the insurgents), and the practical impossibility to capture Warsaw at that particular time. Assisting the Warsaw Uprising did not fit into the Soviet strategic tempo, there was no co-ordination of efforts between the Home Army and Zhukov's staff, and thus militarily the Uprising was doomed to fail.

These notes are fully consistent with Zhukov's detailed description of the operations directed at Berlin. All operations are carefully planned, and very little room is left for improvisation or revision of plans once they have been drafted. Hence, Bor-Komorowski's failure to co-ordinate his efforts with those of Zhukov's 1st Byelorussian Front was not purely a matter of procedure, but was an essential condition for providing support to the Uprising. Zhukov emerges as a technocrat who thinks in purely operational terms. Thus, when discussing the halt of the troops in the Warsaw sector, Zhukov advocates a move to defensive positions, given the degree of exhaustion and depletion of the Red Army troops. When asked by Stalin whether a continued offensive in the Warsaw area would be feasible, he answers that it would cause too many casualties and would yield little strategic benefit. This probably meant the death sentence for the Warsaw insurgents. The fact is, however, that Zhukov uses *exclusively military arguments* for his decision. The image of the Red Army, sitting arms crossed on the banks of the Vistula watching the Nazis slaughter the Warsaw people, is far away. Zhukov was particularly wary of crossing the Vistula, fearing that the Germans might put up heavy defences and inflict terrible losses on the Red Army. In all his moves during the counter-offensives since Stalingrad, such operations are consistently dealt with in a very careful way, Zhukov being particularly apprehensive about exposing flanks of his army to enemy counter-attacks. The same goes for capturing major cities. Always there is a period of halt and preparation prior to taking a city. So, when the Red Army stopped in front of Warsaw, it just *might* have been a matter of military logic, of established Red Army procedure.

The second Soviet source are the memoirs of a diplomat, Valentin Berezhkov (Berezhkov 1982), an aide to the Soviet minister of foreign affairs, Molotov. Berezhkov took part in all the major diplomatic events of the Second World War, including the Soviet–German Pact of 1939 and the conferences of Teheran, Yalta, and Potsdam. He spends a whole section discussing the Warsaw Uprising (356–365), recognising that it was an event of major significance in the diplomatic affairs surrounding the Second World War.

Berezhkov's account is more than Zhukov's punctuated with Soviet jargon ('reactionaries', 'revolutionaries', 'bourgeois', etc.). At the same time, he provides us with a verdict of at least shared guilt. He stresses the fact that Poland had been assigned to the Soviet sphere of influence during the Teheran Conference, and that, consequently, Roosevelt also contributed to the undermining of the Polish government in London. Berezhkov draws a picture in which the Soviet government consistently sticks to the terms of the Teheran agreements, supported by repeated confirmations of these terms by Roosevelt. So there were, in Berezhkov's account, no ambiguous messages given by the Soviets. The Soviets emphasised the need to reach an agreement between the

London émigré government and the Polish communist government, and they saw the latter as the most representative body, 'best informed about conditions in Poland' (356).

What, then, about the Uprising? Berezhkov gives an account in which the Polish émigré authorities attempted to boycott the effectiveness of the activities of the communist government, thus trying to create a *fait accompli* in which the émigré organisation could claim to represent the Polish people. Realising that this strategy would clash with Moscow's and Washington's decisions about the future of Poland, they 'hastily took a number of countermeasures, chief among which was organising the Warsaw uprising' (359), which coincided with the visit of the London émigré leader, Mikolajczyk, to Moscow. 'Reactionary groups in Poland hoped that the uprising in Warsaw would strengthen Mikolajczyk's position at the Moscow talks' (360).

As soon as the Soviets were informed about the Uprising, they made it clear that it was doomed to fail. Stalin himself told this to Mikolajczyk, and a Soviet communiqué to the British government reaffirmed it. Berezhkov also elaborates on the military impossibility of supporting the Uprising in a way which fully corroborates Zhukov's version. The Red Army was exhausted after a 40-day offensive and the Germans had put up new and stronger reinforcements. Despite that, units were sent to assist Bor-Komorowski and material support was parachuted. Also, part of the failure was due to the Polish command's refusal to coordinate actions with the Soviet units. The Soviet units suffered heavy losses and withdrew, while air support continued until the capitulation of the Home Army.[10] Berezhkov calls the Uprising an 'unconscionable gamble of the émigré government' (363), and, contrary to Dziewanowski's thesis that the Soviet actions were inspired by political motives, suggests that the *Polish* actions were inspired by political rather than by military motives.

These two Soviet sources present us with a perspective which is radically different from that presented in the 'background facts' offered to the workshop participants. Zhukov stresses the *military* logic behind the Soviet actions in the Warsaw area, and Berezhkov imputes political scheming to the *Polish* leaders. Both sources contradict the thesis established in Dziewanowski's and other authoritative accounts of the Soviet refusal to assist the insurgents as being inspired by a political agenda. The fact of the matter is that there exists a widely accessible Soviet account of the Warsaw Uprising, a Soviet voice, one that at least deserves to be mentioned and to be investigated. If the issue is still controversial, should both sides in the controversy not be given equal credit?

Of course, one can object that these two sources are biased, or typical instances of 'propaganda' (a recurrent theme in Galasinski's 1997 discussion of Filatov's speech). But this then begs the question as to why and by what standards one would call Kennan, Eisenhower, Dziewanowski, and others 'unbiased', or why *our* version would be an instance of 'information', and *theirs* of 'propaganda'? The question is, therefore, not which perspective is true and which is false. It is rather *whose* perspective we adopted and granted authority when we accepted Dziewanowski's version of history as the background facts necessary to know what the speeches talk about. The question is relevant, for we now know that there are different perspectives, each of which should be tested as to their historical plausibility.

### Synchronisation: the viewpoint of post-communism

I would venture that the background we were given is that of the post-communist, post-Soviet, post-1990 'new order'. The version of history in which the Soviet voice is all but eliminated characterises the political–ideological environment that emerged in the early 1990s, and in which we analyse discourse produced on a historical topic involving the Soviet Union as an actor. We were asked to speak from that position in history, and to produce our assemblage of historical facts accordingly.

In the example of the American war veteran we saw how 'vox populism' became the point where synchronisation took place. This point characterised the system with which he associated himself, and it characterised the historical position of that system. We see similar things here, only, the point where we see synchronisation taking place is a particular, technical, notion of an autonomous text-artefact, which is seen as the object of discourse analysis. Instead of everyday rationality, we used professional vision (Goodwin 1994). Such autonomous notions of text are liable to synchronisation, in fact, they may perhaps be anachronistic in themselves: a purely momentary chronicle of events, with referential links between the chronicle and the events, and to be analysed as just *on* history, not *from* history.

## 6.6 CONCLUSIONS

In previous chapters, I have emphasised how people can speak from different semiotic worlds, from within different economies of signs and general conditions of sayability and hearability, orienting to different norms and rules, often not consistent with the norms and rules of the interlocutors. This, I argued, was a problem of inequality in mobility of semiotic resources: some resources could easily move from one space to another, both socially and geographically, while others appeared to have a very restricted range of mobility. These resources were 'placed', they only functioned in one particular environment. I connected this with issues of choice and determination, arguing that being placed in a particular system imposed all sorts of constraints on what people can do with language.

I extended this argument so as to include history as a factor in inequality. Mobility also applies to perspectives on, and from, history. Every bit of discourse displays what I have called layered simultaneity, it is conditioned by, and refers to, several layers of historical material. But only part of that material is visible and open to individual awareness and experience. Synchronisation occurs in the form of condensation of several historical layers into one, synchronic, layer of history, reflecting a position in history. It includes some historical materials and excludes some others in ways that reflect determination: we see systemic influences operating in the processes of synchronisation.[11]

If we combine these different forms of determination, social, spatial, and historical, we can suggest that people speak *from within a position in the world system*. We shall encounter systemic differences in such positions, reflecting structural differences and inequalities in the world system. This, I believe, could cast new light on two well-established fields of critical scholarship: ideology and identity. The next two chapters will be devoted to an exploration of these topics.

## *SUGGESTIONS FOR FURTHER READING*

Since I believe that everyone in our field should read historical classics, Braudel (e.g. 1981) and Wallerstein (1983, 2001), especially when he discusses Braudel (in Wallerstein 2000) are fundamental. E. P. Thompson (1991) is an excellent introduction to time, culture, and social processes. Ginzburg (1999), especially when read in conjunction with some of his other work, reveals a wealth of methodological and epistemological issues worthy of reflection. The problem of discontinuity and continuity is dealt with in a most fascinating way in Foucault (2003). Simultaneity in discourse is foregrounded in Woolard (1998a), though it is also central to Halliday's view of functions in language (see Kress 1976; Chouliaraki and Fairclough 1999). On problems of time and epistemology, I still find Fabian (1983) illuminating.

# 7 Ideology

## 7.1 INTRODUCTION

Discourse and power: combine the two terms and we think of ideology. Ideology has indeed been a very fertile topic of investigation in CDA (Kress and Hodge 1979; Fairclough 1989, 1992; Wodak 1989; van Dijk 1998) and related branches of discourse analysis (Verschueren 1999). The reasons for this are not hard to find: discourse (or semiotic behaviour at large) has been identified by almost every major scholar as a site of ideology. At the same time, the matter is only apparently straightforward. Few terms are as badly served by scholarship as the term ideology, and as soon as anyone enters the field of ideology studies, he or she finds him/herself in a morass of contradictory definitions, widely varying approaches to ideology, and huge controversies over terms, phenomena, or modes of analysis.

To start with the simplest and most basic difference in definition and approach: there are, on the one hand, authors who define ideology as a *specific* set of symbolic representations – discourses, terms, arguments, images, stereotypes – serving a *specific* purpose, and operated by *specific* groups or actors, recognisable precisely by their usage of such ideologies. On the other hand, there are authors who would define ideology as a *general* phenomenon characterising the *totality* of a particular social or political system, and operated by *every* member or actor in that system (see Eagleton 1991; Thompson 1984 for surveys).

Under the first category we can find the well-known '-isms': socialism, liberalism, fascism, communism, libertarianism, anarchism, and so forth. The category also includes more specific ones referring to the specific 'ideology' attributed to an individual or a 'school', such as Marxism, Leninism, Maoism, Stalinism, Rooseveltism, Gaullism, Mobutism, and so forth. And the suffix '-ism' can sometimes be replaced by nouns such as 'school' or 'doctrine', as, for example, in 'Monroe Doctrine', the 'Truman Doctrine', the 'Chicago School', and so on. They also include particular *positions within a political system*, 'factions' so to speak, such as 'conservative', 'progressive', 'revolutionary', 'reactionary', 'racism', 'anti-semitism', 'sexism', 'classism', etc. Such 'ideologies' characterise actors who adhere to them. A 'socialist' is someone who subscribes to the set of symbolic representations we call 'socialism'; a 'racist' is someone who subscribes to racism; a 'conservative' socialist is someone who, within the complex of 'socialism' subscribes to a particular ('conservative') interpretation of the socialist lines of actions. Such ideologies are often codified – there are 'basic' texts supporting them – as well as explicit and historically contingent: they have a clear origin (often in the writings of a seminal author) and a pattern of development (e.g. through institutionalisation: political parties or movements), and, like Mobutism, the Monroe Doctrine, or Maoism, they may disappear (see Freeden 1996). Ideology in this first sense stands for *partisan* views and opinions, it is sensed to represent a particular bias characterising specific social formations with specific interests. Hence the widespread colloquial usage of 'ideological' as counterfactual, biased, partisan.

The second category is less easy to describe. Authors would emphasise that ideology stands for the 'cultural', ideational aspects of a particular social and political system, the 'grand narratives' characterising its existence, structure, and historical development. This is the sense of ideology often attributed to the work of Antonio Gramsci (1971). Authors in this second category would emphasise that ideology cannot be attributed to one particular actor, not located in one particular site (such as a political party or a government), but that it penetrates the whole fabric of societies or communities and results in normalised, naturalised patterns of thought and behaviour. For such authors, ideology is common sense, the normal perceptions we have of the world as a system, the naturalised activities that sustain social relations and power structures, and the patterns of power that reinforce such common sense. Authors articulating such views include Pierre Bourdieu (1990), Louis Althusser (1971), Roland Barthes (1957), Raymond Williams (1973, 1977) and Michel Foucault (1975).[1] Often, only one '-ism' is accepted: capitalism, seen as the overall system in which contemporary societies develop. And capitalism is a prototype of such ideological processes: it has become so natural and normal as a frame of reference for thought and behaviour that it is not perceived as a system with ideological attributes.

Roland Barthes (1957: 225), with characteristic irony, notes that there is no single parliament in Western Europe in which we can find a

'Bourgeois party', while most parliaments would count members of the 'Socialist party' or the 'Labour party'. He adds:

> the bourgeoisie has erased its name in the transition from reality to representation . . . it has subjected its own status to an act of *ex-nomination*; the bourgeoisie defines itself as *the social class that does not want to be named*. (*ibid.*, my translation, French original)

The centre of capitalism, the bourgeoisie, is a neutral, unmarked, self-evident centre. Ideology, or at least, the overarching ideology which defines the others, is in the system itself, and precisely this all-encompassing ideological character of capitalism makes its ideological nature and characteristics invisible. They are 'normal' and 'normative': other 'ideologies' are measured against the ideological zero-point, capitalism.[2] The ideological enemy, in Barthes' view, is thus not liberalism, Gaullism, or communism, but '*l'ennemi capital (la Norme bourgeoise)*' (1957: 8), the invisible and self-evident systemic core which we fail to recognise as ideological because it is *our* ideology.

Seen from that perspective, the two senses of ideology are not each other's opposite or contradiction. Barthes directs us towards a view in which ideology is *layered*, stratified, something that has varying dimensions and scopes of operation as well as varying degrees of accessibility to consciousness and agency. We see similar distinctions in Voloshinov's work, when he separates 'established ideologies' from 'behavioural ideologies' (Voloshinov 1973: 90–92), in which the former is both the crystallisation of and the motive for the latter. This insight is very useful and it resonates with many of the arguments on polycentric-stratified orders of indexicality and layered simultaneity developed elsewhere in this book. It will guide us through the discussion in this chapter. If we are not facing contradictory definitions but different aspects of the same thing, we need to find a solution for the whole thing.

I shall try to offer some suggestions on how to conceive of the relationship between ideology and layered simultaneity in discourse. The outcome will be a view in which various simultaneous ideologies operate in discourse, providing differing layers of sharedness, coherence, and historicity to discourse. Since discourse is intrinsically historical, it is intrinsically ideological, but again different aspects of this are of a different order. In this exercise I hope to bring together several existing views on ideology, in an attempt to show how they address not different objects but different aspects of the same object. I shall start with a brief *tour d'horizon* of such views.

## 7.2  THE TERMINOLOGICAL MUDDLE OF IDEOLOGIES

Apart from the two main differences outlined earlier, between views of ideology as closed, named and specific objects, on the one hand, and views of ideology as general, totalising phenomena, several other differences should be noted in the field of study.

### Cognitive/ideational versus material

A first distinction is between ideologies as primarily *cognitive/ideational* phenomena versus ideologies as *material* phenomena or *practices*. In the first view, ideologies would primarily be particular sets of ideas, perceptions, received wisdom; in the latter, ideologies would be defined as ideas produced by particular material conditions or instruments and performed in certain ways. In the second view, authors would emphasise the particular social formations, instruments of power, and institutional frames within which particular sets of ideas are promulgated. Obviously, the most useful authors suggest that ideational and material forces interact, heeding Marx's old saying that ideas become material forces as soon as they are appropriated by the masses.

Many approaches that define ideology in the sense of closed, particular objects (as '-isms', in other words) subscribe to the cognitive/ideational ('idealist') view and define, for instance, socialism as a 'socialist' complex of definitions, ideas, and values, rhetorical patterns, canonized texts, and views of society and of human beings (Freeden 1996). Many approaches in the totalising school, however, also conceive ideologies as primarily ideational, as 'normalised' ideas, concepts, associative connections between causes and effects, and so on. Thus Paul Friedrich (1989: 302), reviewing several major sources of scholarship, defines ideology as 'a set or at least amalgam of ideas, rationalizations, and interpretations that mask or gloss over a struggle to get or hold onto power, particularly economic power, with the result that the actors and ideologues are themselves largely unaware of what is going on'.

An extreme example of the cognitive/ideational approach to ideology is Teun van Dijk's socio-cognitive view. Van Dijk defines ideologies as

> the 'interface' between the cognitive representations and processes underlying discourse and action, on the one hand, and the societal position and interests and social groups, on the other hand. . . . As systems of principles that organize social cognitions, ideologies are assumed to control, through the minds of the members, the social reproduction of the group. Ideologies mentally represent the basic

social characteristics of a group, such as their identity, tasks, goals, norms, values, position and resources. (van Dijk 1995: 18)

In other words, ideologies are 'group-schemata' in the cognitive-linguistic sense of the term: abstract cognitive complexes located in the minds of members of groups, based on accumulated experience and socialisation, and organising the way in which these members think, speak, and act:

> As basic forms of social cognitions . . . ideologies also have cognitive functions. We have already suggested that they organize, monitor and control specific group attitudes. Possibly, ideologies also control the development, structure and application of sociocultural knowledge. (van Dijk 1995: 19)

So when it comes to explaining how ideologies become ingredients of structures of power and control, van Dijk's solution is straightforward: people control *themselves* by means of the ideologies they have in their heads, and they do so *as a group* because the ideologies are group ideologies. Van Dijk insists that

> [i]deologies in our perspective are not merely 'systems of ideas', let alone properties of the individual minds of persons. Neither are they vaguely defined as forms of consciousness, let alone 'false consciousness'. Rather, they are very specific basic frameworks of social cognition, with specific internal structures, and specific cognitive and social functions. (van Dijk 1995: 21)

In other words: ideologies are even more abstract and fundamental than propositionally articulated ideas, they are the underlying 'deep structures' of social behaviour.

How such very deep cognitive patterns end up in people's heads, and end up there as collective phenomena is a question van Dijk leaves to others.[3] This is where materialist approaches may be helpful. Louis Althusser (1971) strongly emphasised the role of 'ideological state apparatuses' in the production and reproduction of ideologies. By 'state apparatuses' he understood the whole complex of institutions *below* the level of the state, but working in conjunction with the state or serving state interests. Such apparatuses include the church, schools, the media, interest groups – in short what is often called 'civil society'. And they generate ideological 'interpellations': appeals to individuals to act in particular ways, ways that reflect dominant ideologies. In contrast to the cognitive/ideational approach, Althusser emphasises 'a social process of address, or "interpellations", inscribed in material social matrices' (Therborn 1980: 7). In other words, ideology needs to be understood as processes that require material reality and institutional structures and practices of power and authority.

This corresponds to views such as those of John B. Thompson (1990). Thompson claims that modern First-World societies have undergone a drastic change in the way in which ideological processes develop. This change is due to the rise of modern mass media, and no ideological process today can be understood without taking into account the way in which messages, images, and discourses are being distributed and mediated by the mass media. Consequently, the symbolic or the ideational has become far more of a commodity than before, and the dynamics of ideology should be interpreted likewise. No idea is in itself 'ideological'; it may become ideological as soon as it is picked up by power-regulating institutions such as the media and inserted into the ideological reproduction system they organise. Thus, the media seem to have the power to construct deep ideological messages out of trivial, sociologically insignificant events or phenomena. The message may be shallow but the modulation of the message through the mass media converts it into a message of enormous importance. Consequently, Thompson warns us against 'the fallacy of internalism' (1990: 24), the idea that effects of messages can be 'read off' the messages themselves, that the power of ideologies lies in the message alone, that we, for instance, can understand Lincoln's charisma by analysing the grammar of his speeches. We need to investigate the ways in which the message is organised, mediated, modulated, and reconstructed by the ideological actors using it.

Thompson, Althusser, and others do not deny the necessity of an ideational or cognitive component in ideologies, but they emphasise the fact that something more is required to understand ideologies: attention to the material, political, and institutional environments in which they operate. Ideas operate alongside and inside material conditions and institutions; it is the conjunction of both dimensions which lifts particular sets of ideas to the level of ideology. This basic insight can, of course, also be found in Bourdieu's work as well as in that of Foucault. Foucault systematically emphasised the interrelation between a specific 'épistème' – a complex of *savoir*, of knowledge – on the one hand, and sets of practices and institutional conditions on the other. The 'panopticon' which Foucault described and discussed in *Discipline and Punish* is a case in point. Foucault argued that the panoptic architecture of modern prisons – a star-like shape in which all prisoners could be observed by their guards from one central point – generated a particular kind of knowledge through institutionally organised and materially enabled practices of seeing, observing, and disciplining. It was both the product of and the instrument for such new forms of surveillance-by-knowledge (Foucault 1975; cf. also 2001b: 190–207). Bourdieu and Passeron's (1977) notion of 'reproduction' stresses the connection between institutional educational practice and the construction of 'legitimate' knowledge, i.e. knowledge that relates and refers to the dominant culture (i.e. the culture of the dominant). Bourdieu summarises it succinctly: 'educated people owe their culture – i.e. a programme of perception, thought and action – to the school' (1971: 199), and consequently, the education system, often a state-organised or controlled institution, culturally (or ideologically) reproduces class stratification:

> The school's function is not merely to sanction the *distinction* . . . of the educated classes. The culture that it imparts separates those receiving it from the rest of society by a whole series of systematic differences. (1971: 200)

A safe position, consequently, may consist in adopting a view of ideologies as materially mediated ideational phenomena. Ideas themselves do not define ideologies; they need to be inserted in material practices of modulation and reproduction.

## Whose ideology and why?

Another difference encountered in the literature on ideology relates to the scope of ideologies. As mentioned above, there are authors who suggest that ideologies are general, all-pervasive, and defining of a 'society' or a 'system', and there are authors who distinguish between several, group-specific ideologies. Such group-specific ideologies would be, for instance, class ideologies, gender-ideologies, ethnic group ideologies, and so forth. Such differences cross-cut the general difference between the idealist and materialist main schools outlined earlier, but they raise issues of function and agency.

In the 1930s, Karl Mannheim (in Burke 1992: 95) already introduced the distinction between 'total' conceptions of ideology and 'particular' ones, whereby the total conception roughly corresponded to what in anthropological terms would be called 'worldview', a general pattern of beliefs and ideas characterising a social formation. The particular conception of ideology stood for ideology as *instrumental* to the aims and purposes of specific actors, for ideology as a tool of power. Whereas a 'total' conception of ideology would emphasise that ideologies are *in se* neither positive nor negative, but 'just there', the particular conception would emphasise the ways in which ideologies can become real agents of power and change.

The study of ideology owes much to Marxism, but in core Marxist writings both conceptions can be found. Marx and Engels defined ideology in *The German Ideology* in terms germane to the 'total' conception. In fact, the bourgeoisie is often characterised in such terms (see Barthes' remarks above, but see also Marx's *Eighteenth Brumaire*). Similarly, Marx would identify the working class as characterised by 'false consciousness'. The workers had ideas and perceptions of their life-conditions that were at odds with their objective position within the capitalist system. Thus, they would believe that they shared interests with their employers – interests such as the productivity of the enterprise, the profit margins of the capitalist entrepreneur – whereas, in reality, their interests were fundamentally incompatible with those of capital. This false consciousness was an effect of the incorporation of the workers in the 'total' ideology of capitalism. Therefore – and here we move into the particular conception of ideology – workers needed to acquire a different consciousness that reflected their real situation and would mobilise them against capital. Class consciousness formed by socialist ideology would become a weapon against capital, an instrument in the struggle for power.

Lenin as well as Gramsci further developed this 'particular', instrumental conception of ideology. To Lenin in *What Is To Be Done?* ideology was one of the central preoccupations of the socialist movement, for it was through the development of a socialist ideology that the workers would be built into a working class and become a revolutionary force (recall also E. P. Thompson's theses on class consciousness as crucial to the emergence of 'class'). Such an ideology would be particular: it would be the workers' ideology, and it would be promoted and distributed by an 'ideological state apparatus', the party (or elsewhere the labour union), led by a 'revolutionary vanguard' of intellectual cadres (Lenin believed that a revolutionary ideology needed to be brought in from the outside, since workers could not develop such a theoretically grounded ideology themselves). When Antonio Gramsci started making notes in his Italian prison cell, he had this precise and specific, 'particular' problem in mind: how do we start a proletarian revolution in Italy, a society then completely dominated by Mussolini's bourgeois fascists? His prison notes reveal an analysis of bourgeois ideology seen as a total, all-pervasive ideology, but analysed as to its instrumental ('particular') functions and *modus operandi*, as an ideology of domination. And Gramsci's famous statements on ideological hegemony were the outcome of an exercise in which he adopted and adapted the bourgeois instrumentalisation of ideology for the cause of the proletarian revolution (including the development of a class of 'organic intellectuals' who could counter the ideological work of the 'professional' bourgeois intellectuals).

The desired outcome of such an ideological offensive using a class-specific, particular ideology, would be a total ideology. A socialist, working-class ideology would become the ideology of everyone, it would become hegemonic and so mark the end of bourgeois capitalist society and the transition to a socialist one. The pattern of transition thus swings from a total ideology (that of the capitalist bourgeoisie prior to the socialist revolution) over a particular ideology (that of the revolutionary and mobilised working class) back to a total ideology (that of the new, post-revolution socialist society). The difference between total and particular ideologies is a temporal-sequential difference, the different kinds of ideology represent different stages in the process of historical change.

I would suggest that we keep this in mind: that different forms of ideologies may be part of the same historical process, and that differences between them may reflect differences in the social formations characterised by them, their purposes, or their moment of occurrence. Particular ideologies only make sense when seen in relation to other particular ideologies or to total ideologies operating in the same environment within a particular time-frame (cf. Woolard 1985). A description of a single particular ideology – for instance, racism or anti-semitism – should be accompanied by an analysis of its relation to other ideologies, total as well as particular.

## The different faces of hegemony

Hegemony is a key term in many writings on ideology. The term is not Antonio Gramsci's, but Gramsci is the one who theorised hegemony as an ingredient of political struggle. Hegemony, in Gramsci's work, stood for the 'cultural domination' of the bourgeoisie over the rest of society. The bourgeoisie not only controlled the economy and had the monopoly over the state (and, hence, over the instruments of state violence) but it was also culturally dominant. The power of the bourgeoisie, in other words, was 'hard' as well as 'soft', material as well as cultural and ideational. The bourgeoisie ruled by *force* through its control over the state, as well as by *consent* through its control over culture and ideas in civil society. Hegemony, soft power, was the glue that connected other classes to the bourgeoisie. And if a proletarian revolution was to succeed, it would have to occupy both domains of power.[4]

It is remarkable how often hegemony, or ideology in general, has been interpreted as a domain that could be studied in and of itself, rather than in relation to force. And, consequently, it is remarkable how often hegemony is interpreted as generalised, even internalised, consent. Van Dijk's view of ideology as the conceptual framework in which people live and act is, of course, the most outspoken example, but even some readings of Bourdieu's 'habitus' concept, or Raymond Williams' view of hegemony as 'deeply saturating the consciousness of a society' (1973: 8) may give rise to such views of hegemony as total consent. Two general amendments need to be kept in mind.

The first one is the importance of *coercion* in ideological processes. Gramsci already defined a dual strategy for his socialist revolution. Hegemony – power by consent – was one part of it, and it would be used in defining the relationships between the proletariat and potential allied classes such as the peasants. But the second part of the strategy was force, coercion, and this would define the relationships with the enemy class, the bourgeoisie. The reason was that the proletariat could not acquire hegemony at once, given the complete domination of the bourgeoisie over the 'ideological state apparatuses'. So the bourgeoisie needed to be struck by force, while ideology was a tool necessary to form alliances with other classes. This attack on the bourgeoisie – on the state and its ideological apparatuses – would take place as soon as hegemony had been acquired among the allied revolutionary classes.

It is useful to keep this in mind: that strategically deployable ideology is *part of power*, not coterminous with power. In fact, to the extent that we can distinguish between 'dominant' and 'determining' factors in power, hegemony would be 'dominant' and force would be 'determining'.[5] It is also wise to remember that ideological processes such as the ones described by Bourdieu and Foucault involve elaborate coercive practices. The pattern of reproduction of dominant culture described by Bourdieu is sustained by a coercive and disciplining system of education, a kind of totalitarian institution in turn described by Foucault as the locus of capillary power, all-pervasive surveillance, and perpetual punishability. At the end of the day, hegemony may be what it is *because there is a real price to be paid for being anti-hegemonic*. The price may be that one is not understood, not heard, not recognised as a subject, but it may also be that one is ostracised, exiled, killed or jailed, made unemployable, or declared insane. As Foucault has shown, the boundaries of hegemony are well guarded by coercive institutions.

This insight may be useful for distinguishing between oppositional and anti-hegemonic practices, and so help us to understand the relationship between dominant and dissenting ideologies (Woolard 1985). Oppositional practices are often tolerated, while anti-hegemonic practices are often rejected and punished. Here we enter the realm of those ideologies that Roland Barthes identified as 'borrowing from the bourgeoisie': anti-bourgeoisie, dissident, or resistance ideologies that operate within the boundaries of the general hegemony. They are not anti-hegemonic, for they do not challenge the general boundaries of the system. Many forms of anti-racism in contemporary Europe are thus oppositional but not anti-hegemonic because they do not challenge the basic, systemic forms of inequality in which immigrant minorities are captured, but instead appeal to individual tolerance and broad-mindedness of majority members (Blommaert and Verschueren 1998; compare also Wallerstein's analysis of racism: Wallerstein 2000, part 4; Balibar and Wallerstein 1988). The system can redefine its boundaries and thus outlaw forms of dissidence that were previously tolerated. The Cold War period is full of examples of this process of redefining systemic boundaries on both sides of the East–West divide. McCarthyism, for instance, was an utterly coercive redefinition of hegemonic boundaries in the USA. Left-wing political positions that were tolerated, even celebrated, prior to the early 1950s were declared 'un-American', and persons holding such positions were not *convinced* to alter their ideas, but *forced* to do so or suffer the consequences. The long-term result of this coercive redefinition of boundaries was, by all standards, hegemony – anti-communism as the default 'American' (as opposed to 'un-American') political stance in the world. But it was not the result of consent, it was the result of coercion.

A second important amendment, related to the first one, is the point made by James Scott (1990). Scott drew our attention to the fact that a smooth hegemony could hide deeply dissenting views and practices, so-called 'hidden transcripts'. Domination, argued Scott, rests on the enactment of power and powerlessness. Both the slave-master and the slave needed to enact, to perform, their relations of power in order to reproduce it: the slave-owner by acting brutally and avoiding visible expressions of doubt or insecurity; the slave by acting like a docile, subjugated, harmless person. To both parties in this relationship, this enactment constituted a form of protection against the other in a system which was always fragile: there were always fewer slave-owners than slaves on a plantation, always fewer colonisers than colonised in the colonies, while slave-owners and colonisers had the monopoly over violence. But this hegemonic appearance only occurred in such overt moments of enactment. Separately, the parties could maintain deeply different views of themselves, each other, and their relationship. The white colonisers could talk about their fear and insecurity in the confines of the whites-only country club; the slaves could develop elaborate anti-slave-owner discourses and scenarios of reprisal in their slave quarters. So beneath the surface of hegemony may be a world of dissidence and anti-hegemonic discourses, of hidden transcripts. Such hidden transcripts could be forced to the surface in periods of crisis or conflict. The hegemonic appearances could then be broken and the dissident views could be aired.

Scott cautions us against seeing hegemony as a full package of 'software', so to speak. What looks like hegemony may be a matter of 'hegemonic practices' only, a performance not based on an internalisation of the beliefs and ideas that are sensed to guide these practices. Both can be disconnected, and rather than 'orthodoxy' we may face 'orthopraxy' – *doing as if* one shares the beliefs and ideas, performing hegemonic acts without subscribing to the ideology that gives meaning to them. Given the importance of coercion in ideological practices, it is not unlikely that orthopraxy is one, important, mode of ideological process. In strongly coercive systems, one may adopt the required appearances even if one deeply resents them, just because there are no other options. In fact, *orthopraxy may be the beginning stage of every ideological process that uses coercion as an instrument of hegemonisation*: schools, bureaucracy, the law, the labour market, and so on. Perhaps orthopraxy, rather than internalised social-cognitive schemata, is at the core of hegemony in contemporary First-World societies.

Scott also underscores the *behavioural* dimensions of ideology. Rather than being seen as just a set of ideas, ideology could be seen as at least partially constituted of particular, meaningful practices. In fact, taking ideology out of a purely ideational space and bringing it into a more complex and layered space in which ideational, behavioural, and institutional aspects interact along lines of consent and coercion may considerably enhance our understanding of ideological processes. It may explain why someone who supports Greenpeace and votes for the Green party may still seek a job in a private multinational corporation, put his or her savings in the stock market, drive a car, and believe that immigrants should be 'integrated' in 'our' society. Ideology may be that which guides us through different roles and places in society – but then we are talking about different ideologies that operate at very different levels and obey very different rules. Each of those spaces and roles could in its own way respond to different hegemonies, and groups or communities could be defined on the basis of varying bundles of shared hegemonies.

## Mentalities, public opinion, and worldviews

A final set of distinctions, which I shall treat only briefly, is that between approaches focusing on 'mentalities', 'public opinion', and 'worldviews' versus approaches focusing on 'ideologies'. Burke

(1992: 91ff.) mentions the historical congruence between the emergence of studies of 'mentalities' and studies of 'ideologies'. Both must be situated in the period between the First and Second World Wars, but, whereas the emergence of studies of 'mentalities' was largely due to the *Annales* historical school pioneered by Marc Bloch and Lucien Febvre, the study of 'ideologies' emerged from Marxist scholarship, as noted above. Both seem to address very similar phenomena: collective patterns of thought and action, characteristic of a certain regime, span of time, or social formation. It is hard to think of 'mentalities' in the sense described by Marc Bloch (1961, see also 1953), for example, as anything other than ('total') ideologies.

The same goes for 'public opinion'. To the extent that one can grant credibility to any concept of 'public' 'opinion' (in which both parts of the term are empirically examined as to their validity, see Bourdieu 1993), it is hard to imagine such collective, socially structured, ideational phenomena to be anything other than ideologies representing the particular historical and social viewpoint of the respondents of a public opinion poll (in itself an institutional discourse practice that creates such ideologies). In that sense, I also believe that there are good reasons to replace the term 'public opinion', with its cosy overtones of equality and uniform comparability resulting in statistical fractions, by the politically and historically more sensitive term 'ideology'.

The issue of worldviews is slightly more complicated. The study of worldviews emerged, just like studies on mentalities and ideologies, in the period between the two World Wars. It emerged as part of the Boasian paradigm in American anthropology, and it had a precursor in Von Humboldt's concept of *Weltanschauung*. The way in which it was used in anthropology was as shorthand for the 'deep' levels of culture, the kind of implicit, deeply normalised, patterns and principles according to which a culture became a cohesive whole. And language, especially in the works of Boas, Sapir, and Whorf, was seen as a useful entrance into this implicit world of patterns and principles (Hill and Mannheim 1992; Lucy 1985; Silverstein 1979).

Problematic in the anthropological treatment of worldview was the suggestion of closure and stability, the suggestion that 'a' culture could be imbued with 'a' (delineable, coherent) worldview, the patterns and principles of which would be 'known' by every member of such a culture. The problem is similar to the one with 'public opinion' above: it is hard to find empirical attestations of such cultural uniformity, and the suggestion of closure and stability risks lifting something which emerges, changes, and is a field of struggle to a level of uncontestable universal, timeless principle. Thus, Jane Hill and Bruce Mannheim conclude, 'where "world view" would once have served, "ideology" is often heard, suggesting representations that are contestable, socially positioned, and laden with political interest' (Hill and Mannheim 1992: 382).

Let us return for a moment to the issue of language and worldview, central to what became known as linguistic relativism. Later developments in this field gave rise to the notion of language ideologies (a term often used in this book), and the central argument in the study of language ideologies is well summarised by Irvine and Gal (2000: 37):

> linguistic features are seen as reflecting and expressing broader cultural images of people and activities. Participants' ideologies about language locate linguistic phenomena as part of, and evidence for, what they believe to be systematic behavioural, aesthetic, affective, and moral contrasts among the social groups indexed. That is, people have, and act in relation to, ideologically constructed representations of linguistic differences. In these ideological constructions, indexical relationships become the ground on which other sign relationships are built.

Thus we see how the older Boasian notion of worldview, mediated through Sapir's and Whorf's nuanced views of connections between linguistic forms and 'deep' cultural patterns and principles, has developed in a mature view of an ideologised semiotic world coupled to an empirical programme of investigating links between aspects of such ideological complexes. A particularly worthwhile topic of investigation is the relationship between linguistic ideologies and other, socio-political, or cultural ideologies – the question of how linguistic ideologies can and do become instruments of power as part of larger ideological complexes (Kroskrity 2000; Blommaert, ed. 1999; Jaffe 1999; Bauman and Briggs 2003). The second illustration below will offer some suggestions in that direction.

## 7.3 POLYCENTRIC SYSTEMS, LAYERED IDEOLOGIES

The terminological differences discussed above seem to me to be the result of differences in looking at what is fundamentally the same thing. When these different perspectives collapse in the use of a single term – ideology – all kinds of battles over the meaning of that term can and do emerge. It may be more productive to focus on the different perspectives rather than on the term, and I propose that when thinking about ideology we focus on the who-what-where-why-and-how of ideology. Accepting that 'ideology' may be a term that can cover processes and practices at several levels of consciousness, of different scope and scale, and with different effects, we need to find out how such different ideological processes work and interact. There are several ways of doing this. My suggestion is to go back to the model of voice developed in chapter 4 of this book, and see whether it can be useful for (re)structuring this field.

Let me start by recapitulating the essence of this model of voice. I started with sketching a view of functional relativity, emphasising that the same semiotic actions or processes could mean very different things in different environments. Shifts across environments involved shifts in function, the attribution of different meanings and values to the same semiotic action, object, or process. I then moved on to argue that we could conceive of semiotic behaviour as guided by orders of indexicality, stratified patterns of social meanings often called 'norms' or 'rules'. I connected these orders of indexicality to centring institutions: real or imagined actors perceived to cause to emanate the authoritative attributions to which one should orient in order to have voice, i.e. in order to make sense under the criteria imposed by the orders of indexicality. And, finally, I argued that the semiotic life-world of people can best be seen as a polycentric, stratified system. In every act of semiosis, there are a variety of centring institutions at play, but not all of them are equally salient, accessible to conscious orienting, or equal in scope, range, and impact. Some centring institutions – the small peer group, the family – have a narrow scope, while others such as schools, the church, political movements, or the state had a far wider scope.

The connections between indexicality and ideology are, I believe, abundantly clear. Indexicality is one of the points where the social and cultural order enters language and communicative behaviour. When I answer a request from someone in my workplace environment who is more senior than myself by 'yes sir', I am not only formulating a 'positive' reply, but the use of the term 'sir' marks my answer as a 'polite' answer. But what does this mean? It means that my answer signals an act of deference, a recognition of the stable social status differences between myself and my interlocutor. And, since I would probably not be the only one to use this expression in similar situations, I am inscribing my unique act of communication in a social tradition, in a structure of behaviour that reflects at a microscopic level the general social stratification in society (see Ochs 1990, 1992). In other words, I am displaying effects of 'capillary power' in the sense of Foucault, and apart from orienting to my interlocutor and the norms that define my particular relationship with him, my utterance also orients to common institutional (e.g. workplace, school) norms as well as to general social ones that characterise the kind of stratification of a society such as mine over a (long) span of time. I am displaying hegemony at all these levels of action. My utterance identifies me, or at least, it identifies the social and cultural position from where I speak. It sets me off as a member of a particular workplace culture as opposed to members of other such cultures, where, instead of 'sir', 'John' or 'Jim' would be used. It also sets me off as a member of a particular type of stratified society in contrast to members of societies where forms of address such as 'brother' or 'comrade' would be used in similar circumstances. To my friends in Tanzania in the 1980s, for instance, the use of 'sir' would have invoked orders of indexicality known to characterise *other* societies: colonial Africa or the capitalist world. In their own socialist society, *ndugu*, 'brother', would be the appropriate term of address in similar situations.

But imagine me using the same expression in responding to a request from my wife. In that case, the expression would be ironic in the sense that norms are invoked that are not immediately applicable to the situation at hand, but allow a particular set of attributions to it: my wife is pictured as 'my boss', I am pictured as her subordinate in a stratified, hierarchical chain of command. In other words, I am orienting to an order of indexicality which is 'normally' alien to the particular situation, but nevertheless meaningful when invoked in relation to it. This again is likely to be hegemonic behaviour, for the role- and meaning-reversal could not be effected without the availability of hegemonic associations that connect particular utterances to particular social patterns and structures. So even in an act of apparent defiance of norms – I am not supposed to picture my wife this way, and doing it is marked, unusual, and therefore densely meaningful – I am, in fact, responding to these norms by flouting them, reversing them, or performing a *bricolage* of several norms. Ideology offers semiotic opportunities through the availability of multiple meaningful batteries of indexicality.

This means that we can conceive of ideological processes in very similar terms as the ones defined for voice. We can see them as operating in and through polycentric and stratified systems, in which different ideologies are at play at different levels and in different ways, but operating in the kind of layered simultaneity described in the previous chapter. They are thus open to the same kind of synchronisation as the one we saw in the previous chapter: the various layers of ideology can be collapsed into one, synchronic layer, in which all kinds of differences can be found. Perhaps some of the terminological muddle in the field of ideology is the result of such synchronisations: people investigating phenomena that involve ideological layers of a different order, but collapsing them into one object which then comes to stand for 'ideology', period.

The degree of congruence or contrast between ideologies at different levels allows us to infer various kinds of meanings.[6] In the example above, the senior member of my workplace environment may perceive me as a 'good employee' because of the congruence between the various levels of ideology invoked in my utterance: interpersonal, particular workplace, my workplace *vis-à-vis* others (i.e. *our* workplace), social stratification, my society as opposed to others (i.e. *our* society), everything fits and is in accordance. My wife, however, may perceive me as a 'bad husband' because of the incongruence between various levels: the stratified workplace environment invoked by my utterance, with all its associative meanings, does not fit the interpersonal, home environment in which it is produced. So the same utterance becomes fundamentally different due to different ideological framings. We see stratification: the interpersonal level is invaded by invoked orders of indexicality that operate at higher levels, i.e. the workplace, society at large. And we see layered historicity: the various layers of ideology take us gradually away from the one-time event into slower layers, aspects of society that have been there for longer spans of time, such as the use of 'sir' and its connections to particular features of society. Ideology is that which makes history semiotically meaningful in discourse, for ourselves as well as for others. The more we move up through the layers, the less we seem to be able to exert control or agency over them, and the high levels – for instance, the level where my Tanzanian friends would spot a significant difference between my world and theirs – are hardly visible, not consciously addressed.

Thus, in line with what has been said in previous chapters, ideology as part of meaningfulness comprises conscious, planned, creative activity as well as unintentional reproduction of 'determined' meanings. It also comprises processes at various levels ranging from the individual to the world system, passing through different degrees of awareness, speed and capacity of development, and capacity to create innovative practices. In other words, it simultaneously comprises 'particular' as well as 'total', or 'established' as well as 'behavioural' ideologies, but they operate at different levels, offer different opportunities for people, and are of a different order in analysis. And hegemony may lie not so much in single, unified sets of ideological elements, but in connections between various sets.

I have arrived at a point where discourse offers us opportunities for an analysis that addresses simultaneity – the occurrence of a single, unique discursive form – as something in which we see, through index-ical links, various layers of socially meaningful elements. The various layers are meaningful because they derive from different ideologies that operate at different levels of historicity. This may explain why the same chunk of discourse may be simultaneously understandable for many people, yet receive very different interpretations by these people, depending on whether the work of interpretation is done in the same event as that of production, later, much later, by someone else than the original interlocutor, in a different contextual space, from a different historical position, from a different place in the world, and so forth. It may explain why the works of Plato, Nietzsche, and Proust are still given new interpretations, why reading a particular text may suddenly shed a completely new light on dozens of previously read texts – in sum, why discourse always displays both continuity and discontinuity in meanings attached to it.

I shall now provide two illustrations, both addressing the interplay between different layers of ideology as well as the way in which continuity and discontinuity are managed. In both cases, political rhetoric will be the genre I shall investigate, and Belgium will be the setting for this rhetoric.

## 7.4  SOCIALISM AND THE SOCIALISTS

In what follows, I shall try to substantiate the remark made above that hegemony may reside in connections between various sets of ideological elements. This means that rather than single 'ideologies' (such as, for example, 'socialism'), we have to look at *combinations*, complexes of ideological elements often seemingly incongruous with one another, but brought in action – 'articulated' or 'entextualised' – as a single 'ideology'. My target will be some pieces of discourse produced by the Belgian-Flemish Socialist party in the context of what they called 'ideological congresses'. The texts are *explicitly* labelled as 'ideological' by their authors; they are supposed to articulate *the* 'socialist' ideology of this party.

The Flemish socialists (SP) are a social-democratic party which emerged from of the Belgian, unitary (and bilingual) Belgian Socialist party (BSP-PSB). Their main views can best be described as 'supply-side socialism' (Thompson 1996); or Third-Way socialism (Giddens 1998; De Vos 2003): a lukewarm socialism fully subscribing to market capitalism and striving to safeguard (what is left of) the welfare state. In the 1990s, in the wake of disappointing electoral results and a corruption scandal, the party embarked on a wholesale 'renovation campaign', involving a change in personnel and style – more mass-media advertisement campaigns, more politics of personality, more aesthetics in the presentation of party materials and messages – as well as an ideological *aggiornamento*. The data used here are taken from the preparatory texts of the 'ideological congress' of 1998, the first congress of that sort since 1974. In 1974, the (then unitary) BSP-PSB held another such congress, and I shall examine a few fragments from the congress booklet of 1974 as well (the year will be mentioned with all the fragments).[7]

We shall concentrate on how the SP speaks from a particular position – a *position in the world system*, articulated in a series of statements on the world; and a *position in time*, articulated in a series of differences between the 1998 texts and those of 1974. After that, but connected to it, we shall see how consumerism has seeped through the socialist style of 1998. Let us begin with the first point.

## The modern world

The socialists are embarking on an ideological overhaul, and the reason for this is that the world has changed. It has changed in a particular way, it has improved, potentially for everyone:

> The world has deeply changed over the last fifty years. Never before in the history of mankind did changes come at such a rapid pace. Never before did we see on our planet so many potential opportunities for economic and social development of everyone, for democracy, for the emancipation of women, for the rights of children and so forth. (1998)

The changes have particular effects. They have transformed our society, and, instead of a traditional economy, we now face an economy dominated by flows of information. This economy has penetrated culture, information flows have become the all-defining feature of society:

> If there is one domain in which globalisation is a reality, it is in the domain of information and communication flows. Not only do we witness an explosion of scientific and technological knowledge, but due to the capacities of the electronic highway, tele-text,[8] CD-Rom and the Internet, there is now more information available for everyone. (1998)

We can already catch a glimpse of the world as seen by the SP. This world is the globalised world characterised by a tremendous affluence of information and knowledge, made available through new information technology. This revolution has created a new economy, a new capitalism, and it generates more opportunities for more people than ever before. These opportunities are not purely economic, but also political and social: they include democracy, women's rights, and rights for children.

A rosy image indeed, and probably a more or less accurate image of Belgium, one of the wealthiest countries on earth. But it is hopelessly inaccurate for most other parts of the world, where these new technologies have not penetrated, and where globalisation has not resulted in more prosperity for all, more democracy, more rights for women and children. So we see how the SP speaks from a particular position in the world system: that of an affluent First-World country which benefits enormously from the new developments in worldwide capitalism. The rest of the world is modelled onto us: what works in Belgium is supposed to be a universal recipe for progress and development, economic as well as social and political. The developments qualified as due to globalisation are seen as *progress*, as an improvement of a previous state. And the socialists see their main task as being able to respond to these new opportunities.

Consequently, capitalism is not an enemy. It is obviously not easy to be an anti-capitalist in a country which ranks among the handful of countries in the world which owes everything to capitalism and is treated very well by capitalism. So the socialists differentiate between good and bad capitalism. Good capitalism is the capitalism which characterises our own society; bad capitalism is the capitalism that dominates other parts of the world.

> People do not get the same opportunities everywhere, their potential remains underdeveloped, their capacities remain underused. That is not our society. We revolt against *that* capitalism. We want to change it step by step. That is how a modern socialism works. (1998)

Note how the problem is framed as one of under-used potential. The failure of ('bad') capitalism lies in the fact that the potential of people elsewhere remains underdeveloped. We see a comparative orientation in this statement: capitalism here, in Belgium, is imagined as a force which apparently develops the full potential of people. A capitalism which does not accomplish this is a bad capitalism, against which socialists will revolt because it results in something which is not 'our society'.

We shall see further on how the SP frames its political reaction to this. But a field of action has been sketched. The SP operates *inside* capitalism, as a political movement aiming at spreading *this, our* capitalism, to the rest of the world. Capitalism is not bad in itself, it has bad modes of occurrence elsewhere in the world. Flemish socialists will fight against these bad modes of occurrence, not against capitalism in general, for new developments in capitalism (namely, globalisation) generate unprecedented opportunities. The SP can take this position and make it acceptable to its Flemish constituency (or rather, its Flemish political *customers*) because it is a position which reflects our own social, economic, and political realities. It is easier to project those onto the rest of the world than to announce to the people that our state of affairs is exceptional and indicative of huge inequalities in the world. But the effect is localism: the scope defined by the SP for itself is Flanders, nothing else. The field in which it wants to perform is globalised, capitalist Flemish society. Socialist internationalism has vanished, it has been replaced by blunt Eurocentrism.

## Modern socialism

There was already a reference to 'modern socialism' in one of the fragments above. The SP clearly marks a discontinuity between 'old socialism' and 'modern socialism'. The central thesis runs as follows. The world has changed, there is a new economy and a new social and political pattern that has grown out of it. Consequently, socialism has to adapt to this new environment. Old-style socialism is no longer a valid response to economic and social pressures, one needs a new socialism: Rust-Belt socialism needs to be replaced by e-socialism.

But how did this old-style socialism sound? Let us have a look at some fragments from the 1974 texts. First, the socialists in 1974 still saw themselves as a movement opposed to capitalism:

> [The socialists] fight for the total transformation of society and want to replace the capitalist system by a socialist system. (1974)

Capitalism has changed – the 1974 socialists acknowledge this, but nevertheless:

> Compared to nineteenth-century capitalist society, neo-capitalism occurs as a system from which the activities of the labour movement have wrestled some benefits. Nevertheless, neo-capitalism does not differ in substance from the earlier capitalism. Profit remains its only motive. (1974)

And the 1974 texts contain elaborate critiques of market capitalism as it existed in those days. They emphasise the deterioration of the situation of the Third World and of the environment:

> It would be a huge mistake to think that we can protect nature without altering the economic system that generates its destruction. Materialism and liberalism indeed considerably contribute to the destruction of nature. (1974)

They also emphasise the dehumanising effect of capitalism on the people. There is a fundamental humanism in these texts centring on the concept of 'human development':

> The socialist party does not want to integrate into a society incapable of offering an economic, political and cultural framework in which one can fully develop oneself. (1974)

This humanism is universalist in ambition and scope. It is not confined to Belgium, but it has to be extended to all of mankind; it is a general socialist principle:

> Democratic socialism wants to give everyone equal opportunities in life. It not only aims at the well-being of the individual and the community, but it also perceives social and cultural self-development as the highest human ambition. (1974)

The tone is obviously antagonistic: the socialists in 1974 stand in opposition to capitalism because capitalism is an anti-human system preventing the development of humanity – not only economically but also socially and culturally. There is an expression of refusal to compromise on these matters, for the issue is not one of modes of occurrence but of fundamental differences between *systems*. What is needed is 'a total transformation of society'.

This old-style socialism is categorically rejected by the SP in 1998. Anti-capitalism is no longer an option, as we saw above, and anti-capitalist socialism is negatively qualified in phrases such as:

> The days of the rigid dogmas are over (1998)

> If we continue to hold on to traditional socialist recipes . . . (1998)

It is clear: modern socialism is a socialism that rejects the old, binarised, and polarised contrasts between capitalism and socialism as models of society. Due to changes in society, these dichotomies no longer hold, and attaching oneself to them would be tantamount to accepting 'rigid dogmas' or 'traditional recipes'.

At this point, we see how the SP not only speaks from a position in the world system but also in time. When the socialists in 1974 held their congress, they did so against the background of the Cold War. Being anti-capitalist still had some degree of currency in 1974, which it seems to have completely lost in 1998, after the end of the Cold War and in the wake of loud proclamations of victory for worldwide capitalism. As noted above, it is hard to be anti-capitalist in Belgium; more in particular, it is very hard to be anti-capitalist in Belgium in 1998.

The Cold War, however, is also present in the 1974 texts. We saw above how the socialists used the term 'democratic socialism' to describe their own movement. This is again an implicitly comparative statement which invokes *un*democratic socialism as a point of comparison. The 1974 Belgian socialists were virulently anti-Soviet and anti-communist. It is reasonable to suspect that undemocratic socialism was attributed to the Belgian Communist party as well as to Soviet-style worldwide socialism. We should note, in passing, that the 1974 socialists also argued for a synergy in practice between socialism and capitalism. Despite their antagonistic statements with regard to capitalism, they advocated a critical alliance with capitalism, arguing in favour of planned economy, government control and intervention, and strong trade union participation in industrial ventures. The target is to acquire *control* over capitalism ventures, not to take *possession* of them:

> The target of the socialists thus has to be to inspect in different ways whether the actions and behaviour of enterprises are in line with the interests of all, specifically as this has been specified in the [economic] Plan. (1974)

So, in 1974, the basic political position of the socialists was similar to that of the socialists in 1998: they both accept capitalist free enterprise as a partner in society and as a generator of prosperity (though free enterprise was subject to a 'Plan' in 1974). The historical difference is articulated rhetorically through the presence or absence of an opposition between capitalism and socialism, obviously discredited in the early 1990s. The acceptance of capitalism was already hegemonic in 1974 among socialists, the existence of a socialist alternative was no longer hegemonic in 1998. Contemporary socialism is a socialism which no longer sees itself as a possible alternative system.

But this is not the only historical difference. Another striking difference, is that of collectivity versus individuality.

## The individual voice

One striking difference between the 1974 and the 1998 texts is the dominance of individual voices in the 1998 texts. Nowhere in the 1974 texts do we find references either to the leaders of the party, or to individuals as targets of socialist action. The party speaks collectively, as a movement inserted in a worldwide stream of socialist parties.

Let us briefly return to a fragment already given above. It reflects one of the central principles defined by the party, and the party speaks as a party, it speaks as (worldwide) *socialism*:

> The socialist party does not want to integrate into a society incapable of offering an economic, political and cultural framework in which one can fully develop oneself. (1974)

And let us now turn to an equivalent fragment from the 1998 texts:

> What do we want? What do socialists want? A world such as the one we have today, full of insecurity, unsafety and inequality? No, thanks. We want a world in which as many people as possible have a good life, today as well as tomorrow. When people join each other in a fight for a better life, we are their allies. (1998)

The key is completely different here. This is no longer socialism, but 'we', 'socialists'. This collective noun stands for the sum of 'socialist' individuals, who all share similar socialist values and principles. The focus is on individual ethics, not on massive and rock-solid universal-humanist principles:

> The cement and the building blocks [of our actions are]: the ethical values for which we stand, the big changes confronting us, our own peculiar view of society by means of which we can give an appropriate response to these changes. (1998)

Socialism has become a matter of individual political opinion grouped into a loose and flexible collective – the political customers – and the 1998 party has adopted the formats of commercial advertising to get its message across. Instead of the declarative, affirmative style dominating the 1974 texts, the conversational style identified by Fairclough (1989, 1992a) is there in the question–response pattern. The 1998 texts are also replete with references to socialist mayors, government ministers, and members of parliament, political celebrities whose concrete actions are celebrated as examples of socialist policy-making. Moreover, concrete policy actions rather than principles are central in the texts of 1998. Ideology takes on very concrete shapes, as in:

> Apart from that, the government could pay the costs incurred by enterprises for connections to waterways and the railway, just as it subsidises roads that lead to industrial sites. For waterways, the Flemish Government now subsidises the construction of docking facilities; more money has to be made available for that. With respect to the railway, the National Railways now pay for the first 18 meters of track connecting the main railroad and the enterprises. For the National Railway as well as for the Flemish Government, it is a small effort to take charge of all these costs. (1998)

In general, the ideological renewal assumes the shape of a list of concrete policy proposals, sensed to radiate the socialist ethics that now
define socialism as an ideology.

The shift is momentous. We have moved from a collectively voiced
universalist humanism to a personalised ethical stance leading to concrete measures. The latter is fully in line with consumerist culture as
described by Fairclough (1989). We can now bring all of this together.

## Socialists in 1998

Let us summarise what we have seen so far and try to construct some
kind of ideological blueprint out of it. We have to keep in mind that
the core message of the texts is explicitly ideological, it reflects an
ambition to reposition the SP in a political field in which ideologies
stand for marked differences in opinion about political topics. This is
what we get.

1. The socialists speak from and to Flanders. There is no internationalism left in this socialism. The Flemish social model is projected
   onto the rest of the world.
2. They accept 'modern' global capitalism and view it as the engine
   of progress.
3. They reject socialism as an alternative system.
4. Socialism is seen as a collective characteristic of individuals, connected to ethical values and an appraisal of changes in the world.
5. Ideology is first and foremost a matter of concrete actions, not
   of principles.

Interesting socialism: it is strictly local, pro-capitalist, anti-socialist,
based not on an analysis of capitalism but on individual ethics and
not on principles but on practical solutions. Given this 'ideology', the
question is: how come the SP can still call this 'socialism', thus invok-
ing consistency and coherence with the long history of use of this
term?

The answer lies, I believe, in the sort of layering discussed earlier
in this chapter. We can see how the SP produces statements that, at
a variety of levels, connect to existing hegemonies or form a point of
contrast with such hegemonies. The end result is a constellation of
different items, each responsive to 'truths' at one level, and moulded
together into one new compound message. This compound message
(or 'articulated' message in the terms of Laclau and Mouffe 1985; see
De Vos 2003) is 'new socialism', the new socialist ideology replacing
all the previous ones. Let us take a look at some of the layers we can
distinguish.

1. The party embraces a new economic profile for Flanders, based on information and knowledge production and sustained by technological developments. This new economy is manifestly the outcome of a *deep transformation* in the economic makeup of the world system, and it has a long history of becoming.
2. There is an effect of *the end of the Cold War*, visible in the way in which the SP embraces global capitalism as the hegemonic system and defines it as its field of action. We also see an effect in the rejection of socialism as a *systemic* alternative to capitalism, and in the rejection of the 'recipes' and 'dogmas' of socialist predecessors.
3. We see how *recent consumerist culture formats* penetrate the self-presentation as well as the view of society. Individualism, the focus on political celebrities and practical solutions in political rhetoric all testify to a new businesslike hegemony, in which politics is seen as one specialised branch of management (Fairclough 1989, 2000). We also see what we could call the 'commodification of -isms'. The SP uses 'socialism' as a brand name suggesting ideological-intertextual coherence with a long history of use of that term. This, then, suggests authenticity, perduring quality, and eventually also authority: our 'product', socialism, is still the same good old product, and we (the SP) not only assume authorship for its present quality but also for the past qualities of the product.

Needless to say, however, the 'product' has quite drastically changed. Whereas the first factor is an effect of slow history, the latter two factors are influences due to transformations in Western Europe since the mid- to late-1980s. But, apart from that, we see several other layers:

4. The focus on Flanders is an effect of the regionalisation process in Belgium. This process started in the 1960s and culminated in the late 1990s in a series of constitutional reforms providing far-reaching autonomy for the Flemish (and other) region(s). Since that time, political parties are community-specific: there are no 'national' parties anymore, and there is a Flemish Socialist party as well as a Francophone one. In contrast, the socialists of 1974 were still a national party. So part of what we see in the rhetoric of the SP in 1998 is a *de facto* hegemony of Flemish regionalism, with a Flemish party communicating only to Flemish citizens.
5. The party also talks as a party in power. The socialists, at the time of the 1998 congress, were part of the Flemish and Federal governments. The emphasis on personalities, most of them with

executive functions and track records, speaks to that. They have conducted business for some time, and this business needs to be highlighted.

6. Finally, we see several indications of how the SP takes a position *vis-à-vis* other political parties within its field of action – the 'peculiar view of society' in one of the fragments above. The acceptance of a 'modern' globalised society dominated by information and knowledge industries, for instance, was something the SP shared with all other major parties in Flanders, and it was a matter of government doctrine. Speaking out against this model of society would amount to disloyalty to the coalition partners in the government, and it would jeopardise the SP's chances of being partners in future governments too. At the same time, the emphasis on exclusion as a feature of 'bad capitalism' and the rejection of such capitalism marks the SP off against the centrist parties in Flanders – Liberal as well as Christian Democrat – who subscribe to a rather aggressive market capitalism.

So in sum, we see how the 'socialist ideology' of 1998 is a patchwork of separate responses to different pressures and influences, connected, in effect, only by the act of calling it 'an ideology'. The pressures come from different sides: some are local, some are European, some global; some have to do with differences within the socialist tradition; some with differences between socialists and other political movements. The product is a pragmatic, operational complex of individual responses – in fact, a collage of different hegemonies. And it can now, through synchronisation, be presented by the party as one 'hegemony': the new socialist doctrine for the twenty-first century, the ideology that defines the modern socialist.

## 7.5 SLOW SHIFTS IN ORTHODOXY

The kind of layering and fragmentation examined above allows for multiple interpretations. Similar texts can be inserted into very different ideological alliances, and this will be the topic of this section. At the same time, the illustration I wish to offer here should also illuminate the interplay between linguistic ideologies and larger social and political ideologies, and address John Thompson's 'fallacy of internalism' (1990: 24), a fallacy in which the power of ideologies is believed to be found in the texts and symbols of that ideology. I want to illustrate how a particular linguistic ideology can become an instrument obscuring important political shifts. The linguistic ideology is that of the 'fixed text', the belief that small textual modifications do not matter much, that a slightly modified or reworded version is still 'the original text'. This is one face of Thompson's internalism: the idea that a text is a closed, immutable unit that can and should be explored in itself, for 'all' the meanings can be found in it. What we shall see here is how one textual item, the term 'integration', moves across various political spaces and gets repositioned politically by minor textual revisions. What we should learn from this is that small changes in texts matter to the extent that they go hand in hand with important re-placings or reframings of the text in a political field.

My target is the concept of 'integration' as used in Belgian political rhetoric. Integration is the central concept in Belgian integration policies (see Blommaert and Verschueren 1998). It is supposed to carry political and societal consensus and, as we shall see, it is a wonderfully flexible concept. Noel Thompson (1996: 37) accurately notes how

> [o]ver-arching concepts . . . have their value both in determining the ground upon which political debate takes place and broadening the basis of support for the party which successfully employs them.
> There is considerable electoral virtue in a concept open to disparate interpretations and satisfying a variety of political tastes.

'Integration' is such an overarching concept. Before embarking on the analysis of the different repositionings of the term, I shall have to say something about a well-known form of political discursive practice: the debate.

## Metadiscourse and the 'debate'

In the field of politics, struggle and contestation are generically captured under the label of 'debate'. The political process develops through a series of debates involving a variety of social actors: politicians and policy-makers, experts, interested members of the public, the media. In liberal theory, debates are the points of entrance for civil society into policy making: they are (seen as) the moments during which the polity gets involved in shaping policies. And, for our purpose here, it is crucial to note that this shaping process is mainly a process of shaping textual tools often captured under terms such as 'public opinion': interpretations of policies, illustrative applications of policy statements to various areas of social life and social experience – a variety of forms of entextualisation of policy texts.

Though there may be a prototypical perception of political debates, it is hard to provide conclusive criteria for identifying them, both in terms of discourse event-type (identities of participants, genres, time-span, setting, etc.) as in terms of their relation to the outcome of decision-making procedures. In light of the textual nature of the process, it would be accurate to characterise debates as historical episodes of textualisation, as histories of texts in which a struggle is waged between various texts and metatexts. This struggle is characterised by an asymmetry in textual authority, which distinguishes 'policy-makers' from 'non policy-makers' (opposition parties, the media, the public), and which is expressed in attempts at redefining by the latter and gaining control over a (constructed) space of allowed interpretations by the former. The policy-makers ultimately decide which attempt at redefining by other parties will be considered a legitimate, acceptable amendment, and it is they who assign metatextual labels to the other parties' interventions. They can qualify them as 'left' or 'right', associate them with particular pressure groups or interest groups, downplay the general validity of the position taken by particular actors, and so forth, and so determine which entextualisations offered during the debate will result in a 'revision' or an 'update' of the policy proposal.

Underlying is an ideology of *fixed text*, controlled and manipulated by the policy-makers but, as we shall see, widely shared by the other participants in the debate, and culturally anchored in a widespread belief in 'the fixity of text, the transparency of language, and the universality of shared, available meaning' – what Collins defines as the ideology of 'textualism' (Collins 1996: 204). Collins shows how textualism alongside schooled literacy and the conversational asymmetry which characterised the 'normal order' of classroom interaction between teachers and pupils 'can be seen as important elements of a complex ideological and institutional substrate that underlies early literacy training in our society' (1996: 206). What Collins thus identifies belongs to a well-known complex of language ideologies in which singularity is preferred over diversity (*the* language); in which the abstract and denotational is preferred over the contextual and indexical; in which varieties of language are hierarchically ranked and each accompanied by qualitative, social, cultural, and cognitive evaluations (Silverstein 1977, 1979). It is the complex of ideas about language that is, in fact, to paraphrase Hymes (1996: 26), one of the big 'problems to be overcome with regard to language'. It is the locus and instrument of power, of inequality, of permanent struggles between those who control it and those who (believe they) need it.

The main textual tool for policy-makers is a text-artefact perceived as a stable, clear, and precise semantic unit. Texts are adopted, confirmed, revised, submitted, voted on, and so on, and the adoption of a text suggests the creation of maximum semantic transparency ('literal' meaning), clear-cut applicability to a variety of (assumedly well-defined) social practices, ideological and social alignment (reflecting the 'consensus' over these matters), and, finally, also coherence (or, at least, continuity) with previous policy actions and policy actions in other domains (the policy of *this* government) and contrasts with others (the policies of the previous governments, the opinion of the opposition, and so on). The actions of opposing actors in the debates are, consequently, inspired by a *reading* of the text-artefact,[9] and aimed at a *re-writing* of certain parts of the original text-artefact. The anchor-points in the debate are often text-structural elements: clauses, phrases, particular wording patterns, specific terms.

This ideology of fixed text underlies the construction of a space of allowed interpretations. It is assumed that the text itself is clear and transparent, and that the limits of its meaning can only be stretched so far. It also allows metatextual qualifications such as 'left' or 'right' on the basis of perceived traditions of intertextuality, in which particular groups in society are seen as systematically 'reading certain things into' clear, transparent texts. The Left and the Right are, in this context, seen as traditions of semantic 'curbing': the 'neutral' texts produced by policy-makers are systematically 'curbed' into a particular ('ideologically biased') direction. In turn, the various actors in the debate boomerang metatextual qualifications onto the policy text, denying its neutrality and adding intertextual associations to the text ('another right-wing decision from a right-wing government'; 'another anti-free-trade decision').

At this point, the importance of metadiscourse in the whole process should have become clear. The debate is a struggle over entextualisations with a strong undertone of textual dogmatism. It uses metadiscursive hierarchies, in which a draft ranks lower than a final version, the written word higher than the spoken one, the collective voice higher than the individual, general statements higher than particular ones, and so on. The end result is not one authoritative entextualisation, but a space of possible entextualisations which can be sanctioned as 'valid'. The issue, for debaters, is thus to insert their entextualisations into that space. In the next section, it will appear that the term integration is constantly 'colonised' and inserted into a variety of discourse strategies, both of a strictly 'defining' nature as well as of an argumentative nature. We thus arrive at a whole set of formulations and reformulations, anchored into an idea of coherence with the fixed text which serves as its source and from which the (re)formulations derive their authority.

## Fragments from the debate on integration ▬▬▬▬▬▬

Let us take a look at some of the semantic adventures of the term 'integration'. I shall discuss two sets of phenomena: (i) the dogmatisation of the concept by the government authorities in dealing with criticism, compared to reformulations of the concept in public discourse by the same officials; and (ii) right-wing appropriation of the term. But, before that, we need to take a look at the text-artefact which functions as the 'source text' of the debate – the 'official' text on which attributes are bestowed such as maximum clarity, social consensus, and so on.

The Belgian 'integration policies' (i.e. explicit policies aimed at treating what was seen as the problems caused by the presence of sizeable groups of permanent immigrants) took shape in the period 1989–1993, when a Royal Commissariat for Migrant Policies (henceforth KCM) headed by the former Christian-Democrat minister Mrs Paula D'Hondt and supervised by Prime Minister Wilfried Martens produced report upon report packed with facts and analyses and ending with dozens of policy proposals. The most crucial document defining integration policies is the first KCM report (KCM 1989): a monumental three-volume œuvre, in which the blueprint for what was to become the official Belgian approach to migrant affairs was sketched, and in which a plethora of demographic, administrative, social-economic, and other basic data were presented.[10]

In this crucial report, the most crucial fragment is the definition of the 'concept of integration' (KCM 1989: 38–39):

> The proposals . . . that will follow, will be inspired by a concept of integration, which simultaneously
> 1. Starts from the notion of 'insertion', using the following criteria:
>     a  assimilation where the public order so demands
>     b  a consistent promotion of an optimal insertion according to the guiding social principles that are the basis of the culture of the host country and that revolve around 'modernity', 'emancipation' and 'full-fledged pluralism' – in the sense given by a modern western state.
>     c  unambiguous respect for cultural diversity-as-mutual-enrichment in the other domains;
> 2. And which is accompanied by a promotion of the structural involvement of minorities in the activities and the objectives of the authorities.

This text obviously has a history of its own (one which has been effectively blackboxed: very little is known of the genesis of this formula). But it is this text which became the source text for an intense debate on its meaning and its range of applicability. The text is authoritative:

the formula has been adopted by the various governments since 1989 as the basis of the 'migrant policies' of these governments. It has never been officially revised or revoked.

## Dogmatisation versus reformulation: manipulating the interpretational space

Officials responsible for the production of the concept of integration have given proof of considerable flexibility in using the concept they authored in a variety of contexts. Two main strategies can be distinguished: (a) whenever the concept of integration was attacked, in particular whenever *parts* of the concept were criticised or whenever the *practice* of integration policies was attacked, the concept was dogmatised; (b) in a variety of other contexts, mostly in public speeches, vulgarising writings, or intervention during public debates, the concept was lexically or argumentatively reformulated. Both strategies form a dynamic of entextualisation, which causes a *variety of authoritative versions* of the concept of integration to float around in the debate. The versions are authoritative because they were produced by people strongly involved in the production of the source text. The effect is vagueness: despite the suggested clarity of the concept of integration (there is only one 'original' version, accepted by the Belgian government and sanctioned by parliament), the central actors in the field of migration policies create other, different versions of the same concept, thus adding new authoritative entextualisations of the concept. The concept of integration thus becomes a user-friendly concept, open to manipulation by groups or individuals who want to impose their own agenda on it, and who find ammunition in the reformulations of the concept given by authoritative actors.

### Dogmatisation

In line with the ideology of fixed text, one of the consistent elements in reactions to criticisms was to refer to the original text of the 1989 KCM report. In it, so it was suggested, were the only true meanings of the key terms and concepts. Further on, we shall see that often these references to the original concept of integration display important textual and semantic differences with the source text. But the process is clear: a critique of the concept is countered by a dogmatised reading of the concept, in other words, by a retreat behind the ideology of fixed text.

When in the winter of 1992–1993 some controversy arose about the validity of the concept of integration, fuelled by a critical analysis published by Jef Verschueren and myself (Blommaert and Verschueren

1992, 1998) on the contextual semantics of the concept (the *way of speaking* of integration, in Hymesian terminology), the KCM chief of staff, Johan Leman, emerged as the main defender of the concept. One of the central arguments of our analysis, in which pragmatic aspects of language such as presuppositions and implicatures were central, was that the 'structural involvement' part of the concept of integration was *in the practical usage of the concept* made conditional by the aspects of cultural adaptation. Immigrants would only be granted full rights when they gave sufficient proof of cultural adaptation was the outcome of our analysis. In a published refutation of our thesis, Leman (1993) emphatically stressed the importance of reading the text 'as it is', in its full integrity, devoid of innuendoes, implications, or other forms of guesswork. Leman quotes the full text of the original concept, italicising the phrase 'and which is accompanied by', which initiates part 2 of the concept, to underscore the non-conditionality of structural involvement by cultural adaptation. He then adds, in a passage which could qualify as a credo of textual dogmatism packed with metapragmatic qualifications such as 'in extenso', 'literally', 'in its totality', 'precisely rendered', 'literal quotation', and 'what is on the lines' (1993: 133):

> By the way: why couldn't this fragment, a key fragment in the November report of 1989 and printed in bold face, not be quoted *in extenso* and *literally*? Why can't this fragment be found *anywhere* in its totality and *precisely* rendered? In a 250-page book, which aims primarily at criticising the policy aspect of the concepts used, a literal quotation of what is 'on the lines' surely wouldn't have constituted a crime against linguistic pragmatics? (emphasis in original)

The line of argument is clear: a faithful quotation of the dogmatic version of the concept of integration would have thrown a different light on our critique. It would prove how wrong we were in suggesting that full involvement of migrants was conditioned by cultural adaptation. Put simply: we used the wrong *text*, or we wronged the right text, and we went beyond the limits of allowed interpretation. The original (fixed, source) text was far better than the ones we used and, consequently, our critique was misguided. It is a highly suggestive argument which invokes elements of intellectual honesty, integrity, and methodological correctness. The ideology of fixed text is projected onto critics as a normative frame defining truthfulness, fairness, and correctness, thus sketching a moral code for conducting the debate – at least, when developments in the debate call for such a projection. Note how our interpretation is metadiscursively qualified as illegitimate largely on textual grounds: we did not pay enough attention to the (pure, transparent, literal) source text, and, hence, what we say can be qualified as beyond the boundaries of allowed interpretation.

## Reformulations

We have seen how Leman rebutted our critique against the unilateral character of the integration concept by pointing towards the fact that, in the source text, the first part (the demands made to migrants) was complemented by a second part on structural involvement from migrants in official matters. The crucial text-structural element was *conditionality*. In our view, structural involvement was in practice conditioned by the demands of 'insertion', i.e. migrants could gain access to socially desirable functions only if they gave sufficient proof of 'integration'. Leman rebutted this claim, insisting that 'insertion' and 'involvement' went hand in hand. The textual anchor for his argument is the nonlinear ordering of the various parts of the concept of integration: part 1 is subdivided into three subparts, and then followed by part 2. Our claim was that, in effect, the four elements (i.e. the three elements of part 1 and the one element of part 2) were seen as one single, linear package, in which structural involvement was conditioned by the other elements.

We had evidence for our claim. In a variety of contexts in which the concept of integration was presented to the public, the original two-part structure was forgotten and the four elements were indeed juxtaposed linearly. Let us have a look at two reformulations given by the Royal Commissioner, Mrs Paula D'Hondt, herself. In an opinion article in the daily newspaper *De Standaard* (1–2 February 1992: 7), she wrote:

(1) Integration of migrants in our society has been defined by us as *insertion*. We have concretised this concept in four points. One can find these four points in our first report of November 1989: in the first two points, we demand things from migrants, in the other two, we are open to them.

   1. We demand assimilation where the public order is concerned. That means that migrants have to respect the Belgian laws, with no exception, all of them, just like any Belgian.
   2. We demand that the fundamental social principles of our society be respected by everyone, so also by migrants: the emancipation of women, as we understand it; mutual tolerance; our language, and so forth.

3. Apart from these two very important things that we demand from migrants – and more cannot be demanded from people in a law-abiding society, regardless of whether they are migrants or Belgians – we are open to what those people can contribute: in the artistic, cuisine, linguistic, cultural and other domains. There, we assume that mutual enrichment is not only possible but even desirable, a condition for progress.
4. We also say that sufficiently competent people from migrant circles should be involved in the objectives and the activities of the authorities, because this is the only road to emancipation, just like it was for women.

The version of the concept of integration given during a speech on youth work (*Jeugdwerk in intercultureel perspectief*, Leuven, 23 October 1992) reads:

(2)  1. Therefore, 'insertion', for migrants, means:
A complete assimilation to the Belgian law. The Belgian law is everybody's law on our territory, regardless of whether he [*sic*] is a migrant or a Belgian.
2. A complete respect for the orienting, fundamental ideas of our western society. And that means that my [*sic*] concept of integration is not neutral! It includes, for instance, the knowledge of the regional language. Also, the separation between Church and State, as it has been shaped here, remains primordial. Also, the emancipation of women, as we understand it; and the reciprocity among people as we understand it.
    But it also means – and that is the proposed respect for minorities:
3. that, once the two first conditions have been met, there will be openness, and even promotion, of mutual cultural enrichment.
4. that there will be a promotion for people from the minority groups who have complied exemplarily with the first three criteria, in the sense that they would fulfil exemplary functions in important societal niches.

Two points can be noted with regard to these two reformulations. First, the complexity of the original concept has been reduced, both lexically and structurally. Lexically, the whole concept is now called 'insertion', whereas in the original formulation, 'insertion' only pertained to the first part of the concept. Structurally, the four elements have indeed been linearly ordered, and the two-part and subordinate structure of the original concept has given way to a much simpler version, propagated, it should be recalled, by the Royal Commissioner herself. Secondly, and contrary to Leman's dogmatised reading, there is a clear and explicit conditionality for the structural involvement of migrants in these reformulations. In example 1, this conditionality remains hidden in the phrase 'sufficiently competent people' – competence, in effect, being equated to 'integration' – but in example 2, it is made topical in the third and fourth points mentioned by D'Hondt.

But these text-structural operations do not exhaust the repertoire by means of which sociopolitical power asymmetries can be discursively articulated. It may be interesting to note how, in example 2, a peculiar and strongly reductionist concept of 'culture' is being used: the culture of migrants is reduced to art, cuisine, music, and other surface domains covered by a restricted use of the term 'culture' (one that obviously does not include 'deeper' societal values, likely to clash with 'our' orienting fundamental principles). Also, in both examples some emphasis is put on 'our language', Dutch. This emphasis on language proficiency was absent from the original formulation, but it fits into the normalisation of Herderian 'one language, one culture' perceptions in an increasingly nationalist climate in Belgian–Flemish politics, in which the use of Dutch is commonly perceived as the main index of cultural adaptation. In both examples also, some stress is laid on the phrase 'as we understand it' in connection with the meaning and the practice of some of the so-called fundamental social principles. In connection with the emphasis on language as a salient criterion of cultural adaptation, and on a superficial filling of the 'culture' of migrants, this leads to cultural closure: our culture is a closed unit, which should not undergo any transformations due to the presence and the 'insertion' of migrants. The condition for accepting migrants, and for respecting their culture, is that our own culture should remain untouched.

The important point in these two examples is the way in which a concept which, on the one hand, is used in a very dogmatic way, can become reformulated in other circumstances in ways that are far from innocent. The conditional relation between cultural adaptation and structural participation, as can be judged from D'Hondt's reformulations, was certainly part of the reproduction of the source text by its main architects, even if it was emphatically denied in other contexts. The fact is that the existence of multiple versions of the concept, apparently only differing in details and degrees of transparency, creates a potential for power in a wide variety of contexts. For one thing, it allows factions in society who would tend not to agree to a 'soft' reading of the concept of integration to rally behind a 'harder' reading of the concept, offered not by dissidents, but by the policy-makers themselves, as if it were one and the same thing. (This is why the KCM could claim, in its final report, that 'The concept of integration developed by the KCM has been accepted by almost everyone, be it in a different formulation' (1993: 15).) By reformulating the concept, D'Hondt (and others) create new parameters for allowed interpretations of the concept. The identity of the producers – here, the Royal Commissioner herself – simultaneously entextualises these reformulations as mere re-enactments of the source text. In other words, despite the clear difference in textual structure and possible lines of actions contained in the various formulations, they can still be presented as the 'true' authoritative text-meaning of 'integration'. At the same time, the small textual changes allow for important ideological re-placings, as we shall see.

Another point of critique against the concept of integration was the intrinsic culturalisation involved in the 'insertion' process sketched in the concept. This point is, I believe, amply vindicated by the reformulations given above, in which the emphasis on culture and the avoidance of socioeconomic, material relations are quite clearly articulated. Yet, officials have repeatedly tried to indicate that, in contrast to their own preference for 'culturalist' usages, the concept of integration should, in fact, be seen as a primarily socioeconomic, rather than a cultural notion. Such reformulations are often guided by motives of rhetorical alignment, i.e. they are dependent on the particular audience or occasion for which they are being produced. Again, two examples can be given. The examples are taken from notes made during public debates in which I participated together with officials in charge of migrant policies. Example (3) is a paraphrase of a statement by Johan Leman during a debate in Antwerp (14 June 1995):

(3)    One has to read the concept of integration in the context of a policy document made in 1989. Today, we'd rather speak of a concept of emancipation. I don't care about the name; the point is: we had to obtain a parliamentary majority for our policy, and the concept proved to be a handy mobilising instrument. The original concept contained four parts. For as far as the 'orienting fundamental principles' goes, I myself was upset by the kind of referents given to this. And I wouldn't use a term such as 'modernity' anymore. In general, this element was too vaguely put.

Example (4) is a paraphrase of the definition of the concept of integration as given by one of Leman's senior collaborators during a public debate in Roeselare (23 September 1993):

(4)  1. Assimilation to the public order
  2. Encourage (not force) the acceptance of emancipation, pluralism etc., because these values generate social opportunities
  3. Accept that others are different, including in the domain of religion (Islam)
  4. Participation to power.

Note, again, how both speakers present the concept as containing four (not two) equivalent parts. In both examples we also see how the emphasis is drawn away from culture or culture-related domains, and placed on power and socioeconomic upward mobility. Leman speaks of 'emancipation' instead of 'integration', adding that, to him, both terms do not make a lot of difference. They do, of course: emancipation is a term nested in the semantic and rhetorical tradition of the Belgian labour movement (notably the trade unions) and feminism, in which it acquired a distinct socioeconomic and power orientation. It is highly questionable whether the feminist movement would agree to the kind of 'emancipation' concept offered to immigrants. But the debate was organised by a section of the socialist trade union, and the term 'emancipation' certainly had a positive appeal to the audience because of its recognisability in terms of the union's own history. Also, Leman now rejects the term 'modernity', saying that it was too vague, and – implicitly – that terms such as 'modernity' allowed for unwarranted interpretations. Modernity, in the sense used in the concept of integration, primarily pertains to values and social norms (pluralism, tolerance, male–female equality, church–state separation . . . ), and the concept was given a distinct evolutionist and culturalist dimension in reformulations such as those of D'Hondt quoted above. So, if there were 'unwarranted' interpretations, the government itself had offered some space for them in reformulations of the concept.

In example (4), the 'softness' of the concept stands in sharp contrast to the versions given by D'Hondt in examples (1) and (2). Whereas D'Hondt was unambiguous with regard to the unilateral nature of 'insertion', the speaker in example 4 talks of 'encouraging (not forcing)' the acceptance of the basic principles of the host society, and of the need to 'accept that others are different', adding a reference to Islam. Islam, to D'Hondt, was rather less the object of acceptance of difference. Repeatedly during her career, she referred to Islam in stigmatising terms. In the speech from which example (2) was taken, she, for instance, states (after having noted that her concept of integration allows for 'the development of cultural life' among migrants):

> But conversely, it is the case that a fundamentalist variant of Islam
> cannot be accepted, at least not here. An Islam that integrates
> [itself] can.

The degree of difference that should be accepted on the basis of the
concept of integration apparently differs in the versions of D'Hondt
and Leman's senior collaborator. The latter also uses the phrase 'participation to power', a left-wing, benevolent reformulation of the original
'structural involvement in the objectives and activities of the authorities', and he adds a rational, functionalist argument to the second
element of his concept of integration: migrants should adapt to the
guiding principles of our society, because that would create better
opportunities for them. In other words, and note the colonialist twist
in this argument, cultural adaptation will generate prosperity; absence
of cultural adaptation will keep people in underprivileged positions.

What we see in all this is how central actors in the process of ideological production and reproduction themselves construct a sort of
semantic accordion with regard to the key concept they promote. But
all these reformulations are seen and presented as mere *replications* of
the fixed text. Thus, the reformulations offer a potential for alignment
to other social actors, who can pick up the directions hidden in any
one of the various versions of the concept of integration produced by
the authoritative voices in that field, and transform them into ingredients of their own vision on the issue of migration. The authoritative
reformulations so determine – dialogically and through the various
mechanisms of alignment – the space of allowed interpretation in
the debate. As such, it is not surprising that D'Hondt's doctrine was
acclaimed both by the right wing and by the left wing, be it on very
different grounds and embedded in very different views of society and
ideological lineages, as we shall see below. The vagueness created by
the various authoritative reformulations of the concept thus became –
intentionally or not – a very fine instrument for creating a political consensus precisely by offering a space of textual homogeneity
onto which very different ideological affiliations can be projected. The
term 'integration' can be made central to a variety of different hegemonies.

## Right-wing appropriation

The Belgian integration policies started from the acceptance of the
lasting presence of groups of immigrants in Belgium and the concept
of integration was meant to define the conditions under which their
presence would be accepted and managed. This basic assumption is not

shared by parts of the Belgian right wing, who view the presence of immigrants as undesirable *per se* or acceptable only under very strict conditions. Yet even these right-wing groups have adopted the term integration and have inserted their entextualisations into the space of allowed interpretations. Note that I do not want to suggest that left-wing appropriation of the concept would be less relevant or worthy of comment, nor that right-wing appropriations of the term are 'worse' than any other form of discourse manipulation. I shall focus my attention exclusively on right-wing appropriation only for reasons of expository clarity and space, as an illustration of how an ideology of fixed text can allow far-reaching political and ideological repositionings of the text.

The next example documents a case in which integration is used in an apology of what can at best be called a very biased decision taken by a local politician. The setting is the town of Sint Truiden in 1994. Sint Truiden lies in the heart of an agricultural area which attracts groups of foreign workers for the harvest season. In the early 1990s, a group of Sikhs from India had settled in Sint Truiden and they had become the object of recurrent racist aggression. In the summer of 1993, a fire bomb was thrown at a house populated by Sikhs. In the winter of 1993–1994, the social welfare service of the Sint Truiden town council decided to reduce the welfare allowance to Sikhs, on grounds that they lived with seven or eight in one house and that 'they don't eat meat anyway' (*ergo* they don't need much money). The mayor of Sint Truiden, a flamboyant Christian Democrat named Jef Cleeren, was invited onto a TV talk show to explain that decision. At a given moment during the talk show, the following sequence occurred:

(5) *Interviewer*: I'd like to discuss the argument you used, that they live with so many in a house and need less . . .
*Cleeren*: THEY have to be able to *integrate themselves* like our people; when there are ten people living in a house [owned] by the local population then there is a regulation for asylum seekers, for the foreigners, they have to adapt to OUR culture, to our regulation and to our norms and not the other way round.

Apart from the incoherence of the (heated) argument, what strikes the observer is that Cleeren refers to integration as his source of legitimacy. But what does integration here legitimise? A measure taken on the grounds of two racial and ethno-cultural stereotypes: (a) Sikhs can live with less money than Belgians, because they don't eat meat; in other words, whereas the law dictates that every human being residing on Belgian soil is entitled to an equal degree of welfare support from local authorities, Cleeren decides that the cultural and religious traditions of one group of inhabitants makes them eligible for a disprivileging treatment; (b) Sikhs create ghettos, and ghettos are a source of danger and annoyance. He does recognise that his council's measure is a form of punishment, but the punishment is intended to do well: it should encourage Sikhs to adapt to our (i.e. Belgian) customs and norms, and it should encourage them either to leave Sint Truiden or to break up their ghettos. Apparently, to Cleeren's mind, these two goals are compatible with 'integration'.

Let us take a closer look at how Cleeren structures his 'integration' case, for it documents the way in which integration is inserted in a completely different rhetoric using different registers and ideological frames from the ones used by more immigrant-friendly actors. Not surprisingly, the whole utterance is structured around an opposition between 'us' and 'them', intonationally marked by heavy stress on 'they' and 'our'. 'They' are qualified by negative statements: they have to integrate themselves and adapt themselves to our culture, norms, etc. (implicature: they are *not* integrating and adapting themselves); they cause overpopulation; and they violate the regulations of the city council. The 'us' is qualified neutrally, in terms of norms and regulations. 'Us' is the seemingly unquestionable yardstick, by means of which others' behaviour is evaluated. The relationship thus defined between the majority and the Sikhs is completely unilateral: we are the providers of norms and regulations to which they have to adapt. If they don't, there is a problem of integration.

Also striking is the grammatical perspective in which 'integration' is put: it is made reflexive (integrate *themselves*), so that the full responsibility for the process lies with those who have to undergo it, and so that an element of volition is introduced in the semantics of the term (if they are not integrated, that means that they don't *want* to integrate themselves). The reflexive use of integration appears over and over again in the rhetoric of the moderate right wing, each time with the implicit elements of responsibility and volition heavily stressed. It is a perfect lexical-semantic frame for a strategy of blaming and reproaching: migrant problems are *their* problems; they cause them and they should solve them. Secondly, integration is explicitly made synonymous with unilateral 'adaptation' to our culture, norms, and regulations, 'not the other way round'. This is one of the standard entextualisations of integration, one that has gained currency among the right-wing participants to the debate. It is exegetically justified, but only partially: it selects the first part of the KCM 1989 definition of 'integration', and forgets the rest. A partial acceptance of the source text (in the form of echoes, quotations, or other forms of replication) can suffice as a strategy, for it suggests full acceptance of the source text. Note how this connects to the ideology of fixed text: in the eyes of its promoters, reformulations of the concept of integration are *per se* innocent, as long as the 'essence' or 'core' of the text appears to have been adopted. The point is, however, that integration can be used as a defensive weapon in cases such as these, where racism underlies the political decisions taken by Cleeren's council and where a history of racial violence further sustains an intertextual pattern of racist framings. Cleeren's decision and public statements were, of course, denounced by government officials (saying that they were 'ill advised' and 'less than careful', referring to Cleeren's style and timing), but no one challenged the connection he made between the discriminatory treatment of Sikhs and the argument of integration.

Even the radical right-wing has appropriated integration, and uses it as an ironic strategy to criticise integration policies. The radical right wing, and most prominently the Vlaams Blok party (one of Europe's largest extreme right-wing parties), provides a coherent but radically different entextualisation of integration, mobilising a genuine *theory* of intercultural relations as its basic textual and intertextual frame. In the view of the Vlaams Blok, integration is fundamentally impossible, and the most desirable solution for the 'migrant problems' would consist of sending foreigners back to their countries of origin. But they sustain this view with a cultural theory which can best be described as a radical version of relativism or Herderianism. All cultures are equal; but all cultures function perfectly only within the confines of their historical region of origin. Transgression of cultural boundaries, for instance through migration or intermarriage, leads to the distortion of a natural order and therefore to conflicts. Consequently, there is no problem with the culture of the Turkish and Moroccan migrants in Belgium other than the sheer fact that they are in Belgium. Their culture is not inferior to that of the local majority, it is just not the culture that belongs in Belgium. This sophisticated line of argument allows the Vlaams Blok to avoid charges of racism (usually based on extremely narrow interpretations of racism as a theory of racial superiority). They are conspicuous in avoiding references to cultural superiority and inferiority, and they motivate negative statements *vis-à-vis* migrants in terms of the elaborated cultural theory sketched above.

Given this basic rejection of the possibilities of coexistence of cultures within one region, the way in which the Vlaams Blok uses integration in skirmishes with the government is essentially ironic and aimed at exposing the fundamental weaknesses of various authoritative entextualisations of the concept of integration and the (presumed multiculturalist) philosophy behind it. Consider this extract of a debate in the Flemish parliament (*Vlaamse Raad, Beknopt Verslag*, 17 February 1993: 8). The Vlaams Blok spokesman, Filip Dewinter, challenges the Flemish minister of education on a recent decision which allowed Muslim girls to wear a scarf in state schools:

(6)   Of course this matter touches on more than just wearing the scarf. The Flemish Government with this new approach plays in the hands of the Islamic fundamentalists. This is an obstacle for the integration of second- and third-generation migrants. Even in certain North-African countries, the scarf is only worn among very traditional groups of the population. Allowing the scarf impedes integration. By allowing the scarf, the Minister in fact admits that integration is an illusion. In that sense he comes close to the views of the Vlaams Blok. Only, we are much more consistent, and we conclude from this that only a policy of repatriation makes sense. The Vlaams Blok advocates the reintegration of foreigners in their own community. In view of this we want to build a separate education system for them, which could prepare them for their repatriation.

This is a very clever piece of political rhetoric, in which Dewinter appropriates arguments used in authoritative versions of integration (namely, the rejection of fundamentalism, see above), associates these arguments with the concrete case at hand (namely, wearing the scarf as a sign of fundamentalism), then jumps to conclusions which highlight the virtues of the Vlaams Blok's view (namely, the illusion of integration and the greater consistency of their repatriation and 'reintegration' policy), and inserts the minister's decision into the Vlaams Blok logic. It is an embarrassing piece of rhetoric: many politicians find it very hard to react against objections such as these, in which their own doctrine (i.e. their own ideology of fixed text) is ironically turned against them. Quite a few of them, moreover, would agree to Dewinter's initial assumptions: that wearing a scarf signifies sympathy for Islamic fundamentalism, and that Islamic fundamentalism is an obstacle to the integration of Muslim migrants in Belgium. As we have seen above, the authors of the concept of integration themselves were less than clear with regard to how Islam fitted into the picture of integration, and they themselves raised (and thus legitimated) doubts about the 'integration-enhancing' potential of Islam. The right wing exploits this element in the space of allowed interpretations and uses it to construct its own coherent, but radically different, concept of integration. The irony can be constructed around a 'colonisation' of the mainstream trope 'scarf wearing = Islamic fundamentalism = anti-integration'; this trope is entextualised in another set of arguments, it is made to signify other things, and so the dispute appears to be one of *consequences* rather than one of diagnosis.

## Conclusions: the slow shift in orthodoxy

The crucial point in the discussion of the various examples is the interplay between an ideology of fixed text and a set of discourse practices which extend or alter the source-text or create paradoxes and contradictions in entextualisations of a concept of 'integration'. The lexical label 'integration' is inserted and re-entextualised in various discourses, but the ideology of fixed text (strongly associated with the use of a particular lexicon) creates an impression of coherence and allows for the recuperation of various entextualisations in new ones (for instance, the recuperation of a labour-movement entextualisation into the policy-makers'). The use of the term 'integration' (like 'socialism' in the previous section) creates a hinge of intertextuality, masking other discontinuities. *Ideological heterogeneity is both enabled and made invisible by textual homogeneity.* Linguistic ideologies – the ideology of fixed text – and wider social and political ideologies closely interact.

Note that the ideology of fixed text seems to be shared by all the participants in the debate. It allows the right wing to produce legitimate entextualisations based on a partial adoption of the source-text, notably by quoting the lexical frame (the term integration itself) as well as by borrowing certain stock arguments produced by authoritative actors (in particular, by the authors of the source text themselves).

It is this impression of stability and closure, created mainly by the lexical re-enactment of an ideologically fixed text, which allows for a gradual and hardly noticed shift in political orthodoxy. The debate goes on, and at first glance (i.e. adopting the ideological grids used in the debate) the parties do not change their minds or policies. Looked at from a perspective of entextualisation, however, the doctrinaire semantic core was left as soon as it was entered into the debate. From that moment onwards, it became a mere trope or argument in the debate, and the 'original' text moved on and assumed new shapes all the time, allowing political and ideological repositionings of considerable moment and consequence. Depending on time, cause, and audience, new arguments may be incorporated, registers may be adopted, terms or arguments can be borrowed. As long as some ingredients of the source-text can be maintained, a closure of topic and a streamlining of the debate can be effected. Utterances can be metadiscursively

qualified as part of the debate, as constructive or oppositional contributions to the debate, as legitimate or illegitimate interpretations of the
meanings contained in the source-text. Power resides in this interplay
between an ideology of fixedness and practices of re-entextualisation,
for it is precisely through this interplay that authority in the domain
of interpretation of texts can be managed and channelled.

## SUGGESTIONS FOR FURTHER READING

A very useful general introduction to the field of ideology is Eagleton
(1991). Various excellent discussions can be found in John Thompson
(1984) and his (1990) *Ideology and Modern Culture* is an excellent, readable
text on ideological processes in contemporary First-World societies. Of
course, the classics such as Gramsci (1971) or Althusser (1971) should be
read, though preferably in conjunction with some important commen-
taries on them, Anderson (1977) and E. P. Thompson (1978), respectively.
And the approaches of Foucault (1975) and Bourdieu (1990) should be
included in the reading list as well. Scott's (1990) book on hegemony
and resistance is important as an amendment to overly consensual
treatments of hegemony. Giddens' (1998) text on modern socialism is
both an analysis and an object of analysis for anyone interested in the
topic. Fairclough (2000) provides a necessary counterpoint. Blommaert
and Verschueren (1998) offer a road map for the Belgian debates on
integration.

# 8 Identity

## 8.1 INTRODUCTION

Identity is who and what you are. That sounds simple and straight-forward, and in everyday life, we find ourselves continually involved in identity rituals. Dating or developing friendships involve intricate narratives about one's self and requests for such narratives from the interlocutor – a matter of 'getting to know one another'. Meetings will start with a sequence in which everyone present tells his or her name and a couple of biographical and/or professional items sufficient to situate one's self in relation to the group and the occasion (when the meeting is professional, one is not likely to start off by saying 'Hi, I am so-and-so and my marriage is falling apart'). In highly bureaucratised societies we have to flash our identity every time we enter into contact with administrative bodies, and in the job market, a written genre called the CV together with several other modes of talking about one's self play a crucial role. When we go to watch a sports game, we are likely to shift into another identity gear and wear caps, T-shirts, and banners with 'our' team's logo or colours. On the day of our country's independence or of our king's birthday, we get the day off because we are citizens of that country. And when abroad, we discover ourselves talking a lot about that country, living up to its stereotypes, defending its values and virtues, and in return receiving flak because of the mistakes it made or makes.[1] When in Africa, I am also likely to be struck by the fact that the colour of my skin is different from that of most of the people around me, and I would become aware of the fact that, compared to many people there, I am a very wealthy person.

These are simple everyday rituals, but the examples above already indicate that identity is many things. The 'who and what you are' is dependent on context, occasion, and purpose, and it almost invariably involves a semiotic process of representation: symbols, narratives, textual genres such as standard forms and the CV. In fact, identity is semiotic through and through, and every act of semiosis is an act of identity in which we 'give off' information about ourselves (Le Page and Tabouret-Keller 1985). Such acts are of tremendous complexity, for they involve a wide variety of situating processes: situating the individual in relation to several layers of (real, sociological) 'groupness' and (socially constructed) 'categories' (age category, sex, professional category, but also national, cultural, and ethnolinguistic categories), situating this complex in turn in relation to other such complexes (young versus old, male versus female, highly educated versus less educated, and so on), and situating this identification in relation to the situation at hand, making selections that result in 'relevant' identity.

There is a tremendous amount of literature on identity, distributed over several social-scientific disciplines. Often such literature addresses particular kinds of identity such as gender, race, ethnic or national identities, with recent foci on diasporic and globalised network identities (Roosens 1989; Martiniello 1995; Romanucci-Ross and De Vos 1995; Castells 1996, 1997). In discourse-oriented studies, we have witnessed a lot of work on gender identities (Butler 1990; Wodak 1997; Cameron 1992; Cameron and Kulick 2003; Kulick 1998), on race (e.g. Hewitt 1986) and class (e.g. Willis 1981), and on particular articulations of identity such as racism (Wodak and Reisigl 1999; van Dijk 1987, 1991, 1993b; Wetherell and Potter 1992). The complexity of the field is quite tremendous, as identity questions invariably lead to highly problematic group concepts such as 'culture' or 'society' (with 'speech community', 'ethnicity', 'network', 'community', and 'nation' in between), and remarks on identity can be dispersed over work on such identities proper as well as on racism, anti-semitism, nationalism, and feminism, and even on intercultural communication and translation studies.[2]

Rather than trying to 'break into' this enormous body of work, I intend to focus on the way in which some of the points raised in the previous chapters could be applied to the field of identity. I shall argue that we may benefit from taking a semiotic angle on identity, for it will show how a wide variety of widely used concepts – culture, ethnic group, language community, society, nation – can be reconceived and reconceptualised as analytical tools. When starting from a semiotic point of departure, such concepts are empirical, that is, they cannot be used a priori any more. Very little can be taken for granted with regard to presumed stable identity categories as soon as we concentrate on semiotic practices as the points where identities are produced.[3]

But there are two points we wish to keep in mind while embarking on this exercise: one which reflects a consensus in scholarship; another which stems from the discussions in the previous chapters.

1. Almost any significant author in the wide field of identity studies would argue that people don't *have* an identity, but that identities are constructed in practices that *produce, enact,* or *perform* identity – identity is identification, an outcome of socially conditioned semiotic work. Thus, Judith Butler (1990) emphasised the 'performative' nature of gender identity, arguing that gender identity is something that is continually performed and enacted (see Hall and Bucholtz 1995; Wodak 1997). Roosens (1989) demonstrated how a seemingly stable identity category such as ethnicity can be (and often is) the result of conscious and elaborate processes of 'ethnogenesis', and Hobsbawm and Ranger (1983) famously made the same case for national identity. In one of the most thought-provoking studies on the topic, Don Kulick (1998) demonstrated how Brazilian male transsexuals performed highly complex and ambiguous identity work involving a perpetual tension between gender and sexuality. In an attempt to be the perfect object of homosexual desire, male homosexuals would transform and adorn their bodies in such a way as to be the perfect sexual partner while articulating not a desire to be female but a desire to be an attractive partner in male–male homosexual activities.

What we have to remember from this is that labels that presuppose identity as a sociologically stable attribute of groups are usually less than reliable. It is safer to start from a performance perspective which emphasises that identity categories have to be enacted and performed in order to be socially salient. This argument brings me close to that of Conversation Analysis, where identity categorisation is seen as exclusively a matter of practical enactment in interactional events (Schegloff 1999; Antaki and Widdicombe 1998; see D'hondt 2001, 2002 for a nuanced discussion). But I shall amend it in the next point.

2. I have to underscore some of the arguments developed in the previous chapters. There, I emphasised that meaning – including the attribution of identity categories – is a dialogical practice in which the uptake of one's semiotic acts may be as consequential as the structure of the semiotic acts themselves. In other words, in order for an identity to be established, it has to be *recognised* by others. That means that a lot of what happens in the field of identity is done by others, not by oneself. I know of only very few individuals who would self-qualify as 'arrogant bastards', 'liars', or 'cowards'; yet many people carry such identity labels around, they have been stuck on them by other people. The fact is that, regardless of whether one wants to belong to particular groups or not, one is often *grouped* by others in processes of – often institutionalised – social categorisation called *othering*. There is a difference between 'achieved' or 'inhabited' group identity and 'ascribed'

categorical identity, and both kinds involve different semiotic practices and occur under different conditions.

Such processes are semiotic, of course, but they need not be inter-personal, and this invalidates the claim of Conversation Analysis that identities are not relevant until interactionally oriented towards by immediate participants in conversations. Identities can be there long before the interaction starts and thus condition what can happen in such interaction. A conversation between a Turkish immigrant and a Belgian police officer may not show any interactional traces of active and explicit orienting towards the categories of 'Turkish immi-grant' or 'police officer'. But both parties in the interaction are in all likelihood very much aware of each other's identity, since these categories as well as particular attributions of these categories and typical relationships between them have been pre-inscribed in the interaction. Identities can also be attributed afterwards, by parties not involved in the interaction. In bureaucratic practice, for instance, people become a particular type of bureaucratic identity, a 'case' (a refugee, an urgent case for social welfare, someone entitled to a pen-sion, a criminal) after officials have scrutinised facts and accounts of facts provided earlier during interviews and on forms and written statements (Hall and Slembrouck 2001 provide an excellent example). There are, in effect, particular social identity categories that can only be bestowed on people *after* identity-performing acts have occurred: a hero, a coward, a saint are all retrospective evaluative, ascribed identities.

In conjunction with this, it may be worthwhile reiterating that peo-ple are not entirely free in semiotic work; they are determined in the sense outlined in chapter 5. That means that they carry with them different capacities for articulating inhabitable group identities and attributing ascriptive categorical identities, capacities that may work well in one environment but fail in another. Globalisation processes probably only intensify processes that are general in nature: the fact that, as one moves around through various social and spatial environ-ments, group and categorical identities change and become less clear cut or less well understood by those involved in acts of categorisation. That is why we tend to produce stereotypes about our country of ori-gin abroad, thus providing narratives of identity the ingredients of which are probably very irrelevant at home but reflect, in our minds, what others may (want to) know about us. That is also why the colour of my skin, less relevant as an identity marker in Belgium, becomes a pervasive identity marker in Africa, my accent in English a marker in the United States. It is also the reason why I become a 'discourse analyst' among historians, an 'anthropologist' among linguists, and a 'linguist' among anthropologists.[4]

The greater the distance, the more general and less precise our categories become. We tend to have extremely nuanced and fine-grained categories for that which is closest to us, but may have to revert to simple stereotypes exuding incapacity to perceive all kinds of differences as soon as we move away. Thus, the more people sink in history, the more totalising identity categories become. We speak about 'the Romans', 'the Mongols', 'the Vandals', or 'the Middle Ages' as if we were facing one uniform social formation or historical period. The 'Chinese' are a similarly lumped category, and the Soviets were all Russians. The application of a Sudanese asylum seeker was once turned down by a Belgian judge on grounds that he was 'too black', and 'everyone knows that the Nigerians are the blackest of the Africans'. In the eyes of the judge, this very dark African man *had* to be Nigerian. In the age of globalisation, precisely such issues of distance resulting in an inability to see and understand identities may be a crucial problem.

## 8.2 IDENTITIES AS SEMIOTIC POTENTIAL

In line with the foregoing remarks, I would propose that we see identity not as a property or a stable category of individuals or groups, but as *particular forms of semiotic potential, organised in a repertoire*. People construct identities out of specific configurations of semiotic resources, and, consequently, just as linguistic and semiotic repertoires are conditioned by dynamics of access, identity repertoires will likewise be conditioned by unequal forms of access to particular identity-building resources. And similar differences between the relative value of resources will apply: status identities will require status resources, the kind of resources we associated with mobility, the capacity to perform functions across contexts. Consequently, the capacity to enact such status identities will be unequally distributed, and some people will never be capable of enacting them.

Seeing identities primarily as forms of semiotic potential has two main analytic advantages, I believe. First, it provides us with a clearer view of the relationship between semiotic resources and identities; second, it also allows us to connect the issue of identity to stratification and inequality, and may thus offer us clearer views of how identity can be investigated in the context of globalisation.

## Unpredictable mobility

The first advantage I see is that this perspective allows a *performance-approach to identities*, which focuses on identity as a form of socially meaningful practice. In that way, it precludes the essentialising tendencies so widespread in several identity discourses. In effect, essentialised identity discourses themselves can be seen as one particular form of performing identity, often the prerogative of specific actors. Essentialising ascriptive statements on the 'quality' of students, for instance, are the prerogative of faculty, and a discourse on how good or bad students are this semester is a particular, powerful enactment of inhabited professorial group identity – performing specific forms of 'othering' is an ingredient of many forms of identity performance. Further on, we shall see how a discourse on ethnolinguistic identity is typically produced by, or with reference to, the state. The state there acts as the 'othering' actor defining citizens in terms of an essentialised identity category, while in the same move it defines itself.

The range of identities, as said before, depends on the range of available semiotic resources out of which recognisable identities can be constructed. That means that, in principle, all kinds of identities can be constructed in very flexible ways, and that every semiotic means can be used to construct such identities. The work of Ben Rampton (1995, 1999, 2001, 2003) is exemplary in this respect. Rampton (1995) showed how, in the speech of urban, multi-ethnic youth in London and the South Midlands of England, the smallest ingredients of talk could be turned into consequential identity markers. A single word pronounced with a Jamaican Creole accent could flag alignment by a white British youngster with Caribbean Rasta culture and group identity. Identity work here was not enabled by elaborate bilingualism between local London English and Jamaican Creole, it was based on the appropriation of particular sounds, pronunciations, lexemes, and topics of conversation. Similarly, ethnic minority schoolchildren produced 'German' (or at least: German-sounding and German-resembling utterances learned during German classes at school) (Rampton 1999) as well as imitations of Cockney expressions by a teacher (Rampton 2001) to express relational identities that refer both to their own local in-group identities (pupils in a class) and to macro-identities of ethnic minorities in Britain. Switches into Cockney and 'Posh' – an imitation of upper-class British English – expressed a complex of ethnic, sexual, and social class relations (Rampton 2001, 2003).

In all of these cases, the markers of identity were small and unspectacular at first sight, but, as John Gumperz reminds us, 'what from a purely linguistic perspective may count as minor distinctions can often, for largely ideological reasons, attain great social import as badges of identity' (Gumperz 2003: 110). They were also unpredictable on grounds of general, stereotypical social categorisation. Jamaican Creole can be stigmatised as 'bad English' at higher levels of social perception; in these multi-ethnic peer groups, however, it could carry considerable prestige. And even if school-taught codes such as Standard British English or German 'officially' bear standard associations with particular identities (often middle-class normative identities), 'their uptake can obviously lead in unforeseeable directions', and it would be best to view *all* linguistic resources, at least a priori, as 'unpredictably mobile' in terms of their potential for deployment in identity-performing activities (Rampton 1999: 501).

Rampton directs our attention to the different domains, and the differences between domains, in which identity work can be performed. Society is full of niches in which highly particular identities can and need to be performed, using resources that have no such positive identity-performing values elsewhere. There is no contradiction here with identities and resources operating elsewhere or on higher levels, and more or less widely used metaphors such as 'fragmented identities' do not adequately cover what we witness here. We also do not need to relate everything that happens to overarching identity categories such as ethnic identity or social class (like, for example, in Myers-Scotton 1993). What we are facing are specific identities operating at specific levels, more or less autonomously (and, hence, with enormous degrees of flexibility in the kind of material used in performing them) but referring to categories and values operating at other levels. To illustrate the latter: it is clear that speaking 'Posh' English derives its ironic, distancing effect among members of a particular peer group from higher level stereotypical images of people-speaking-Posh in Britain. The same goes for German: the widespread commanding, stern, disciplined associative attributions of German (articulated, for example, through war movies) become the material out of which the youngsters can build ironic constructions of themselves and their teachers.

One implication of all this is that the niche in which such group identities emerge, operate, and are meaningful can be small, temporary, and ephemeral, with no necessity for institutionalisation or persistence over time. In some of our own research (Maryns and Blommaert 2001; Blommaert *et al.* 2003), we felt compelled to focus on 'speaker position' – a shifting perspective adopted by speakers in narratives and involving shifts in stylistic, epistemic, and affective stances – as the clearest empirical clue for identity. Speakers would speak from different positions in the space of one single narrative event, and they would speak *as different subjects*, enacting different 'roles'. Thus, identity work seemed to be thematically organised, with shifts in identity complementing thematic shifts. This is, of course, reminiscent of Erving Goffman's (1974, 1981) theses about the self being constructed through the performance of everyday social inter-action rituals – 'the self as conversational motivator' in the words of Randall Collins (1988: 57), taking several positions in conversations from which to present oneself. These positions were called 'footing' and they empirically occur in the packaged shifts in stylistic, epis-temic, and affective stance mentioned above. The point is also remi-niscent of conversation-analytic views on categorisation, though with substantial qualifications. In Conversation Analysis, we should recall, identities are seen as primarily produced in talk by direct participants. In a superb paper on this topic, D'hondt (2002) shows how in one con-versation different identities can be produced and made relevant in the interaction, at least if a more flexible and richer notion of context is used than that commonly applied in Conversation Analysis. D'hondt argues that conversationally produced identities are *argumentative*, that is, speakers produce identities from repertoires that fit particular argu-mentative moves.

I suggest we adopt this in principle, but I would add that such reper-toires would display more structure and more constraints than usually accepted in Conversation Analysis. Such structure and constraints, I have already argued, are the product of higher level contexts – con-texts that do not normally become visible in interactions between close peers, but are a matter of substantial analytic concern as soon as we engage in discussions of language and globalisation. And, as a conse-quence, the mobility of resources (or absence of mobility) may be less unpredictable and more structured.

Summarising, by taking this position in which we see identities as forms of semiotic potential, we avoid the reduction of identities to static, established categories that are in themselves, in all likeli-hood, discourses of identity produced by particular actors. We are in a position to replace such imposed categories with a fine-grained analy-sis of how people *practically* identify themselves and others, and how they do so through the deployment of whatever means they have at their disposal. If identity is a semiotic construct, it should be seen in the same terms as semiosis: as organised by topic, situation, genre, style, occasion, purpose, and so on. Such means, however, are ordered in stratified repertoires, and the suggestion of identities as semioti-cally organised does not entail a chaotic and unrestricted world of identifying practices. It entails the dynamics of creativity and determination described earlier; nothing less and nothing more.

## Identity, inequality, and the world system

A second advantage of this perspective is that it allows us to set identities in the framework we sketched before, of *polycentric and stratified systems in which hierarchies in identities can be developed*. Not every identity will have the same range or scope, nor the same purchase across social and physical spaces. Identities, like the semiotic resources by means of which they are enacted, are part of a stratified system, and the particular stratification of identities and their resources will depend on the particular environment in which one lives.

That means that several features discussed earlier also obtain here. For instance, we repeatedly mentioned the non-exchangeability of 'values' for particular linguistic resources across societies. A good mastery of East African English may be valuable and a source of prestige in Nairobi, but it may be the object of stigmatising reactions in London or New York. The same effects can be seen in the domain of identities: a middle-class identity in Nairobi may not be immediately convertible to an equivalent class identity in London or New York; a Rasta in Kingston may be quite different from a Rasta in Moscow; a professor in Jakarta can be different from one at Harvard or the Collège de France. We encounter the fundamental inequalities characterising the world system here as well: socially recognisable, valid identities in one part of the world may not correspond to their perceived counterparts in another part of the world. And the key to the process is indexicality. The indexicalities that provide opportunities for inhabited group identities *there* are different from the indexicalities that provide opportunities for ascriptive, categorical identities *here*.

It is therefore a mistake to project attributions of prestige or stigma as well as of a particular identity potential onto seemingly similar resources all over the world. To give a concrete example: it makes little sense to project prestige, mobility, and a middle-class identity potential onto English worldwide, and neither should we project attributions of oppression or imperialism onto English worldwide (as is the case in much of the literature on linguistic rights, see Phillipson 1992). What happens to resources such as English, their value and identity-articulating potential in one place is not necessarily predictable from what happens to them elsewhere. Let me illustrate this by means of some data from Tanzania.

Years ago, I started noticing the often peculiar varieties of written English used in all kinds of public displays in urban Dar es Salaam,

Tanzania's major city. Such varieties would come to me in the form of signs on doors and walls of shops, bars, and restaurants, inscriptions on the small, privately operated buses that provide mass transportation (the infamous *daladala* – 'dollar-dollar'), advertisements in newspapers, or on billboards, road signs, and so forth. The most striking aspect of these publicly displayed forms of English literacy was the density of 'errors' or unexpected turns of phrase in them. Here is a small sample:

- *Fund rising dinner party* (on a banner in central Dar es Salaam)
- *Disabled Kiosk* (the name of a 'kiosk' – a converted container that serves as a small shop – operated by a disabled man)
- *Whole sallers of hardwere* (sign at a hardware shop)
- *Shekilango Nescafé* (the name of a café on Shekilango Road in suburban Dar es Salaam)
- *new Sikinde tea (room)* (the name of a café, note the brackets)
- *Sliming food* (in an advertisement for a health shop)
- *Con Ford* (written on a bus)
- *Approxi Mately* (written on a bus)
- *Sleping Coach* (written on a long-distance bus)

Clearly, these inscriptions are packed with information. They reveal a problem with the distribution of linguistic resources: Standard English with its codified referential meanings, on the one hand, normative literacy conventions for English, on the other. Seen from the angle of monoglot normativity (Silverstein 1996b), the people who wrote and used these inscriptions display incomplete insertions in economies of literacy and linguistic forms. In that sense, they testify to some of the crucial problems of language policy in Tanzania: the lasting prestige functions attributed to English combined with the extremely restricted access to its prestige-bearing, standard varieties (the latter completely subject to access to post-primary education).[5]

But there are other aspects to this. It is clear that the producers (and consumers) of these signs orient towards the status hierarchy in which standard, Euro-oriented English occupies the top. This is an orientation to a transnational, global hierarchy, reinforced by the state's ambivalent and meandering stance on English. There is an orientation to English as a code associated with core values of capitalist ideas of success: entrepreneurship, mobility, luxury, female beauty. The use of English is sensed to index all of this. But, at the same time, it indexes this not in terms of internationally valid norms (e.g.

standard varieties of written English), but in terms of *local* diacritics. The man who commissioned the *disabled kiosk* sign probably did not imagine himself as an international businessman, but he did imagine himself as a businessman in Dar es Salaam (or even more specifically, in the Magomeni borough of Dar es Salaam). And at this point a new space of meaning-attribution is opened. We have an act of communication which at once orients towards transnational indexicalities and to strictly local ones, and the effect is that the English used in these signs has to make sense *here*, in Magomeni – but *as English*, i.e. as a code suggesting a 'move out' of Magomeni and an insertion into transnational imaginary networks.

This is a transpatriation of sign-complexes which offers a tremendous semiotic potential for users to construct inhabitable group identities. They can produce strictly local meanings of great density and effect. The man who wrote *Con Ford* on his bus was simultaneously advertising the brand of his vehicle, alluding to the local folk-category of 'conmen' – smooth talkers and ladies' men – and boasting the standards of comfort in his bus, while also displaying his wit and capacity to perform word play in English. The same goes for the owner of the *Shekilango Nescafé*: an anchoring in the local topography goes hand in hand with a display of knowledgeability of prestigious, European brand names (Nescafé), a suggestion of a degree of sophistication and a European-touch-of-class for his business, and a flair for finding well-sounding names for things. And as for the authors of *fund rising* or *sliming food*: they target an audience who would focus on the total value of the English display rather than its normative correctness, and so offer them a space for identifying with high-class, internationalized categories of activities. It is the value of English and of literacy *in Dar es Salaam* that has to be put central.

So we are not really witnessing an invasion of an imperialist or killer-language here. What we are witnessing is a highly complex, intricate pattern of appropriation and deployment of linguistic resources whose values have been relocated from a transnational to a national set of indexicalities. It is a *Tanzanian* bourgeois (or bourgeois-aspiring) resource. This set of indexicalities will obviously only work in Dar es Salaam. As soon as these bits of English start to travel, the orthographic or pragmatic errors in them start dominating the perceptions of meaning and function, and different ascriptive categorical identities may emerge. But this is the point: semiotic potential is tied to places and their characteristics, and determined by the inequalities between that particular space and others.

Now that this framework is sketched, I shall comment on two different aspects of identity, both of which, in my view, connect with long-standing problems in research. I shall first offer some comments on the issue of ethnolinguistic identity, a category very deeply enshrined in the study of language. Next, I shall turn to a neglected area of research related to identities: space and semiotisations of space. I shall argue that space may offer important empirical inroads into the practice of identity-work. After these discussions, I shall provide a case analysis of globalised identity work.

## 8.3   WHAT IS LEFT OF ETHNOLINGUISTIC IDENTITY?

Few concepts appear as stable, uncontroversial, and intuitively correct as that of ethnolinguistic identity – an identity expressed through belonging to a particular language community and articulated in statements such as 'I speak Dutch', 'I am British [ergo I speak English]', or 'In Dutch, we call this N'. In the study of language, such statements have been captured under well-established concepts such as that of the 'native speaker', and in the practice of research it has created this category of people we call 'informants' – 'native speakers' also seen as ideal members of an ethnolinguistically defined community.

Technically, ethnolinguistic identity is a complex notion covering both linguistic and 'ethnic' features. An ethnolinguistic identity would emerge at the confluence of a sense of belonging to a language community ('speakers of X') and a sense of belonging to an 'ethnic' community. As for the latter, language usually features among the core criteria for defining ethnicity (Blommaert and Verschueren 1998; Martiniello 1995; Fishman 1999), thus causing considerable overlap between language community and ethnic community. Obviously, and as we shall argue below, every ingredient of this complex of features represents a major empirical problem as soon as we start investigating it in practice. Notwithstanding this complexity, ethnolinguistic identity is perhaps one of the most stable and most widespread notions in the study of language, as well as in the politics of language. Language policies almost invariably take an explicitly or implicitly defined notion of ethnolinguistic identity as their point of departure: 'since our people are French, the French language shall be used in all aspects of public life'. Political struggles over ethnic or cultural minority rights almost always involve ethnolinguistic identity as one of the most convincing arguments in favour of minority status. And in recent years, the branch of sociolinguistics devoted to linguistic minority rights uses ethnolinguistic identity as its core defining instrument (see, for example, Skutnabb-Kangas 2000).

The stability of the notion of ethnolinguistic identity has been questioned since the days of Labov (1972). In fact, Labov's demonstration of grammar, structure, and coherence in the speech of young African-Americans amounted to a frontal attack against easy, uniformising, and homogeneistic associations between 'being American' and 'speaking (standard, middle-class) American English', showing how a part of the American 'nation' spoke a different language, not a bad variety of the same language. Simultaneously, Dell Hymes (1968) demonstrated that the concept of 'tribe' – perhaps one of the most dominant notions of human community in the history of Western thought, and almost always tied up with ideas of ethnolinguistic homogeneity – was fraught with linguistic problems. Tribes are seen as groups of people with a name ('Sioux', 'Bamileke', 'Dayak', 'Guarani'), distinguishable because of a common language and a common 'culture', i.e. common traditions and particular forms of social organisation. Such a view, Hymes argues, is based on a 'one language-one culture' assumption, namely 'the ethnographic world can be divided into "ethnolinguistic" units, each associating a language with a culture' (1968: 25). The next move is to assume that this 'language' is the medium of communication within that culture (and thus defines the group using it *as* a group).

In relation to this, Michael Silverstein (1996b, 1998) distinguishes between 'language community' and 'speech community'. The distinction is fundamental to our understanding of linguistic identity processes. Language communities are 'groups of people by degree evidencing allegiance to norms of *denotational* . . . language usage' (1998: 402, italics added) – people, in short, who believe that they speak the 'same Language'. A speech community, in contrast, should be defined in terms of *indexicality*, as soon as we 'recognize an implicit normativity to such indexical semiosis as informs and underlies communicative acts of identity and groupness' (1998: 407) – people, in short, who produce, share, and exchange orders of indexicality. If we bring this distinction to bear on Hymes' argument, we see how ideas of ethnolinguistic uniformity make both notions – language community and speech community – coincide. Support for this is usually provided by investigations of the degree of shared lexicon between different dialects, a tactic based on an assumption in which shared 'words' account for mutual intelligibility and, hence, for communicative unity. Empirically, however, the degree of shared lexicon proves to be a weak indicator of communicative unity. Languages may be shared without significant amounts of communication going on between speakers, and vice versa. Thus, as soon as we replace language by speech and differentiate between language community and speech community, the one language–one culture connection becomes very shaky and 'the relations between the units classified by linguists as languages, and the communicative units of ethnology, are problematic' (Hymes 1968: 30).

In fact, Hymes suggests to see language (i.e. the linguistic 'denotational code' concept) 'not as a constant, but as a variable' (*ibid.*) in defining cultural entities, and to focus on communicatively salient linguistic varieties such as codes and ways of speaking instead, replacing the notion of 'speakers of a language' by that of 'users of a particular (specialized) code within a repertoire' (1968: 32). In sum, '[i]n order to determine communicative relationships among persons and groups, one must begin with persons and groups, the codes they share, and the purposes to which the codes are put' (1968: 37). In other words, Hymes suggests, we focus on 'speech community': a group defined on the basis of practical sharedness of sociolinguistic (indexical) norms and rules. Such speech communities can be multiple and overlapping, single individuals being involved in several speech communities at the same time, and moving through different sets of speech communities throughout their lives. Seen in this way, speech community is an empirical construct that can only be made by observing practices 'from below'. It is hard to imagine how it can be used deductively as something that follows organically from a description of linguistic norms and rules. Yet, that is how speech community has often been used in linguistic and sociolinguistic work, deductively – communicative behaviour is seen as predictable because of ethnicity – and as a synonym for language community.[6]

When given this linguistic and deductive orientation, speech community is a pretty useless concept if we intend to understand how groups emerge from and rally around communicative practices. As Rampton (1998) notes, it contains precisely those suggestions of homogeneity, uniformity, and territorial boundedness that formed the empirical weakness of the one language–one culture assumption. As we have seen, Rampton focuses our attention on 'deterritorialised' and 'transidiomatic' linguistic resources (cf. also Jacquemet 2000), and the way in which they become crucial ingredients of repertoires and of identity-constructing communicative practices. When practices are emphasised, almost any conventional notion of language as a group marker becomes questionable.

But then how do we explain the pervasiveness of such static and homogeneistic notions of ethnolinguistic identity? My suggestion is that we see it as a particular discourse on language, a discourse in which a statified and homogenising notion of (shared) language is used in order to demarcate an equally statified and homogenising notion of common identity: that of the language community. This has effects both on the capacity to construct inhabitable group identities (defining oneself as a member of the 'nation', for instance) and on the capacity to construct ascribed categorical identities (defining others as non-members, for instance). Such a discourse is clearly and often explicitly language-ideological, and, more often than not, it is organised by the *state* or by ideological state apparatuses in Althusser's sense, resulting in the patterns of symbolic domination and *méconnaissance* described by Bourdieu (1982, 1991). When it is not organised by the state (as, for example, in the case of minority issues, see Jaffe 1999; Heller 1999; May 2001), it is organised *with reference to* the state, often as a denial or a critique of the state ideology, and often also aimed at a self-definition of language community. In other words, I suggest that we see ethnolinguistic identity primarily as a construct at the state level, within a polycentric and stratified system in which the state assumes an intermediate position between infra-state and supra-state levels.

This suggestion is worth elaborating, I think, for one of the widespread ingredients of discourses on globalisation and late modernity is a denial of the state as an important actor in linguistic and cultural processes. Modernity, it is assumed, was characterised by an emphasis on state formats for organising the polity with the 'nation' as its desired outcome. The main actor in these processes was the 'nation-state'. In late modernity however, and due to the processes we call globalisation, the nation-state seems to become less and less of a factor in determining people's identity, networks, and practices. It is a view I intend to qualify.

One error consists in equalling 'state' with 'nation-state'. It is remarkable how often authors use the collocation 'nation-state' as a blanket descriptor for what they believe is the common, default form of statehood in modernity. Every modern state is consequently supposed to be a nation-state; if not, it is atypical. But what is a 'nation-state'? It is a state characterised by successful nationalism, i.e. by the outcome of an elaborate political process of forging a uniform, 'modern' nation. In other words, a nation-state is a *specific*, a *very* specific kind of state, and not every state is a 'nation-state' just by virtue of being a state, nor should it be. Both terms are different and need to be kept separate: a state is a formal, institutional construction with features I shall discuss below; a nation-state is one particular form such a state can assume, but this requires very specific actions and developments.

I am of course willing to accept that the processes we call globalisation have an eroding effect on *nationalism* in the 'classical' sense, as, for example, described by Hobsbawm (1986). Even in states characterised by a high degree of emphasis on cultural and linguistic uniqueness and uniformity, we would see that transnational and transidiomatic linguistic and cultural practices flourish and cannot be kept under control by the state. Speaking for myself: the Flemish part of Belgium where I live is a region characterised by an outspoken linguistic and cultural homogeneism. It is one of these few states where language (in my case Dutch) is seen as defining every aspect of being Flemish. The country has the most elaborate language laws in the world, and linguistic purism is one of the most dominant language ideologies in public life. Language laws compel me to do my teaching in Dutch, and students can obtain a degree if they have completed a fully Dutch-speaking programme. But almost all the readings assigned to my students are in languages other than Dutch, notably in English and French. My own academic writing is a trilingual affair, with Dutch, English, and French as my languages of publication. Most lectures by visitors to our department are in English or French. And when I switch on the TV to watch one of our government-supported Flemish broadcasting networks, almost all of the entertainment programmes are in English – series, movies, documentaries, some talk shows. Flanders would probably qualify as a 'nation-state', yet we see that globalisation results in dense multilingualism as a norm, even in domains which, by law, are defined as monolingual (as is the case in university education), and are indeed often perceived as such. Contemporary states cannot, or can only with absurd efforts, 'step out' of globalisation, and no state can nowadays impose with political or economic impunity the kind of massive homogenisation characteristic of the 'modern' nation.[7]

So the *nation*-state may be on its way out. But that does not mean that the *state* is on its way out in the era of globalisation. On the contrary, if we follow Wallerstein's (2000, 2001) approach, we would have to see the practical operation of the world system as controlled by *inter-state* relations. States need not be completely 'sovereign' in the classical sense of the term (which is, incidentally, also the sense often used by the state itself), they are interconnected within the world system, and they have to respond to pressures from above and from below, from transnational as well as from intra-national developments. And even if we see individual states sacrificing parts of their traditional sovereignty in favour of task-sharing interstate organisations such as the EU or the UN, this does not mean the *end* of such states. It may very well be the case that much of what we identify as 'nationalism' in recent decades is, in fact, a new form of 'statism': the state searching for reinforced authority in symbolic fields such as culture and language because of the gradual erosion of authority in 'hard' domains such as the economy, monetary affairs, social policies, international relations of defence. The state is now inserted in a wider and more complex pattern of power and decision-making, and it has to share several of its functions with other actors (cf. Ferguson and Gupta 2002).

In the field of language, and in particular with regard to the construction of state discourses on identity, the state is, and remains, a crucial actor. I see three main factors:

1. The state is a switchboard between various scales. In particular, it is the actor that organises a dynamic between the (transnational) world system and (national) 'locality'. The state often orients towards transnational centring institutions: capitalism, democracy, an international work order, transnational images of prestige and success, models of education, and so forth. It often also orients to transnational models of language and language use: literacy, the relative value of 'local' languages versus 'world' languages, and so forth. The dynamic is two-way, and contrasts between 'us' and 'the rest of the world' are at the core of many state activities.

2. Closely related to this first factor, the state organises a particular space in which it can establish a regime of language perceived as 'national' and with particular forms of stratification in value attribution to linguistic varieties and forms of usage. Thus, the state is one of the main organisers of *possible sociolinguistic contrasts* within a particular space: it allows others to create differences between their norms and those that are valid nationally (e.g. those that are transmitted through the education system). Civil society, for instance, will typically organise itself in contrast to (or modelled on) the state. The state is, wherever it exists, a centring institution with a considerable scope and depth. And the state is very often the actor that uses 'language' in the sense of 'language name' (English/French/Chinese', etc.) as its 'central value'.

3. An effective state can contribute a materiality to its role as a centring institution and impose its authority on others. The state has the capacity to provide an infrastructure for the reproduction of a particular regime of language: an education system, media and culture industries – each time a *selective* mechanism

which includes some forms of language and excludes others. The state, in other words, has the capacity to exert substantial control over the two dynamics of access discussed in earlier chapters: access to symbolic resources, and access to spaces of interpretation and value-attribution. The state has coercive instruments usually exclusive to the state: the legal system and the law enforcement system. So the state is often a *determining* force in the sociolinguistic landscape, in contrast to other centring institutions whose effect can best be described as *dominant*.

In sum, there are good reasons to attribute a special position to the state as an actor in the construction and reproduction of orders of indexicality within stratified polycentric systems, enormous differences between states with regard to effectiveness, scope, and range of activities notwithstanding (Ferguson and Gupta 2002). There will be cases where the state's authority appears to be overruled by that of others: the real centres to which people orient can be religion, political organisations, neighbourhoods, media, or other civil society actors (cf. Haeri 1997; Stroud 2002, but see Spitulnik 1998; Blommaert 1999b). This should not be denied, but my point is that the actions of such non-state actors need to be understood *with reference to the state*, which remains a centring institution at one particular level. There is never just one centre, but a whole collection of centres, and orientations to one centre (the church, particular grassroots organisations) derive value from the position of that centre *vis-à-vis* others. The precise scope and range of action of the state are an empirical matter; what we cannot do, I'm afraid, is to eliminate it from analysis or to treat it in purely idealistic terms. Even very 'weak' states can be very strong as frames of reference and points of contrast (and, hence, as meaning-attributing centres) for all sorts of non-state activities.

So what with ethnolinguistic identity in such a model? It will emerge as one particular kind of identity operating at one level: that of the state and relations to the state. It will consequently be one kind of semiotic opportunity people have: that of articulating something that indexes their position within and *vis-à-vis* the state, marking all kinds of contrasts with indexicalities operating both at higher and at lower levels of the polycentric system. It will also, and simultaneously, have to be seen as a discourse of power and (often) of coercion *by* the state or its apparatuses *about* the (ascribed) ethnolinguistic identity of its citizens. It will co-occur with all kinds of other identities in the kinds of layered simultaneity repeatedly mentioned before, sometimes more or less harmoniously and sometimes in conflicting ways that are not necessarily perceived as such. Thus, when I do my teaching, apart from several particular local orders of indexicality characterising my relations with students, programme, and institution, I also orient to the state when I deliver my lecture in Dutch, and to the transnational orders of discourse that characterise my professional universe whenever I point towards a book or an article written in English or French. For those intent on checking my loyalty to the state, there will be a clear articulation of ethnolinguistic identity, but only at one level and inseparable from other articulated identities.

Does this matter for discourse analysis? I believe it does. For one thing, ethnolinguistic identity is a feature of our analytic metadiscourse, and whenever we say that a particular stretch of discourse is 'in English', we project ethnolinguistic identity categories onto the discourse and its participants. For instance, we would start introducing distinctions between 'native' and 'non-native' varieties influencing or characterising the discourse. My argument here has been that we should not be naïve in this, for we are dealing with a heavily loaded and highly problematic category of identity. Second, a refined notion of ethnolinguistic identity is necessary to understand the centring institutions to which people orient while communicating. We infer notions of community membership whenever we impute ethnolinguistic categorisations onto discourse and its actors; it should be clear that such notions of community are, again, highly problematic and that an off-hand treatment of this issue might result in a flawed analysis of the sets of norms and expectations people orient towards in discourse. We often use ethnolinguistic categorisation as something we do in the 'preliminary' stages of analytic work, something that precedes 'real' discourse analysis ('ah, this text is in French . . .'). It should be part of the analysis.

## 8.4 SPACE, PLACE, AND IDENTITY

A second set of comments I wish to offer is about the importance of space in understanding identities. Several scholars before me have noted the importance of space and spatial references as organising motifs in narratives, emphasising how space provides a framework in which meaningful social relationships and events can be anchored and against which a sense of community can be developed (e.g. Johnstone 1990), how it can become the overarching motif in historical and identity narratives (e.g. Collins 1998; Feld and Basso 1996; Masquelier 2002; Thomas 2002), or how communication develops within densely semiotised spaces, so that people always speak *in* a place

(Scollon and Scollon 2003). Space can be filled will all kinds of social, cultural, epistemic, and affective attributes. It then becomes 'place', a particular space on which senses of belonging, property rights, and authority can be projected.

Adopting the idea in its most general form, we can say that identities often contain important references to space or incorporate spatial locations or trajectories as crucial ingredients. But, strangely, most of the literature on identity makes hardly more than cursory references to space in relation to identity. In what follows, I shall offer a few suggestions for incorporating spatial aspects in analyses of identity.

Let us begin by noting the deep connectedness, in practice, of what we understand by autobiography and space. Autobiographical narratives invariably contain references to 'where one is from' ('I was born in [place]') and to itineraries followed during one's life. As Barbara Johnstone (1990) so sensitively describes, such spatial anchorings are crucial in the organisation of senses of self and the definition of meaningful relations to others. Johnstone's materials were gathered in Fort Wayne, Indiana, a small town in 'Middle America'. Johnstone demonstrates how being from *that particular* place organises references to other parts of the US (the major cities, the South) and allows the crystallisation of packages of moral, cultural, and social attributions around Fort Wayne as a site of human activity. It organises the moral economy by means of which judgements of people and activities are made. And it becomes an ingredient of a semiotic matrix by means of which 'members' and 'non-members' can be identified and granted various kinds of attributive qualities: character, style, preferences for food, even specific modes of behaviour (e.g. in dating or marriage), and political preferences. This, obviously, connects with older sociolinguistic findings on accent. Accent, we now know, is a sociolinguistic feature that tells far more than just regional origin: it invokes the wider complex of features mentioned above. Lippi-Green (1997) discusses the manifold ways in which accents in American English can be, and are, used to portray people politically, culturally, socially, and ideologically. Apart from regional descent, accents thus suggest places and rankings on several other highly sensitive scales in society. And Johnstone (1999: 515) shows how the use of an identifiable Southern accent by Texan women can signal 'a display of gentility, it can indicate closeness and friendship, it can set a Southerner apart from others, it can be used to manipulate men, and so on'.

Interesting in this is to see how, very often, attributions are based on centre–periphery models. People seem to have an acute understanding of what is central and what is peripheral. If someone introduces him/herself by 'I work at the University of Western Kentucky', versus someone who says 'I work at Yale', the difference between these utterances is not purely spatial-referential. It is a difference between *value-attributions to the place*, and such attributions are organised along centre–periphery models: Yale is more 'central' than Western Kentucky. Having a 'central' accent in English or a 'peripheral' one may be a significant difference. Many Belgians would exhaust themselves trying to acquire what they perceive as American accents of English. Nobody makes any effort at acquiring, say, Nigerian or Indian English. And when an American addresses a Belgian, the Belgian will have the impression that his own Belgian English is 'bad'. But when a Nigerian addresses a Belgian, the Belgian will have the impression that the Nigerian speaks 'bad' English. The difference between the two varieties is rather trivial linguistically, but huge in terms of social value and purchase in the world. It is the world system coming down on language again, as we have seen above. Thus, place defines people, both in their own eyes and in the eyes of others, and such definitions of belonging are mediated through ethnodialectal indexicalities. And obviously, when people get displaced, their discourses become deterritorialised – disconnected from their usual spaces and inserted in new ones governed by new rules. This we have seen in several of the examples throughout the chapters of this book. But there is more.

People speak *from* a place. Given the deep connections between forms of language and particular places, the use of specific varieties 'sets' people in a particular social and/or physical place, so to speak, and confers the attributive qualities of that place to what they say. So, for instance, in a conversation one may switch from a standard variety into a regionally marked variety and back. The shift invokes the differences attributed to the spaces typically associated with the varieties. The regionally marked variety will place the speaker in the region associated with the variety, and it will confer all kinds of indexical values on the utterance, values we associate with the particular region. The shift back into the standard variety then marks a 'move out' of that particular place and back into another one. The shift across varieties and places may also involve delicate shifts in epistemic or affective stance (Biber and Finegan 1989), general style, footing, or key, all of which reflect – iconically – characteristics of the place. In the illustration in the next section, we shall discuss aspects of this process in detail. For the moment, we can suffice by saying that the attributive qualities of spaces, projected onto speech varieties, allow for an enormous semiotic potential through which people can articulate far more different identities, subjectivities, and speaker positions than previously assumed. What we see is that, along with a repertoire of speech varieties, a repertoire of associative, indexically salient, speaking positions develops and becomes a battery of meanings. When in globalisation processes transnational movements become more intense, we can expect such phenomena to characterise more and more of social interaction, and we can also expect the repertoires to become more complex, less transparent, and more densely layered.

Space interacts with cognitive, moral, emotive frames within which people situate themselves and from and to which they speak (Blommaert *et al.* 2003). This results in seemingly fragmented utterances in which people 'shift place' frequently and delicately, and each time, in very minimal ways, express different identities. Such identities, consequently, can be seen as generated by particular topics or discursive moves – Goffman's footing. In Maryns and Blommaert (2001), for instance, we saw how a man from Sierra Leone spoke as an 'administrative subject' whenever he spoke about Belgium, as a victim of violence and atrocities whenever he spoke about Sierra Leone, and as a victim of racism whenever he talked about contacts with Belgian officials. The shifts in speaking position – inhabited identities – came in packages of shifts across different language varieties, different styles, and different epistemic and affective stances. We are facing small shades of identity (often distinctions within established big categories) that may matter very much for those who produce them in discourse. In the next section, I shall offer a proposal for how to analyse such delicate shifts.

## 8.5 THE WORLD SYSTEM IN ACTION

In what follows I shall again analyse and discuss a piece of globalised discourse. The data we shall investigate are a fragment from a radio show on UCT Radio, the radio station operated from the University of Cape Town in South Africa. The show is a reggae programme, deejayed by a young man who calls himself Ras Pakaay. Listeners can call in to request particular songs. The show was broadcast on Sunday afternoons, and this recording was made in December 2000.

We are facing a rather typical globalisation product here: a mass-media format in which one of the transnational, globalised art forms *par excellence*, reggae music, is staged in Cape Town, the southern tip of Africa. The audience is a mixed one, composed both of black and white South Africans from the Cape Town region, most of them rather young. And the show is done in what counts as English, though, as we shall see, this is far from a simple proposition.

I shall focus in my discussion on the main point of this chapter: identity as semiotic potential. We shall see how globalisation offers discursive opportunities for the deejay and his listeners, and how the deejay can move across various thematic spaces by means of a variety of discursive shifts that also indicate shifts in identity. Let us have a look at the transcript first. There are four parts in the fragment. The fragment begins with Ras Pakaay commenting on the song he just played (part 1). Next, he engages in anecdote telling (which will be rendered in the transcript by an ethnopoetic organisation of the lines) (part 2). After that he enters into a telephone conversation with a female listener (part 3). A conflict occurs, and Ras Pakaay terminates the phone conversation (part 4).

Ras Pakaay uses at least four identifiable linguistic varieties in the fragment: 'Standard English', 'Black English', 'Township English', and 'Rasta Slang'. I use scare quotes for these varieties, because they have to be seen and understood in terms of local repertoires, accents, and potential for realisation. Thus, the 'Standard English' utterances bear a marked South African black accent, and the 'Black English' varieties (imitations of Hip-Hop North American black accents) also sound eminently South African. When Ras Pakaay shifts into Rasta Slang, we hear an attempt towards producing Jamaican Creole accents, blended with some 'typical' Rasta lexemes. In the transcript, I shall use roman for the 'Standard English' fragments, underlined for the 'Black English' parts, and bold to indicate Rasta Slang. There is a one-word shift into 'Township English', which I mark in bold italic. I shall also provide glosses in phonetic script for heavily marked utterances.[8] Note that we are talking about small *linguistic* differences here – differences in accent and style – but they will be shown to be big *sociolinguistic* and *discourse-strategic* differences.

## Transcript

*Part 1*

{music}
R. definite he is.
{creaky voice}
**I'm a noo sssssssmoke** [s:mo:k]
**No chronic to bother no one** [no kronik. tu bo:də nowaɲ). . .
but=**I man** [maɲ] . . .
Yes: my brethren.

you must {laughin voice, dragging intonation} <u>ha=</u> (   ) with a smoke
[smoᵃk] <u>you know=</u> I had a smoke [smo:k]
<u>I tell you my brethren</u> {end laughin voice}.


{style shift: fast, neutral declarative style}
While it =am. time is=has goneh twelve minutes pas the hour of five
o' clock on UCT radio wonderful point five ef em studio.


*Part 2*

{style shift: slow, truncated speech, creaky voice}
<u>I just had a brethren right</u> **now** [no:ᵂ].
<u>he's actually calling</u> **all the way** [o:l də we:ᵃ] from **Heideveld** [hiᵃ:dəfeld]
   <u>I say</u>
      yo Ras Pakaai gone to heave'.
      *Bush *Band
  <u>an=I say</u>
      <u>my brethren I do have</u> **Budj Band**


and I say   yo.
  <u>Why do wanna come live on air</u>
   <u>I said allright allright allright</u>
<u>and then az' I was preparing to pu' the man</u> [man] 'pon line.
<u>the man</u> [maɲ] got *cut [kot] off with Ras Pakaai.
{style shift: neutral, declarative style}
<u>but then on that very same</u> **note** [noᵃt]
beautiful listeners of this=e show
we have. a caller on the line {technical sound}
. . .


*Part 3*

**cottin edge hoi**

F. hello?
R. hello <u>yo live on air</u> [ɛ:]
F. OK
R. {fast} yea who'm I speaking to everythin is all right thanks and how
   'bout you?
F. yeah I'm fine
R. yeah. an=
F. (=   NAME)

R. {laughing} hehehe [NAME]. everythin is all right. I know you're
    calling from **all the way** [o:l də we:ª] .what am calling now **all the**
    **way** [oª:l də we:ª] from **Khayelitsha** [koyəlisha] is that right
F. yeah
R. allright..how may I help you
F. yeah OK I would like to uhm if you just wanted(ed) to play mh. this
    song for *me please
R. What song you'd like me to play for you
F. [= by Luciano
R. by? Luciano
F. [=yeah
R. well. {laughing voice} I don know what's happenin' with Luciano
    today.. Ehm what a song you'd like me to play for you
F. =Kiss me again=ja
R. **Kiss me again olmos' I gat Jah** . I'm definitely gonna play that song
    for you my sisterene allright? . And who'd you like me to play the
    song for
F. for   my*se:lf
R. for yourself?.   Oh really. {laughs} hahahahha an you=
F. yeah      =what you *laughin {laughing voice} at me (about)?
R. ehhr?


*Part 4*

F. {serious style, falling intonation} why you laughing at me?
R. {serious, flat intonation} no I'm not laughin' my sisterene *otherwise*
    [a:dawais] I thaught you would ehm actually want to play the song..
    or want me to play the song for somebody else or:. for some people
    **dem** seen?
F. = just for myself
R. =just for yourself.. so you just sitting at home?
F.                                           yeah
R. =listenin' to reggae music, with Ras Pakaai on UCT radio
F. yeah
R. {fast, creaky voice} (   [kom tru yu]) **my sisterene sha me do dat**
    (   ) **all right?**
F. okay
R. **yeah give thanks** [tʃanks]
F. (   )
R. {laughing} **thanks for callin my sisterene all right?. and**=e **keep**
    **dem things under control** [kəntroªl]. I don know
    {jingle}

Let us take a closer look at what happens in this fragment. The first thing we notice is the connection between shifts in linguistic varieties and specific parts in the fragment. The connection appears to be mainly thematic. Whenever Ras Pakaay talks about the world of reggae – song lyrics, Rasta values and atmosphere – he shifts into Rasta Slang. We see this in part 1 when he recaps the theme of the song he just played; in referring to the place where the listeners' calls are made from (Heideveld and Khayelitsha, both townships in Cape Town) in parts 2 and 3; the song title the female caller has requested in part 3, and, of course, towards the end of part 4. The anecdote he tells in part 2 is predominantly in Black English, though some lexical shifts into Rasta Slang occur ('Budj band'), and the telephone conversation with the girl as well as the announcements of the time and the station are predominantly in Standard English.

These are relatively general correspondences which should not obscure the finer shifts occurring in several parts. *Part 1* starts in Standard English, then a shift occurs into Rasta Slang when Ras Pakaay quotes from the song lyrics. A third shift occurs immediately afterwards: the song just played was about smoking marihuana, and Ras Pakaay confesses to his listeners that he too has had 'a smoke'. He produces this confession in Black English and with a giggling voice and a dragging intonation, suggesting a slightly intoxicated state of mind. But then a fourth shift occurs: Ras Pakaay shifts into Standard English again, and produces a formulaic, rapidly spoken statement on the time, identifying his radio station.

*Part 2* starts with a style shift. Ras Pakaay shifts back into Black English mixed with markedly Rasta Slang lexemes, slows down the pace of his speech, and starts placing strong sentence stress on certain words, using creaky voice. He tells an anecdote of a man who called him during the previous song, requesting a song. When Ras Pakaay asked him to come live on air, the line was cut off. We see shifts into Rasta Slang in 'right now' and in 'all the way from Heideveld', as well as in the reference to the Reggae group requested by the caller ('Bush Band'). A final, small shift occurs towards the end, in 'that very same note', after which Ras Pakaay engages in another activity: announcing a caller on the line. This announcement is made in Standard English.

*Parts 3 and 4* are the most complex parts. In *part 3* Ras Pakaay welcomes the caller in Black English ('yo live on air') but then shifts into Standard English. The caller mentions her name and Ras Pakaay repeats it. He continues in Standard English but shifts shortly afterwards into Rasta Slang, when he mentions the place where the caller is from. The utterance here is identical to the one he produced earlier in part 2: 'all the way down from [place]'. The conversation goes on from there in Standard English. The girl requests a song title, which Ras Pakaay reiterates in Rasta Slang ('kiss me again olmos' I gat Jah'). He then asks who the song is for, and the girl answers that it is a song she wants to have played for herself. There is surprise in her voice when she gives her answer: a strong stress on the second syllable of 'myself', and a lengthened, dragging vowel in the second syllable: 'my*se:lf'. Ras Pakaay starts laughing, and this is where a small conflict emerges: the girl giggles and asks him 'what you *laughin at me (about)?', reverting the question–answer pattern established during the conversation.

*Part 4* is the conflict-and-repair sequence prefaced towards the end of part 3. Ras Pakaay did not catch the girl's question and the girl reiterates it, in a flat and serious intonation. The sequence, thus far, is in Standard English. Ras Pakaay responds in a very serious, flat, and declarative intonation, and he responds at length. Two small shifts occur: a one-word shift ('otherwise') into Township English – a markedly different accent from the Standard English one thus far used by Ras Pakaay, and a one-word shift into Rasta Slang in 'dem'. The girl reacts, and there is a brief, friendly exchange between Ras Pakaay and the girl in Standard English. He then mentions 'listenin' to Reggae music on UCT radio', and this triggers both a style shift and a code shift into Rasta Slang. Ras Pakaay shifts gear, speaks faster and in an excited voice, and produces Slang phrases such as 'kom tru yu', 'give thanks', and 'keep dem things under control'.

There is dense stylisation going on in this fragment, and if we introduce space into the analysis, we may get a clearer picture of that. The finer correspondences between shifts and discourse functions can be related to an iconic pattern of spatial and identity features. Several such spaces and identities are at play here:

1. There is, first, an identity of *reggae deejay* at play, connected to a transnational, globalised cultural space, that of reggae and Rasta-farianism. Ras Pakaay iconicises this space and identity through shifts into Rasta Slang. This variety connects his discourse to the globalised genres. The same goes for Black English. The use of a particular intonation contour, some lexemes such as 'yo' and some grammatical patterns ('why do wanna come live on air') connects his speech to transnational 'Gangsta English' and Hip-Hop culture. He speaks *in* South Africa, but not *from* South Africa. He uses the voice of an international black youth culture. But this voice is also a *masculine* voice: the talk produced in these varieties is distinctly 'tough' and virile, with references to illegal behaviour (smoking marihuana). So space, identity, linguistic variety, and style come in one package here.

2. Another space is *UCT radio*, the radio station of the University of
Cape Town. UCT is an affluent university predominantly populated by upper middle-class white students. Ras Pakaay is probably a student at UCT, and his being black makes him a member
of a privileged minority of black students who obtained a place
at this prestigious university. Here, we enter the realm of the
history of class stratification in South Africa: the identity articulated here is a *class identity* and Standard English iconicises this
class identity. As everywhere in the peripheries of the world,
Standard English is a rare commodity in South Africa, tightly
controlled both by patterns of race stratification and by patterns
of access that often have to do with education trajectories. Standard English marks this elite space, and Ras Pakaay systematically uses it whenever he refers to UCT radio. He also uses it as
his 'default' code in the interaction with the girl. The style he
uses in this variety is 'neutrally' conversational: it is a friendly
yet non-egalitarian (elite) code.

3. The girl is from Khayelitsha, a black, poor township where Xhosa-
speakers predominate. This is a third space: that of *the black townships*. The girl triggers the identity categorisations here by sponta-
neously giving her (ethnically marked) name to Ras Pakaay. She
metaphorically drags Ras Pakaay out of his elite UCT space as
well as out of the (equally exclusive) transnational reggae space,
and drags him into the township which, in all likelihood, is
his space of origin. Class is again an issue here: the girl ascrip-
tively identifies Ras Pakaay as a *black South African man from the
townships*, thus denying the asymmetries previously established
by Ras Pakaay's use of elite and exclusive codes, Black English
and Rasta Slang. Another probable aspect of this is *gender*: Ras
Pakaay finds himself in a male–female conflict, which needs
to be repaired by reverting to 'original', 'authentic' codes. Ras
Pakaay obviously gets drawn into this: in trying to repair the
conflict with the girl, he briefly lapses into Township English
('otherwise'). Ras Pakaay is twice made to speak 'from within the
township', once when he responds to the girl's name, another
time when he shifts into Township English in order to repair
the conflict. But, interestingly, in order to get out of the conflict (and out of the township), he shifts into the asymmetrical codes again, Standard English and Rasta Slang. He moves
back into the privileged, safe spaces over which he has full control: that of his elite university and that of the globalised reggae
world.

The delicate multilingualism we see in this fragment appears to be governed by orientations to space. These spaces organise the particular indexical order that steers the deployment of elements from the multilingual repertoires. We see orientations to transnational centres as well as to social spaces within South Africa, all in one fragment. We also see stratification: the transnational and national elite codes clearly afford better opportunities for Ras Pakaay to conduct his preferred business, and the space of strict linguistic, ethnic, and class 'origins' is dispreferred. In short, we see the hierarchies of the world system simultaneously at work in this one small fragment, including distinctions between centres – transnational reggae culture and local elite membership – and peripheries – the black township.

This stratification is an effect of both local South African (even Cape Town) dynamics as well as transnational ones, and of slow processes (the spread of transnational cultural genres such as reggae, and the commercialisation of such genres in a worldwide media industry) as well as of faster ones (e.g. the presence of a black Township boy at UCT, which is an effect of the disappearance of Apartheid). These developments result in semiotic potential for Ras Pakaay: a potential to produce fine-grained distinctions in identities organised in a repertoire, and to deploy them strategically in interaction. The identities produced here defy simple categorisation: we are facing delicate shifts that include cultural, class, gender, and ethnic aspects occurring in a variety of combinations. Ras Pakaay speaks in a very masculine, dominating voice whenever he speaks Black English and Rasta Slang; this outspoken masculinity disappears as soon as he shifts into Standard English, but he remains a member of an elite class; this elite identity vanishes as soon as he engages in the conversation with the girl, who proves to be a member of his geographical, ethnic, and social 'group-of-origin'. We are confronted with packages of identity features occurring in a variety of permutations, and all indexed by big and small discursive shifts. These shifts, it should be stressed, are not merely forms of code-switching. The shifting from one linguistic variety to another is part of a bigger package which includes shifts in the space from which one speaks, identity shift, and style shifts.

In theoretical terms, what we have encountered here can be summarised as stylisation (in the sense of Rampton 1999), but within a polycentric and stratified system which defines both the repertoires of speakers and the indexical validity of moves in discourse. The material mobilised in this stylisation process is astonishing in scope and variety. This is in accordance with Rampton's emphasis on the 'unpredictable mobility' of linguistic resources in view of identity effects. At the same time, these resources display *different* effects, depending on their connections with particular – ordered – indexicalities. That the transnational and local elite codes carry more weight than the strictly local ones should be no surprise, even if Rasta Slang would have little purchase in social life outside the niche of Rasta subcultures, and even if all of this has to be seen as tied to local, South African, value-scales. There is structure and stratification in this mobility.

A second theoretical implication is that 'identity' becomes a matter of details. This has been said repeatedly above, but I hope to have shown empirical substance for this claim. Large categories such as 'male' versus 'female', 'black' versus 'white', 'upper class' versus 'lower class', and so on tell only part of the story. What occurs in discursive work are delicately organised packages of identity features indexed in talk, with rather intensive shifting between such packages, which are infinitely small in the eyes of the analyst but may be very important to the participants in the interaction. The performance of identity is not a matter of articulating *one* identity, but of the mobilisation of a whole *repertoire* of identity features converted into complex and subtle moment-to-moment speaking positions.

## SUGGESTIONS FOR FURTHER READING

The work of Ben Rampton has been a major source of inspiration for this chapter. Read especially his *Crossing* (1995) as well as some of his equally important articles (e.g. 1999, 2001, 2003). The 'acts of identity' model is sketched in LePage and Tabouret-Keller (1985). The conversation-analytic view on identity is outlined in Antaki and Widdicombe (1998), although I would recommend reading of D'hondt (2002) – an important critical appraisal of conversation-analytic approaches. Kulick's book on Brazilian transvestites (1998) should not be underestimated as to its theoretical consequences. Goffman (1981) again emerges as an important source of important and nuanced statements on the 'staging' of identity. On ethnolinguistic identity, Silverstein (1996b, 1998) has offered recent important observations. Johnstone (1990) is one of the best books on how space and place get converted into experiential narratives. Scollon and Scollon (2003) recently offered us an interesting set of observations on the semiotisation of space.

# 9 Conclusion: Discourse and the social sciences

Back to basics. I have started this book by saying that a critical analysis of discourse needs to focus on power effects, and in particular on how inequality is produced in, through and around discourse. In order for this to happen, I argued, we need to develop a broadly based approach to language in society, in which the contextualisation of discourse is a central element. If we take context seriously, we have to investigate it seriously. This meant to me that we had to adopt an eclectic register of approaches and methods capable of grasping the full complexity of discourse as a site of inequality. The core of this was ethnography: a perspective on language as intrinsically tied to context and to human activity. I added to this a wide variety of insights from linguistics, pragmatics, and (prominently) sociolinguistics. The ambition was to arrive at a framework that could answer questions raised by a wide range of data, not restricted to the common forms of spoken or written language and not restricted to analyses of data with which the analyst is socially and culturally familiar. If globalisation is accepted as a context in which discourse is produced nowadays – and many scholars subscribe to this – we need to get rid of some of our age-old assumptions of sharedness, community, function, and so forth.

Based on these assumptions I have followed a trajectory that took me from a commentary on Critical Discourse Analysis to a critique of existing notions of context as used in prominent trends in the critical study of language. The main objection I had against these trends was their use of a restricted notion of context, strongly centred on linguistic and textual explicit forms, and overlooking the modes of production and circulation of discourse, including all the epistemological and methodological implications of this. I drew a sketch of a theory of linguistic inequality, which focused on the existence of polycentric and layered systems within which language and other forms of semiosis become socially meaningful and from which discourse derives its effects. This attempt involved 'stepping out' of linguistics as an approach privileging textual-linguistic artefacts, and 'stepping into' society, its history

233

and structure, as the locus of study of linguistic inequality. A critical analysis of discourse needs to begin long before discourse emerges as a linguistically articulated object, and it needs to continue long after the act of production. These theses were elaborated in a series of comments on choice versus determination, in which I argued that one of the problems with discourse analysis was its assumption of choice for participants in communication. Against this assumption I pitted a view in which, especially under conditions of globalisation, one needs to take into account the significant constraints imposed on people in communication, constraints that found their origins in the structures of their societies and the differences in structure between societies. This was further developed in a chapter on history, in which this aspect of determination was elaborated as an effect of history, and in which discourse was seen as intrinsically and invariably produced from a particular historical viewpoint, a point in time as well as in space: a point in the world system. The stratified layering we encounter in discourse is an effect of multiple, but different (i.e. non-equivalent), influences operating on communicating people. These influences create simultaneity in discourse: all kinds of influences operate at the same time in the same communicative event. But they do not operate in the same way. Simultaneity involves stratification, with some influences that are more immediate than others, more visible, and more open to conscious exploration, negotiation, and manipulation. This stratification is a crucial site of inequality, for it is governed by asymmetrical patterns of access. Such patterns operate both within and between societies, and in the age of globalisation, differences stemming from the way in which such patterns function across the world become more and more an ingredient of our object of analysis.

I finally took this view of layered simultaneity into two fields of application: that of the study of ideologies and that of identities. Both domains are central to a lot of Critical Discourse Analysis, and the preoccupations of language scholars are shared by many scholars in other social-scientific fields. In the case of ideologies, I arrived at the conclusion that a view based on layered simultaneity allowed us to see ideologies, in practice, as packages of diverse elements tied together by factors that have little to do with textual or philosophical coherence and more with the occasion, the particular point in time, and the actors involved. Ideologies proved to be multifaceted, and a textual analysis of ideologies requires a historical analysis as well. In the field of identities, similar conclusions were reached. Rather than the established 'big' categories such as 'man'–'woman', 'black'–'white', 'upper class'–'lower class', and so forth, we saw how people organised repertoires of identities tied to semiotic resources strongly depending on spatial positioning – the position from which one speaks – and allowing the production and semiotisation of fine shades and distinctions in identity work. Similar constraints operate here: not only are the semiotic resources subject to unequal patterns of access but repertoires of identities are also conditioned by differential access.

I am aware of the fact that I have moved far away from what is often understood by discourse analysis. But in my defence I would say that this was the whole point. To the extent that we still believe that discourse is a linguistic object, the meaning of which can be fully tapped by deploying the rules of linguistic analysis, we shall never get there. The phenomenology of our object – the contextualised nature of language – compels us to recognise that linguistics offers us just part of the answers. If we see discourse as contextualised language, and take this dimension of contextualisation seriously, we shall be forced to develop a linguistics that ceases to be linguistic from a certain point onwards, and becomes a social science of language-in-society. We shall be forced to deploy concepts of considerable elasticity, adaptable to new data and new forms of analysis *which will be forced upon us*. Transformations in the world will continually push us towards revisions of our old and established instrumentarium, and the fact that a particular analytic recipe worked in the past does not offer us any guarantees that it may work in the future. There can be no theory of the critical analysis of discourse – but there can, and should, be a permanent will to think theoretically while we work practically. And while doing this it is advisable to see our disciplinary toolkits as repertoires from which elements can be chosen and combined, depending on the specific problem that needs to be solved.

There were several specific problems I set out to solve in this book, or at least to attempt to solve. There was a challenge I defined for myself, to bring discourse analysis in line with globalisation, seen both in phenomenological terms – new patterns of communication emerging as part of globalisation processes – and in terms of the body of theory produced on globalisation in the social sciences. The latter forces us to reconsider 'old' patterns of communication in light of theories that stress interconnectedness, global structures of inequality, and so forth. This challenge, I argued, forces us to reconsider our own theories, for they too often assume a kind of locality in vision and definition of phenomena which we can no longer afford. This locality very often stems from, and is fuelled by, a habitual pattern of work in which one studies phenomena from one's own society and thus projects features of one's own society on phenomena that escape or defy such features.

A more versatile discourse analysis is required, one which takes difference *and* inequality as points of departure, rather than sharedness, closure of contextual spaces, and familiarity with norms, rules, and their consequences.

This kind of discourse analysis questions the macro-levels that often invisibly control discourse work, and it questions them actively for they matter at the lowest levels of discourse production and exchange. And this questioning is something we can accomplish by drawing on some of the unique methodological instruments we have developed in our fields: close analysis of situated social events, contextualised at a variety of levels and in ways that allow empirical inspection, and supported by a mature theory of meaning as a social process centred on indexicality. This framework, I firmly believe, offers us some purchase. We were, for instance, able to provide an alternative view to theories emphasising fragmented subjectivities, the chaotic nature of social life, and meaningful symbolic behaviour, and other postmodern catchphrases. Instead, we could offer a view of multiple, stratified layering in social conduct, in which multiple ideological and identity positions are at play simultaneously, not in a chaotic or random way but structured and to some extent predictable. We were also capable of providing a more precise view of the global spread of 'languages' such as English, and their effects across the world. Rather than just global uniformity and linguistic imperialism, the spread of globalised languages, varieties, styles, genres, and formats results in complex patterns of the reshuffling of repertoires, offering new semiotic potential when used in one place and new obstacles to understanding when used in another place. In both cases, global sociolinguistic processes result in opportunities for, and restrictions on, the deployment of particular forms of discourse. Thus, again, we must look into macro-processes in order to understand micro-processes.

A second challenge I defined for myself, but one which I shall only briefly mention here, was to destereotype discourse analysis as an analysis of a limited range of linguistic phenomena. Too often, discourse analysis is still text linguistics, and too often, we tend to look for clear cases of 'discourse' – particular types of data and contexts. And we also tend to differentiate discourse analysis from, for instance, sociolinguistics, pragmatics, Conversation Analysis, and so on, claiming (more than arguing) that each focuses on different objects and applies different tactics in doing so. It is the safety of particularism that I wanted to subvert by offering a far wider approach to discourse. When we see discourse in more general terms, as (any form of) meaningful semiotic conduct, then we find ourselves facing the task of analysing more things in more ways. This takes away the comfort of clarity that comes with sticking within well-defined boundaries. But it offers opportunities as well: opportunities to treat different sets of data; opportunities to combine eclectically insights from every available approach to language in society, semiosis, or social conduct. I find this a richer and more interesting field to dwell in than rigidly defined habitual orthodoxies of scientific exploration.

It was my stated ambition to offer a series of reflections of some use to scholars from other disciplines. This, of course, raises complex and often debated issues of the nature and practice of interdisciplinarity. I do not believe I can add much to these debates, but some observations can be made with regard to our own role as scholars of language. First, I believe we need to revise our own basic assumptions so as to be in a position to offer something significant to others. Concretely, we have to abandon the old linguistic wisdom that one linguistic form has one function or meaning. As long as we maintain this old wisdom, we are and remain a rather useless ally to the other social sciences. If we replace it with a conception of discourse as characterised by layered simultaneity (thus defining it as intrinsically historical), we are offering other social scientific disciplines an object open for exploration from a variety of angles, and other disciplines will help us to understand this object.

Secondly, we need to revise our established tactics of questioning. A discourse analysis which offers perspectives for interdisciplinary dialogue consists in using linguistic and discourse-analytic disciplinary techniques to answer non-disciplinary questions. In effect, discourse analysis should be a social science that utilises linguistic technique to answer social-scientific questions. It is such an interrogation of our data, our objects of inquiry, that may construct a discourse *for* (not *by*) anthropologists, sociologists, historians, and political scientists. All of this, I fear, is necessary if we intend to arrive at a discourse analysis that can contribute to a critique of social systems as well. This, again, is not an affair that can be solved by conventional questioning and examination – we need to go further.

The view on interdisciplinarity I advocate here is strongly inspired by Dell Hymes. More than three decades ago, in the wake of the development of what we now call ethnography of speaking, Hymes said that in order to arrive at interdisciplinary dialogue,

> linguistics and anthropology [should] revise their conventional scope and methodology, so that matters now let fall between them are seen as indispensable to both. (1971: 32)

Because

> No amount of combination of disciplines as presently constituted . . .
> asking just the questions each normally asks, will serve. (1971: 50)

I believe that the truly intellectual challenge for discourse analysis is precisely that: to reconfigure our own discipline in a permanent process of self-critique based on observations of the way in which our object of study changes. And change it does; it does so all the time. Voloshinov already said that the word is the most sensitive index of social change. If we accept this, it entails a challenge and a huge responsibility. It means that we do have something to contribute to other fields of scholarship, but that we need to incorporate change into our own repertoires of scholarly practice. A refusal to do that will result in more and more things that fall in between the disciplines as presently established. It will consequently result in analyses of little consequence to other scholars, let alone to the people we hope to serve by them.

# Notes

## Chapter 1

1. Members of the CDA 'school' contributed to this image. See the discussion in the next chapter.
2. Johannes Fabian has, throughout his œuvre, demonstrated that such reiterations alongside critical probing into their reality are both necessary and instructive. See his 1983, 2001 for examples.
3. To give an example: a glance at the list of references in Chouliaraki and Fairclough (1999) reveals hardly any references to American linguistic-anthropological work. The same is true in the opposite direction – see, for example, Briggs (1996). In Chouliaraki and Fairclough, however, one finds references to all kinds of critical discourse-analytic approaches ranging from Žižek (1994) and Kristeva (1986) to Laclau and Mouffe (1985). The more surprising is the absence of references to, for example, Hymes, Briggs, Hill, or other American scholars. Fairclough, interestingly in light of the above, begins his *Language and Power* (1989) with a quote from Boas.
4. This contingent history includes a separation between 'anthropological' views of ethnography and 'linguistic' ones. In both trends we see a narrowing of ethnography. In the former there is a reduction of ethnography to fieldwork, i e a particular phase in anthropological work; in the latter, ethnography is often short-hand for 'contextual background' to linguistic material (see below, chapter 3). In both moves, the immense value of ethnography as a complex of theory, method, and epistemology is overlooked. Fabian (1983, 1990a, 1991, 2001) is an indispensable source for capturing the potential of ethnography, as well as its limitations.

## Chapter 2

1. One of the most balanced and fair assessments of CDA is Slembrouck (2001). The paper also contains a very insightful intellectual historiography of CDA.
2. Panoramic surveys of work can be found in, for example Caldas-Coulthard and Coulthard (1996); Blommaert and Bulcaen (1997).
3. Other programmatic statements of CDA can be found in Fairclough (1992b, 1995); van Leeuwen (1993); van Dijk (1993a, 1993c, 1997); Wodak (1995, 1997).
4. In Chouliaraki and Fairclough (1999) this claim is somewhat softened, and more emphasis is placed on explanation as temporary epistemic gain. At the same time, the Althusserian emphasis on the truth-revealing capacity of social theory is maintained (e.g. Chouliaraki and Fairclough 1999: 33).

## Chapter 3

1. In my discussion, I shall not do justice to the variety of approaches as well as the immense differences of nuance and analytical sophistication within both schools. I shall have to generalise and focus on stereotypical work in that domain in an attempt to raise general issues of which, no doubt, many practitioners of discourse analysis are acutely aware. Suffice it to say here that I am familiar with good work in both schools and that my comments will be applicable to various degrees to work done in those schools. Blommaert (1997a) provides a lengthy and more detailed discussions of 'context' in CDA as well as in CA.
2. In the field of analysis of political discourse (one of CDA's main preoccupations) often also highly simplistic and strongly biased *historical* narratives are given as 'background against which discourse needs to be understood'. See chapter 6 for an extended discussion of such practices.
3. I provide English translations, though not without the warning that these translations obviously cannot do justice to the 'broken' and hence very complicated ways of speaking. I shall use a highly simplified format of transcription here. Symbols used are: '*' for stress on the following syllable; '=' for rapid successions of turns or syllables in self-corrections; '/' for intonationally marked phrase or sentence ends; dots indicate pauses. There has so far not been any systematic research on literacy and written discourse among this group; small samples of writing are presented in Blommaert (1999a, 2003d). Illiteracy and semi-literacy are clearly widespread among the group of African asylum seekers, and many of them need to seek assistance from lawyers or welfare workers for their paper work. The data were collected in late 1998 by students of the African studies programme, Ghent University, in the context of a fieldwork project supervised by me.

## Chapter 4

1. A lot of work in pragmatics can serve as an illustration of this; see, for example, work based on the Gricean Maxims, or Politeness Theory (Sarangi and Slembrouck 1992 and Eelen 2001 provide a critique). Orders of indexicality are accepted as (unquestioned) points of departures in such work.
2. Society is full of such centring institutions, and, for example, popular media culture as well as commercials offer an infinite supply of exquisite examples. Needless to say, there are often obvious connections between symbolic economies and real economies.
3. One is reminded here of Erving Goffman's (1974) 'frames', and in particular of his views of 'frames within frames': the fact that particular interpretive universes can be embedded in other ones, and that, consequently, utterances can have *layered* meanings, some of which need to be activated before others can. I share this preoccupation with layered, multiple meanings in one utterance, but, as will become clear further on, I shall place more emphasis on the systemic, political, and historical nature of such layering.
4. This text was given to me by the Canadian historian Bogumil Jewsiwiecki as part of a collection of approximately twenty essays. While a handful of essays were longer and displayed a better command of French and of writing skills, the overwhelming majority of the essays bore the features discussed here.

## Chapter 5

1. This incorporation, I wish to add, has not always done justice to Foucault's work, and I find the discussion in Fairclough (1992a) less than helpful for an appraisal of Foucault's potential value to critical analyses of discourse. Fairclough

manages to read Foucault completely through the spectre of a linguist's concern with textual artefacts. Thus, Fairclough compares Foucault's 'rules' of discourse (Foucault 1969, 2002) to sociolinguistic variable rules (Fairclough 1992a: 40), and the 'absence of text and textual analysis' is equated to 'the absence of a concept of practice' i.e. 'real instances of people doing or saying or writing things' (1992a: 57). Hence, Fairclough's claim that (his own) Textually Oriented Discourse Analysis is likely to 'strengthen social analysis' by offering inspection of linguistic-textual detail, as opposed to Foucault's 'schematism and one-sidedness' (1992a: 61). Fairclough appears to overlook the rather basic fact that Foucault's concern was with 'non-linguistic analyses of statements', more precisely, with developing a strategic model (a 'theory of practice', if one wishes) that could account for discourse, knowledge, truth, and relations of power simultaneously (Foucault 2003, see esp. Arnold Davidson's introduction pp. xix, xxi). Foucault was emphatically not a linguist, and examining compatibilities between Fairclough's and Foucault's programmes requires more than comparing Foucault to standards of linguistic analysis. It is advisable to understand Foucault's *discours*, with its deeply French intellectual semantic pedigree, as something quite different from Anglo-Saxon linguistic interpretations of *discourse*. To paraphrase Fairclough: the 'interdiscursive' differences between both concepts are substantial. I personally keep in mind Jean-Jacques Rousseau's *Discours sur les origines de l'inégalité* rather than an editorial in the *New York Times* as a genre model when I read Foucault's discussions of *discours*.

2. Despite this overall emphasis on struggle and 'subjugated knowledge', Fairclough still finds that 'in the totality of [Foucault's] work and in the major analyses, the dominant impression is one of people being helplessly subjected to immovable systems of power . . . he gives the impression that resistance is generally contained by power and poses no threat'. This is a consequence of Foucault's lack of attention to textual detail, according to Fairclough (1992a: 57). I hope to have made clear that Foucault's primary concern with discourse is to offer units and levels of description in an analysis of historical discontinuity, not of 'immovable systems of power'. See also the remarks in the next chapter

3. Foucault is not clear on the scope of archives. He mentions 'a society, a culture, or a civilization . . . a whole period', adding that it is impossible to describe such archives exhaustively (Foucault 2002: 146).

4. The debates in the New Left belong to the intellectually most stimulating ones in post-Second World War social-scientific history. They turned the *New Left Review* into an indispensable journal for social-theoretical thought and they testify to the transformation of Marxism into a mature social-scientific paradigm.

5. Over the last decade, significant new insights on literacy-as-practice have been produced by the so-called New Literacy Studies, to whose perspective I here subscribe. See Street (1995); also, for example, Gee (1990); Besnier (1995); Barton (1994); Barton and Hamilton (1998); Graddol, Maybin, and Stierer (1991); Baynham (1995); Prinsloo and Breier (1996); Collins and Blot (2003). Collins (1995) provides an overview.

6. None of these features is unexpected: they are present in a great number of 'grassroots literacy' documents from Africa. Blommaert (1999a, 2001b, 2003a, 2003b, 2003c) provides examples and discussion.

7. This is an extreme case of what Hymes (1996: 37) calls 'communicative plenitude': 'meaningfulness expands to fill available means', the fact that available linguistic resources can acquire multiple meanings. But 'plenitude' may not be the best denominator here, for the process develops in a context of scarcity of linguistic-communicative resources. Consequently, the (few) available resources

get inflated with all kinds of new and often unexpected functions, forms of 'meaningfulness'.

8. One could note in passing that precisely some of the errors in the text offer strong suggestions of veracity. The fact that the author produces written replicas of how street names are *pronounced* locally would render the claim that the man 'is from Bujumbura' very plausible.

## Chapter 6

1. One such strange phenomenon is the way in which intertextuality generates incomplete links to previous texts. Engels' *Anti-Dühring* is a well-known book. It has provided lasting fame for a man named Dühring. But very few of the people who have read *Anti-Dühring* have read Dühring's own work, the work that was so enthusiastically and thoroughly demolished by Engels. So, despite the fact that *Anti-Dühring* is explicitly intertextual, the intertextual link is hardly ever activated. A lot of political discourse involves such processes of incomplete intertextuality: critiques of textual materials without making the object of critique accessible, yet presupposing a well-known contents through the intertextual invocation. An example of this is the way in which the US and UK governments talked about 'intelligence reports' on Iraq's arsenals of weapons of mass-destruction during the run-up to the Gulf War of 2003, or earlier, the innumerable references to 'intelligence reports' on Al Qaeda terrorism. Did anyone ever see these reports?

2. Wallerstein's research centre at SUNY-Binghampton, devoted to the study of the world system, is called the Fernand Braudel Center.

3. Eric Hobsbawm's classic *Bandits* (2000) offers a rich account of the sociopolitical contingency of the category 'bandit'.

4. Bourdieu's *Homo Academicus* (1988) is a brilliant analysis of the far-reaching transformation of French universities after the May 1968 revolt, demonstrating the different speeds of development of changes at various levels. The unfinished nature of this process of transformation (and, consequently, the asymmetries between various positions from which one approaches the system) is something that I experience every day. My students address me with terms ranging from 'professor' and 'sir', to 'Mr Blommaert', as well as 'Jan', and 'hey you'.

5. Those familiar with development co-operation practices probably know what I am talking about. We perform such synchronisations continuously, whenever we select Third-World universities as our preferential partners in a network, or whenever we talk about their governments as dragging their feet and not living up to expectations.

6. Hobsbawm calls this the 'Fabrice syndrome': 'There are perfectly sound reasons why participants at the bottom do not usually see historic events they live through as top people or historians do. One might call this (after the hero of Stendhal's *Chartreuse de Parme*) the "Fabrice Syndrome"' (Hobsbawm 1983: 13n.).

7. In some work (available only in Dutch) I called this 'vox populism': a populism that iconicises and thus appropriates the 'vox populi', the voice of the people, and can thus claim a new form of genuinely democratic legitimacy. See Blommaert (2001d).

8. For instance, the very popular *Late Night Show* host, Jay Leno, produced sarcastic jokes on France on an almost daily basis during his shows in that period. The jokes usually capitalised on an image of France as a nation of cowards and incompetent fighters saved by the Americans. One example: in a series of jokes about 'the name of countries before they got their current name', France was 'Germany, until we saved their asses'. Similarly, in early March 2003 two Republican Congressmen decided to rename the French fries in the Congressional cafeteria as 'Freedom fries'.

9. It also becomes a graphic illustration of Foucault's thesis of the pervasiveness of warlike frames in politics: 'the role of political power is perpetually to use a sort of silent war to reinscribe that relationship of force, and to reinscribe it in institutions, economic inequalities, language, even the bodies of individuals' (Foucault 2003: 16).

10. The Soviet contribution in supplying the Warsaw insurgents by air (affirmed both by Zhukov and by Berezhkov) is nowhere mentioned in the Commemoration speeches, nor in Dziewanowski's historical account.

11. Perhaps I should point out that I see no contradiction between my argument and the one developed by Johannes Fabian (1983). Fabian argues that the anthropological Other has been constructed through a 'denial of coevalness', i.e. the denial of a synchronic plane of coexisting realities, and the replacement of such 'coevalness' with achronic evolutionary scales. One could misread this as a denial of synchronisation. But seen from the perspective developed here, the denial of coevalness is the denial of history and the reduction of various historically layered differences to differences within one synchronic-comparative scale. It is, in other words, the denial of layered simultaneity which allows (or even invites) 'universal', timeless, evolutionary distinctions. The denial of coevalness is an act of synchronisation.

## Chapter 7

1. Foucault avoids the term 'ideology' for the totalising and normalising phenomena of 'capillary power' or 'biopower' he investigates. There is, for instance, no entry for 'ideology' in the index to Foucault (2001a) and (2001b). Foucault has no problem talking about *specific* ideologies such as Marxism or particular theories of the state. But the terms he uses to describe these complexes (which we call particular ideologies here) is 'philosophies' or 'political discourses', and he often situates them in relation to longer, slower, deeper processes of the emergence of a *savoir* (see, for example, Foucault 2001b: 953–980, and 2003). Foucault (2003) is perhaps the best illustration of his tactic of situating 'particular' complexes of ideas (Hobbes, Machiavelli) in the larger and slower historical development of a *savoir*.

2. In Barthes' own words: 'ideologically, everything which is not bourgeois is forced to *borrow* from the bourgeoisie' (1957: 226, my translation, French original).

3. Van Dijk merely suggests that 'they are essentially shared by groups and acquired, used, and change by people *as* group members in social situations and institutions, often in situations of conflicting interests between social formations' (1995: 21). Almost every term in this sentence invites substantial empirical investigation, questioning, and qualification.

4. Perry Anderson's *Antinomies of Antonio Gramsci* (1977) is still the best source for understanding the complexity of Gramsci's concept of hegemony. I shall base many of my comments on Gramsci on Anderson's text and shall have to gloss over many of the important points made by Anderson. I refer the reader to his text.

5. I follow Gramsci in this. Cases are not hard to find. The post-1990 'New World Order' has shown us several times that by absence of hegemony for a Grand Narrative of market capitalism and liberal democracy brute power steps in and determines the outcome of events. Note how frequently one is at pains to explain this extreme coercion as part of, and something sanctioned by, a presumed general consensus over the Grand Narrative.

6. Irvine and Gal (2000: 38) propose to call this phenomenon 'fractal recursivity': 'the projection of an opposition, salient at some level of relationship, onto some

other level. For example, intragroup oppositions might be projected outward onto intergroup relations, and vice versa.'

7. The original texts used in the sections 7.4 and 7.5 are in Dutch, and all translations into English are mine.

8. Tele-text is a system of information distribution through the TV cable. It is offered by a number of Belgian TV channels and consists of topically organised pages of text that can be read from the TV screen.

9. Note that the public debate usually often starts as soon as a text-artefact (e.g. a policy paper, a draft bill) has been *made public*. The ideology of 'fixed text' in politics includes a view in which the text only exists when it is made public (i.e. publication transforms the text from a personal, 'unofficial' statement into a statement with societal, hence 'political', dimensions). Leaks about opinions circulating during the preparatory phases, i.e. before the publication *strictu senso* of the text-artefact, are therefore also seen as 'publications' and may trigger preemptive actions from actors in the debate.

10. It may be interesting to note how the 'pure' political dimension of the KCM activities was constantly downplayed by insisting on an 'academic' style and format of writing. The KCM reports are not only seen as policy papers, they are also seen (and were presented) as *scientific* analyses of the 'migrant problem'. A Royal Commissariat is in the Belgian context also a non-political institution more or less comparable to a technical department in a ministry.

## Chapter 8

1. By way of illustration, this is how I introduced myself to a group of students in Chicago, January 2003: 'I am from Belgium. If some of you don't know where that is, don't worry, I'm not offended. It's a small country squeezed in between France, Germany and the Netherlands. We produce great beers, great chocolate, and we invented French fries. We also produced Jean-Claude Van Damme.' Note the concatenation of stereotypes sensed to identify Belgium.

2. The complexity of a central concept such as culture is illustrated in Srikant Sarangi's excellent survey of the way in which 'culture' has been used in language-related research (Sarangi 1995); a similar, equally impressive, exercise on the concept of speech community is Rampton (1998).

3. Ron Scollon (2001) goes a long way in this direction. Revisiting his previous work, Scollon suggests we abandon terms such as 'communities of practice' and use 'nexus of practice' instead: a complete focus on situated activity as the point where social categories, practices, and interpretive contexts are formed and used.

4. I still remember my considerable *déconfiture* when, during my first trip to Tanzania, a student from Rwanda greeted me by saying: 'ah, you're Belgian, so your grandfather whipped mine hé?', imposing upon me a startling, but nevertheless real, identity category.

5. Access to advanced education levels is extremely restricted. Official 1996 statistics from the Tanzanian Ministry of Education and Culture show that less than 4,000 students finished secondary education (offering access to higher education), while more than 700,000 children enrolled in primary schools. That means that only about 0.5 per cent of those who begin primary education eventually finish secondary levels. It was once pointed out to me that the graph of these figures (which I had presented as 'pyramidical') looked rather like a Burmese temple.

6. It is not difficult to find examples of this. A case in point is Carol Myers-Scotton's (1993) account of code-switching in Africa. Myers-Scotton completely collapses language and ethnic group, treating multilingualism as a problematic feature,

and defining the social dynamics of code-switching as heavily based on strategies of ethnic inclusion and exclusion.

7. Of course, this does not mean that states cannot develop and impose homo-geneistic ideologies, notably where immigrants or national minority groups are concerned. See Blommaert and Verschueren (1998).

8. One can note, in passing, that Ras Pakaay would probably not qualify as a 'speaker' of Jamaican Creole. The shifts he accomplishes, consequently, are not enabled by full bilingualism in the varieties between which he shifts. They are topically and stylistically organised. Thus, we have code-switching without bilin-gualism here.

# Appendix: English translation of the documents in chapter 5

Roman = author A; *italics* = author B; **Bold** = author C; (xxx) = unreadable original

[Document 1]
*The president*
The first president who ruled was Michombero in 1966
The second Ndaye Melkior. He ruled for three months (3)
Afterwards he was assassinated by Tutsi soldiers in the
Palace. Ndadae was a (Hutu)
Afterwards came Cypria Mtayamira and he too
Was assassinated in a plane crash together with the one who was president
Of Rwanda habiyarimana while returning from a
meeting In Arusha Tanzania, after that came Sylvester
Ntibantunganya and that one was ousted by Major Pierre
Buyoya but he was not assassinated. - - - - - - - - - - - - -
                    The University is in Mutanga (South)
It is called 'kampis Mutanga'
(xxxx)        various quarters and roads
Nyagabiga is the Tutsi part. In that quarter there are
Many houses of Hutu who live there
Below Nyagabiga lies Bwiza. Below Bwiza lies Buyenzi
Hutu
Bwiza In this part there are many houses of Tutsi
Hutu who live there in great number ~~they are tusi~~
~~Byiz~~ Buyenzi is the Swahili quarter, there
are many Swahili people that you'll get there and many
don't speak French and Kirundi
                    In front of the hotel "Novotel" There are two roads
That go all the way to the university "Kampis Mutanga"

*Important places*
The presidential palace is close to the soccer stadium FFB
Lake Tanganyika is on Avenii de Plage
The FFB stadium is on Avenii de State

246

*Soccer teams*

The national team is called "INTAMBA"

Another team is "Vitalo" *Inter Star*

*Musea (makumbusho)*

The Museu vivant is on Avenue du 13 October

<u>Independe(n)ce (Uhuru)</u>

It obtained independence on 1.7.1972 from Belgium

*Ntanyamira died – 6/4/94*

[Document 2]

*1 16 districts*

1. Bujumbura
2. Gitega
3. Ngozi
4. Kirundo
5. Makamba
6. Kayanza
7. Bururi
8. (Khibitoke) Cibitoke
9. Romonge
10. Rutana
11. Bubanza
12. Ruvubu

*11 cities*

1. Buyenzi
2. Bunza (?)
3. Ngagara
4. Jabe
5. Rohero
6. Kinama
7. Kamenge
8. Kanyosi
9. Mutanga (N)
10. Mutanga (?)
11. Nyagabige

*2 Mountains*

Teza, heha, Twinyoni
Nyambuye, Buhonga
The Bujumbura mountains

*Rivers*

Ruvubu ndahangwa
Kanyosha tusizi
That passes through Buyenzi

### 3 *The government newspapers*
<u>Ubumwe</u> written in Kirundi
Another government newspaper is written in French

<u>Passport</u>

It is called Karanga mundu yellow color and there is a he ad of a Lion

### 4   *Money* it is called: Burundi Franc
1000   a picture of three cows
100   ≪   of prince Luis Rwagasore
50   a picture of a man beating three drums
20   a picture of a man he is half naked and wears a rubega (~~green~~ *red*)
     coins (10) and (five) (5) *a lion*
*xx – a map (green)*

### 5   *Hotels*
NOVotel   close to the FFB football stadium
MERIDIAN
Albatros – *close to Busee Primary School*

### 6   *Important places*
The radio station is in Kabondo
The State House is close to the football stadium
Of Prince Luis Rwagasore

### 4 look• *Money*
5000   has a picture of the national bank and the harbor *(green + white)*
500   (xxxxxxx) Rwagasore

[document 3]

### 7   *National parks*
RUVUGU   and   Kibira

<u>License plates</u> ~~of individuals' cars~~

<u>Individuals' cars</u>
White plates red numbers

<u>License plates of government cars</u>

Red plates white letters
Numbers begin with BR.BN   BD   BU   BA

### *Buses*
The bus company is called OTRACO
The bus stations are on Prince Luis Rwagasore

### *National anthem*
(I know it a little bit) Burundi buachu Burundi buhire
- - - - - - - - - - - - - - - - - - - - - - - - - - - - - -

*8 HOSPITALS<*
1. Rua Khalid *big*
   is in Kamenge
2. rejee Charles   [DRAWING]
   is in Buyenzi
   The Prince Luis Rwagasore Clinic
   Is in town
- - - - - - - - - - - - - - - - - - - - - - - - - -

*9 MARKETS*
Crazy market is on 19 street
Crazy market is on 8 street
Main market is on Shosii Prince Luis Rwagasore Buyenzi

*Post offi ce*
The post office is on the corner of Avenii du Commerce and
Boulevard Lumumba
   Factories
The sigar      factory   is called   Supa machi
The textile   factory   ≪            Kotebu
The tea factory   ≪          CK   BUKIPO

*The beer   factory*
            The beers themselves ~~ny~~ Primus Amstel
*CNDD. (PP. RPB) Tutsi*
*Hutu*

[Document 4]
10

*PARties*
FRODEBU           UPRONA
By the Hutu       by the Tutsi
[DRAWING]         [DRAWING]

*Ethnic groups*
There are three (3) ethnic groups
Hutu 85%   TUTSI 14%   TWA 1%

*11 POLICE*
They wear khaki and marine blue clothes
The police offices are called Sebokuve
Officers to counter chaos are called Jandarma

*TAXI*
Their colors are blue at the bottom and white on top
The dala dalas are called 'bisi' and they have no special colors

## *12 Roads*

1. Prince Luis Rwagasore          [drawing] *highway*
2. Avenii de la Pierre ngenda ndumwe
3. Avenii de la Univasity
4. Avenii du Opital
5. Shosii du people Burundi
6. Boulevard de la Uprona
7. Boulevard Lumumba
8. Avenii du 13 october
9. Avenii du 28 November

## *13 school*

1. Jumuiya is on 8 street
2. Stela is close to the regina Mundi church
3. Athenée is close to the shoe shop
4. Basee is in Buyenzi close to hotel Albatros

## *SEKONDARY*

SAINT ESPRIT is close to the slaughterhouse
   MOSQUE
Is on Rue Tanganyika and rue Packaus
It was built by the government of Lybia

[Document 5]
*Ubumwe, Ibikorwa, Amajambere*
*Umoja, Kazi, Maendeleo*

[Document 6]

1. *prince Luis Rwagasore (XX) 1963 died*
2. *Michombero Michael 1976*
3. *Bagaza jean Baptis 1986–1987*
4. *Buyoya Pierre*
5. *Ndadaye Melkio 1976 (3 months)*
6. *Ntanyamire Cyprias*
7. *Ntibantungunga Silvester (overthrown 1996)*
8. *Buyoya*

[Document 7]

| Independence | Balance | |
|---|---|---|
| | Tutsi | Hutu |
| Umoja | Nyabusoronyo | |
| To | | |

      **GEORGEMICHAEL KAPP**
            **LONDON**
            **UK**

# Glossary

Archive   The totality of all meaningful statements and their rules of production at any given time in a given society. Archives impose restrictions on what can be said meaningfully.

Articulation   The process of communicating a particular complex of meanings.

Ascriptive identity   An identity attributed to someone by others (as opposed to 'inhabitable identity') and including that someone in a socially defined category.

Centring institutions   Real or imagined actors perceived to emanate the authoritative attributions to which one should orient in order to make sense.

Coherence   Grammatical and semantic patterns that connect various parts of discourse into a structured and meaningful whole.

Context   The totality of conditions in which discourse is being produced, circulated, and interpreted.

Contextualisation   Interpretive practices by means of which discourse is connected to and made meaningful in terms of context. Contextualisation imposes particular metapragmatic frames onto discourse and so provides a 'preferred interpretation' for it.

Creativity   The capacity to produce unique meaningful statements.

Decontextualisation   Isolating discourse from its context.

Determination   Processes of a macro-order that impose restrictions on the range of actions people can peform.

Dialogue   Social activities developed between people in which meaning is jointly constructed through interaction. Dialogue contains evaluative procedures, and meaning emerging from dialogue contains value-attributions about statements made.

Discourse representation   Practices by means of which discourse is re-entextualised in terms of particular professional or lay formats. Examples are transcripts, subtitles, visualisation.

Dogmatisation   Restricting the interpretation of a text or utterance to some 'original', authoritative meaning.

Durée   Long history, the history of slow transformations in climate, demography, or general sociopolitical and economic organisation.

Entextualisation   The process by means of which discourse is successively decontextualised and recontextualised, and thus made into a 'new'

251

discourse. In every phase of the process, discourse is provided with new metapragmatic frames.

Ethnolinguistic identity   An identity of being a speaker of some language; e.g. 'I am Francophone' is an articulation of ethnolinguistic identity.

Ethnopoetics   An analytical approach aimed at uncovering 'emic' performative patterning in speech; i.e. forms of patterning that are created and transmitted as part of cultural transmission in some community.

Frame   A contextual scheme: meanings, forms of behaviour, and other semiotic attributes associated with a particular semiotic act. Frames are invoked by discourse and function as preferred spaces for contextualisation. For instance, a formally uttered greeting may invoke a frame of official communication with role-relationships marked by social distance.

Functional relativity   The observation that the same semiotic act may have different functions in different contexts, depending on how that semiotic act is lodged in the repertoires and orders of indexicality valid in those contexts. For instance: the function of handwriting may be different in a highly mediatised, literacy-saturated, urban context and in a rural context marked by very low levels of literacy circulation and production.

Genre   An ordered complex of indexicalities, structuring the precise ways in which particular communicative actions have to be performed and creating expectations in that sense. A letter needs to be written differently from an academic paper – they are different genres.

Habitus   The naturalised adoption of features of social structure that becomes a 'normal' ('habitual' and 'embodied') pattern of behaviour.

Hegemony   The dominance of particular ideologies or sets of ideologies in a particular social environment.

Heterography   The deployment of literacy means in ways different from the orthodox ones.

Historicity   The quality of being historical, i.e. being imbued with features that derive from human intervention over a span of time.

Homogeneism   An ideology in which social, cultural, linguistic, and other homogeneity is presented as the 'best' form of governance.

Iconicity   A semiotic act is iconic when features of that act are sensed to mirror features of the object or process it is supposed to represent. For instance, a slow, dragging intonation contour in narratives may iconicise slow, endless processes.

Idealism   A tradition of social thought in which preference is given to ideational, cultural, or other 'immaterial' or 'soft' characteristics of society, social relations, and social processes (as opposed to 'materialism').

Indexicality   Meaning that emerges out of text–context relations. Apart from (often) having a denotational meaning, linguistic and other signs are indexical in that they suggest metapragmatic, metalinguistic, metadiscursive features of meaning. Thus, an utterance may indexically invoke social norms, roles, identities.

Indexical order   The non-arbitrary, socially, and culturally sensitive way in which indexicality operates in societies.

Inhabitable identity   A self-constructed and self-performed identity (as opposed to 'ascriptive identity') through which people claim allegiance to a group.

Interdiscursivity   Connections between discourses across time as well as synchronically within repertoires. Contemporary political discourse, for instance, shows interdiscursive connections with earlier political discourse as well as with contemporary commercial advertisement discourse.

Intertextuality   Connections between texts (statements, utterances) over time as well as synchronically within repertoires. Every text displays intertextual links with previous (similar or related) texts as well as synchronically with related texts.

Language community   People professing or displaying allegiance to a denotationally defined 'language'.

Language ideology   Socially, culturally, and historically conditioned ideas, images, and perceptions about language and communication.

Layered simultaneity   The fact that the multiple contexts operating in every semiotic act ('simultaneity') are not of the same order but stratified: some being immediate and unique, others being perduring; some being open to conscious elaboration and manipulation, others not.

Literacy   The complex of practices related to the production, circulation, and reception of literate text. Literacy is not coterminous with 'writing', but also involves multimodal communication modes (e.g. internet or mass-media literacy).

Materialism   A tradition of social thought in which preference is given to economic, political, material, and other 'hard' characteristics of society, social relations and social processes (as opposed to 'idealism').

Metadiscourse (metapragmatics)   Indexical levels of discourse. Every discourse simultaneously says something *in* itself (e.g. it describes a particular state of affairs 'out there') and *about* itself, about how that discourse should be interpreted, situated in relation to context, social relations, and so on. Such indexical levels can also be called 'metalinguistic' (i.e. about linguistic structure) or 'metapragmatic' (i.e. about forms of usage of language).

Monoglot ideology   A monoglot ideology emphasises the hegemony of a standardised, singular, denotationally defined 'language'; e.g. 'English only' is a monoglot ideology.

Narrative patterning   Narratives are patterned, i.e. they always display non-arbitrary structures of composition and meaningful arrangement.

Orders of indexicality   Stratified patterns of social meanings often called 'norms' or 'rules', to which people orient when communicating. Such norms emanate from 'centring institutions', and orders of indexicality always form part of a polycentric system; there are always multiple orders of indexicality present.

Orthopraxy   Hegemonic appearances, practices that suggest the performance of a hegemony but are not necessarily directed by an 'orthodoxy', i.e. an acceptance of the performed ideology. Doing 'as if' one subscribes to the hegemony.

Place   Space made socially and culturally significant. People imbue particular spaces (e.g. their neighbourhood, their town, or region) with all kinds of symbolic attributes centring on property rights (*my* town, *our* country), authority (particular norms sensed to dominate conduct in those spaces), and value ('there is no place like home').

Polycentric   A system is polycentric when it contains multiple 'centres' to which people operating within that system can/must orient. In communication, we always orient towards multiple orders of indexicality within a polycentric whole.

Pretextuality   The features that people bring along when they communicate: complexes of resources, degrees of control over genres, styles, language varieties, codes, and so on that influence what people can actually do when they communicate.

Professional vision   Customary, habitual professional practices of perception, understanding, and interpretation. Normative professional-cognitive behaviour.

Recontextualisation   Placing text in a 'new' context, thus adding new metapragmatic frames to the text.

Referential meaning   Denotational, propositional meaning. The 'pure' linguistic meaning of a term or grammatical construction, sensed to relate it to an object 'in the world'.

Repertoire   The totality of linguistic resources, knowledge about their function and about their conditions of use in an individual or community.

Semiosis   Meaningful symbolic behaviour, larger than, but including, linguistic behaviour.

Simultaneity   The observation that multiple layers of context operate in every semiotic act, thus creating simultaneously produced multiple meanings.

Speech community   People displaying shared patterns of indexical meaning-attribution, an (often implicit) adherence to social-semiotic norms and rules.

Stance   Complexes of linguistic and communicative features that identify how someone relates towards what is being said. Stance marks, e.g., that what is being said is 'sensitive', 'delicate', 'important', 'secret', 'scandalous', 'funny', and so on.

Stratification   Hierarchical layering. Something is stratified when it displays several non-equivalent layers.

Stylisation   The use of dense complexes of stylistic features (e.g. poetic and performance features) in communication.

Synchronisation   The process by means of which the different contextual orders operating in 'layered simultaneity' are being reduced to differences on one synchronic scale of distinction.

Systemic   Something which is part of a system and thus not an isolated, arbitrary feature.

Text trajectories  Patterns of shifting and transferring bits of discourse through series of entextualisations; e.g. a patient's oral narrative is written down in scribbled notes by a psychiatrist, who then writes a (prose) summary of it and talks about it to colleagues, who in turn take notes and incorporate elements of the narrative into a published paper.

Voice  The capacity to make oneself understood.

# References

Althusser, L. 1971 Ideology and ideological state apparatuses. In *Lenin and Philosophy and Other Essays*: 121–173. London: Verso.

Anderson, B. 1983 *Imagined Communities*. London: Verso.

Anderson, P. 1977 The antinomies of Antonio Gramsci. *New Left Review* 100: 5–78.

Antaki, C., and Widdicombe, S. (eds.) 1998 *Identities in Talk*. London: Sage.

Auer, P. 1992 Introduction: John Gumperz' approach to contextualization. In Peter Auer and Aldo DiLuzio (eds.), *The Contextualization of Language*: 1–37. Amsterdam: John Benjamins.

1995 Context and contextualization. In Verschueren, J., Östman, J.-O., and Blommaert, J. (eds.), *Handbook of Pragmatics, 1995*: 1–19. Amsterdam: John Benjamins.

Auer, P., and Di Luzio, A. (eds.) 1992 *The Contextualization of Language*. Amsterdam: John Benjamins.

Austin, J. L. 1962 *How to Do Things with Words*. Oxford: Oxford University Press.

Bakhtin, M. M. 1981 *The Dialogic Imagination*. Austin: University of Texas Press.

1986 *Speech Genres and Other Late Essays*. Austin: University of Texas Press.

Balibar, E., and Wallerstein, I. 1988 *Race, Nation, Classe: Les Identities ambigues*. Paris: La Découverte.

Barthes, R. 1957 *Mythologies*. Paris: Le Seuil.

Barton, D. 1994 *Literacy: An Introduction to the Ecology of Written Language*. Oxford: Blackwell.

Barton, D., and Hamilton, M. 1998 *Local Literacies: Reading and Writing in One Community*. London: Routledge.

Bauman, R. 1995 Representing Native American oral narrative: The textual practices of Henry Rowe Schoolcraft. *Pragmatics* 5/2: 167–183.

Bauman, R., and Briggs, C. 1990 Poetics and performance as critical perspectives on language and social life. *Annual Review of Anthropology* 19: 59–88.

2003 *Voices of Modernity: Language Ideology and the Politics of Inequality*. Cambridge: Cambridge University Press.

Bauman, R., and Sherzer, J. (eds.) 1974 *Explorations in the Ethnography of Speaking*. Cambridge: Cambridge University Press.

Baynham, M. 1995 *Literacy Practices: Investigating Literacy Practices in Social Contexts*. London: Longman.

Baynham, M., and Slembrouck, S. (eds.) 1999 *Speech Representation and Institutional Discourse*. Special issue, *Text* 19/4: 439–592.

Bell, A., and Garrett, P. (eds.) 1998 *Approaches to Media Discourse*. London: Longman.

Berezhkov, V. 1982 *History in the Making. Memoirs of World War II Diplomacy*. Moscow: Progress.

Bernstein, B. 1971 *Class, Codes and Control, Vol. 1: Theoretical Studies Towards a Sociology of Language*. London: Routledge & Kegan Paul.

Besnier, N. 1995 *Literacy, Emotion, and Authority: Reading and Writing on a Polynesian Atoll*. Cambridge: Cambridge University Press.

Biber, D., and Finegan, E. 1989 Styles of stance in English: Lexical and grammatical marking of evidentiality and affect. *Text* 9/1: 93–124 (special issue on *The Pragmatics of Affect*, ed. E. Ochs).

Billig, M., and Schegloff, E. 1999 Critical discourse analysis and conversation analysis: An exchange between Michael Billig and Emanuel A. Schegloff. *Discourse and Society* 10/4: 543–582.

Birch, D. 1998 Criticism, linguistic. In Jacob Mey (ed.), *Concise Encyclopedia of Pragmatics*: 190–194. Oxford: Pergamon/Elsevier.

Bloch, M. 1953 *The Historian's Craft*. New York: Knopf.

1961 *The Royal Touch*. London: Routledge & Kegan Paul.

Blommaert, J. 1997a *Workshopping: Notes on Professional Vision in Discourse Analysis*. Antwerp: UIA-GER (Antwerp Papers in Linguistics 91).

1997b The slow shift in orthodoxy: (Re)formulations of 'integration' in Belgium. *Pragmatics* 7/4: 499–518.

1999a Reconstructing the sociolinguistic image of Africa: Grassroots writing in Shaba (Congo). *Text* 9/2: 175–200.

1999b *State Ideology and Language in Tanzania*. Cologne: Rüdiger Köppe.

2001a Context is/as critique. *Critique of Anthropology* 21/1: 13–32. (special issue on *Discourse and Critique*, ed. J. Blommaert, J. Collins, M. Heller, B. Rampton, S. Slembrouck, and J. Verschueren).

2001b Investigating narrative inequality: African asylum seekers' stories in Belgium. *Discourse and Society* 12/4: 413–449.

2001c The other side of history: Grassroots literacy and autobiography in Shaba, Congo. *General Linguistics* 38/1: 133–155.

2001d *Ik Stel Vast: Politiek taalgebruik, politieke vernieuwing en verrechtsing*. Berchem: EPO ['I observe': Political discourse, political innovation and the rise of the extreme right].

2003a Commentary: A sociolinguistics of globalization. *Journal of Sociolinguistics* 7/4: 607–623.

2003b Grassroots historiography and the problem of voice: Tshibumba's 'Histoire du Zaire'. *Journal of Linguistic Anthropology* 14/1: 6–23.

2003c Orthopraxy, writing and identity: Shaping lives through borrowed genres in Congo. *Pragmatics* 13/1: 33–48.

2003d Writing as a problem: African grassroots writing, economies of literacy and globalization. Paper, African Studies Workshop, University of Chicago, March 2003.

(ed.) 1999 *Language Ideological Debates*. Berlin: Mouton de Gruyter

Blommaert, J., and Bulcaen, C. (eds.) 1997 *Political Linguistics*. Amsterdam: John Benjamins.

Blommaert, J., Collins, J., Heller, M., Rampton, B., Slembrouck, S., and Verschueren, J. 2001 Discourse and critique: Introduction. *Critique of Anthropology* 21/1: 5–12 (special issue on *Discourse and Critique*, ed. J. Blommaert, J. Collins, M. Heller, B. Rampton, S. Slembrouck, and J. Verschueren).

Blommaert, J., Dewilde, A., Stuyck, K., Peleman, K., and Meert, H. 2003 Space, experience and authority: Exploring attitudes towards refugee centers in Belgium. *Journal of Language and Politics* 2: 311–331.

Blommaert, J., and Verschueren, J. 1992 *Het Belgische Migrantendebat*. Antwerp: IPrA ['The Belgian migrant debate'].

1998 *Debating Diversity: Analysing the Discourse of Tolerance*. London: Routledge.

Boas, F. 1911 *Handbook of American Indian Languages*. Washington, DC: Smithsonian Institute.

Bolinger, D. 1980 *Language: The Loaded Weapon*. London: Longman.

Bourdieu, P. 1971 Systems of education and systems of thought. In Young, M. (ed.), *Knowledge and Control: New Directions for the Sociology of Education*: 189–207. London: Collier-Macmillan.

1977 *Outline of a Theory of Practice*. Cambridge: Polity.

1982 *Ce que Parler Veut Dire: Une Economie des Echanges Linguistiques*. Paris: Fayard.

1984 *Distinction: A Social Critique of the Judgment of Taste*. London: Routledge.

1988 *Homo Academicus*. Cambridge: Polity.

1990 *The Logic of Practice*. Cambridge: Polity.

1991 *Language and Symbolic Power*. Cambridge: Polity.

1993 Public opinion does not exist. In *Sociology in Question*: 149–157. London: Sage.

Bourdieu, P., and Passeron, J.-C. 1977 *La Réproduction: Eléments pour une Théorie du Système d'Enseignement*. Paris: Minuit.

Boyarin, J. (ed.), 1992 *The Ethnography of Reading*. Berkeley: University of California Press.

Braudel, F. 1949 *La Méditerranée et le Monde Méditerranéen à l'Epoque de Philippe II*. Paris: Armand Collin.

1969 (1958) Histoire et sciences sociales: la longue durée. In *Ecrits sur l'Histoire*: 41–83. Paris: Flammarion.

1981 *The Structures of Everyday Life: The Limits of the Possible (Civilization and Capitalism, Vol. I)*. New York: Harper & Row.

Brenneis, D., and Macaulay, R. (eds.) 1986 *The Matrix of Language: Contemporary Linguistic Anthropology*. Boulder: Westview Press.

Briggs, C. 1997a Notes on a 'confession': On the construction of gender, sexuality, and violence in an infanticide case. *Pragmatics* 7/4: 519–546.

1997b Introduction: From the ideal, the ordinary, and the orderly to conflict and violence in pragmatic research. *Pragmatics* 7/4: 451–459.

(ed.) 1996 *Disorderly Discourse: Narrative, Conflict and Inequality*. New York: Oxford University Press.

(ed.) 1997 *Conflict and Violence in Pragmatic Research*. Special issue, *Pragmatics* 7/4: 451–633.

Briggs, C., and Bauman, R. 1992 Genre, intertextuality, and social power. *Journal of Linguistic Anthropology* 2: 131–172.

Brown, G., and Yule, G. 1983 *Discourse Analysis*. Cambridge: Cambridge University Press.

Bucholtz, M. 2000 The politics of transcription. *Journal of Pragmatics* 32: 1439–1465.

Burawoy, M. (ed.) 2001 *Global Ethnography*. Special issue, *Ethnography* 2/2: 147–300.

Burke, P. 1992 *History and Social Theory*. Cambridge: Polity.

Butler, C. 1985 *Systemic Linguistics: Theory and Applications*. London: Batsford.

1995 Systemic functional grammar. In Verschueren, J., Östman, J.-O., and Blommaert, J. (eds.), *Handbook of Pragmatics: Manual*: 527–533.

Butler, J. 1990 *Gender Trouble: Feminism and the Subversion of Identity*. New York: Routledge.

Buur, L. 2000 *Institutionalising Truth: Victims, Perpetrators and Professionals in the Everyday Work of the South African Truth and Reconciliation Commission*. Ph.D. diss, Aarhus University.

Caldas-Coulthard, C. 1993 From discourse analysis to critical discourse analysis: The differential re-presentation of women and men speaking in written news. In Sinclair, J. M., Hoey, M., and Fox, G. (eds.), *Techniques of Description: Spoken and Written Discourse*: 196–208. London: Routledge.

1996 'Women who pay for sex. And enjoy it': Transgression versus morality in women's magazines. In Caldas-Coulthard, C, and Coulthard, M. (eds.), *Texts and Practices: Readings in Critical Discourse Analysis*: 250–270. London: Routledge.

Caldas-Coulthard, C, and Coulthard, M. (eds.) 1996 *Texts and Practices: Readings in Critical Discourse Analysis*. London: Routledge.

Cameron, D. 1992 *Feminism and Linguistic Theory*. London: Macmillan.

1995 *Verbal Hygiene*. London: Routledge.

Cameron, D., and Kulick, K. 2003 *Language and Sexuality*. Cambridge: Cambridge University Press.

Castells, M. 1996 *The Rise of the Network Society*. London: Blackwell.

1997 *The Power of Identity*. London: Blackwell.

Chilton, P., Mey, J., and Ilyin, M. (eds.) 1998 *Political Discourse in Transition in Europe 1989–1991*. Amsterdam: John Benjamins.

Chilton, P., and Schäffner, C. (eds.) 2002 *Politics as Text and Talk: Analytic Approaches to Political Discourse*. Amsterdam: John Benjamins.

Chouliaraki L. 1998 Regulation in 'progressivist' pedagogic discourse: Individualized teacher–pupil talk. *Discourse and Society* 9: 5–32.

Chouliaraki L., and Fairclough, N. 1999 *Discourse in Late Modernity: Rethinking Critical Discourse Analysis*. Edinburgh: Edinburgh University Press.

Clark, R., Fairclough, N., Ivanic, R., and Martin-Jones, M. 1990 Critical language awareness part 2: Towards critical alternatives. *Language and Education* 5: 41–54.

Clark, U., and Zyngier, S. 1998 Women beware women: Detective fiction and critical discourse analysis. *Language and Literature* 7: 141–158.

Clifford, J. 1988 *The Predicament of Culture: Twentieth Century Ethnography, Literature, and Art*. Cambridge, Mass.: Harvard University Press.

Collins, J. 1995 Literacy and literacies. *Annual Review of Anthropology* 25: 75–93.

1996 Socialization to text: Structure and contradiction in schooled literacy. In Silverstein, M., and Urban, G. (eds.), *Natural Histories of Discourse*: 203–228. Chicago: University of Chicago Press.

1998 *Understanding Tolowa Histories: Western Hegemonies and Native American Responses*. New York: Routledge.

Collins, J., and Blot, R. 2003 *Literacy and Literacies: Texts, Power and Identity*. Cambridge: Cambridge University Press.

Collins, R. 1988 Theoretical continuities in Goffman's work. In Drew, P. and Wootton, A. (eds.) *Erving Goffman: Exploring the Interactional Order*: 41–63. Cambridge: Polity.

Conley, J., and O'Barr, W. 1990 *Rules versus Relationships: The Ethnography of Legal Discourse*. Chicago: University of Chicago Press.

Cope, B., and Kalantzis, M. (eds.), 2000 *Multiliteracies: Literacy Learning and the Design of Social Futures*. London: Routledge.

Darnell, R. 1998 *And Along Came Boas: Continuity and Revolution in Americanist Anthropology*. Amsterdam: John Benjamins.

2001 *Invisible Genealogies: A History of Americanist Anthropology*. Lincoln: University of Nebraska Press.

de Beaugrande, R., and Dressler, W. 1981 *Introduction to Text Linguistics*. London: Routledge.

Deleuze, G. 1989 *Michel Foucault, Philosophe*. Paris: Le Seuil.

De Vos, P. 2003 Discourse theory and the study of ideological (trans)formations: Analyzing social democratic revisionism. *Pragmatics* 13: 163–180.

D'hondt, S. 2001 Conversation Analysis and History: Practical and discursive understandings of quarrels among Dar es Salaam adolescents. Ph.D. diss., University of Antwerp.

D'hondt, S. 2002 Framing gender: Incongruous gendered identities in Dar es Salaam adolescents' talk. In McIlvenny, P. (ed.), *Talking Gender and Sexuality*: 207–236. Amsterdam: John Benjamins.

Dittmar, N. 1996 Correlational Sociolinguistics. In Verschueren, J., Östman, J.-O., Blommaert, J., and Bulcaen, C. (eds.), *Handbook of Pragmatics 1996*: 1–14. Amsterdam: John Benjamins.

Dreyfus, H., and Rabinow, P. 1982 *Michel Foucault: Beyond Structuralism and Hermeneutics*. Brighton: Harvester Press.

Ducrot, O. 1996 *Slovenian Lectures: Argumentative Semantics*. Ljubljana: ISH.

Duranti, A. 1997 *Linguistic Anthropology*. Cambridge: Cambridge University Press.

(ed.) 2001 *Linguistic Anthropology: A Reader*. London: Blackwell.

Duranti, A., and Goodwin, C. (eds.) 1992 *Rethinking Context*. Cambridge: Cambridge University Press.

Eagleton, T. 1991 *Ideology: An Introduction*. London: Verso.

Eastman, C., and Stein, R. F. 1993 Language display. *Journal of Multilingual and Multicultural Development* 14: 187–202.

Eckert, P. 2000 *Linguistic Variation as Social Practice*. London: Blackwell.

Eelen, G. 2001 *A Critique of Politeness Theories*. Manchester: St Jerome.

Eerdmans, S. 2003 A review of John J. Gumperz' current contributions to Interactional Sociolinguistics. In Eerdmans, S., Prevignano, C., and Thibault, P. (eds.), *Language and Interaction: Discussions with John J. Gumperz*: 85–103. Amsterdam: John Benjamins.

Englund, H. 2002 Ethnography after globalism: Migration and emplacement in Malawi. *American Ethnologist* 29: 261–286.

Ensink, T., and Sauer, C. (eds.) 2003 *The Art of Commemoration: Fifty Years after the Warsaw Uprising*. Amsterdam: John Benjamins.

Fabian, J. 1983 *Time and the Other: How Anthropology Makes its Object*. New York: Columbia University Press.

1986 *Language and Colonial Power: The Appropriation of Swahili in the Former Belgian Congo 1880–1938*. Cambridge: Cambridge University Press.

1990a *Power and Performance: Ethnographic Explorations through Popular Wisdom and Theatre in Shaba (Zaire)*. Madison: University of Wisconsin Press.

1990b *History from Below: The 'Vocabulary of Elisabethville' by André Yav, Texts, Translation and Interpretive Essay*. Amsterdam: John Benjamins.

1991 *Time and the Work of Anthropology: Critical Essays 1971–1991*. Chur: Harwood.

1996 *Remembering the Present*. Berkeley: University of California Press.

2001 *Anthropology with an Attitude: Critical Essays*. Stanford: Stanford University Press.

Fairclough, N. 1989 *Language and Power*. London: Longman.

1992a *Discourse and Social Change*. Cambridge: Polity.

1992b Discourse and text: Linguistic and intertextual analysis within discourse analysis. *Discourse and Society* 3: 193–217.

1995 *Critical Discourse Analysis*. London: Longman.

1996 A reply to Henry Widdowson's 'Discourse analysis: A critical view'. *Language and Literature* 5: 49–56.

2000 *New Labour, New Language?* London: Routledge.

(ed.) 1992 *Critical Language Awareness*. London: Longman.

Fairclough, N., and Mauranen, A. 1997 The conversationalisation of political discourse: A comparative view. In Blommaert, J., and Bulcaen, C. (eds.), *Political Linguistics*: 89–119. Amsterdam: John Benjamins.

Feld, S. and Basso, K. (eds.) 1996 *Senses of Place*. Santa Fe: SAR Press.

Ferguson, J., and Gupta, A. 2002 Spatializing states: Toward an ethnography of neoliberal governmentality. *American Ethnologist* 29: 981–1002.

Fishman, J. 1972 *The Sociology of Language*. Rowley, Mass.: Newbury House.
    (ed.) 1974 *Advances in Language Planning*. The Hague: Mouton.
    (ed.) 1999 *Handbook of Language and Ethnicity*. New York: Oxford University Press.

Foucault, M. 1969 *L'Archéologie du Savoir*. Paris: Gallimard.
    1975 *Surveiller et Punir: Naissance de la Prison*. Paris: Gallimard.
    1982 The order of discourse. In Shapiro, M. (ed.), *Language and Politics*: 108–138. London: Blackwell.
    2001a *Dits et Ecrits I, 1954–1975*. Paris: Quarto-Gallimard.
    2001b *Dits et Ecrits II, 1976–1988*. Paris: Quarto-Gallimard.
    2002 (1972) *The Archaeology of Knowledge*. London: Routledge.
    2003 *Society Must Be Defended. Lectures at the Collège de France 1975–1976*. New York: Picador.

Fowler, R. 1996. On Critical Linguistics. In Caldas-Coulthard, C., and Coulthard, M. (eds.), *Texts and Practices: Readings in Critical Discourse Analysis*: 3–14. London: Routledge.

Fowler, R., Hodge, R., Kress, G., and Trew, T. 1979 *Language and Control*. London: Routledge & Kegan Paul.

Freeden, M. 1996 *Ideologies and Political Theory: A Conceptual Approach*. Oxford: Clarendon Press.

Friedrich, P. 1989 Language, ideology and political economy. *American Anthropologist* 91: 295–312.

Gal, S. 1979 *Language Shift*. New York: Academic Press.
    1989 Language and political economy. *Annual Review of Anthropology* 18: 345–367.

Gal, S., and Woolard, K. (eds.), 2001 *Constructing Languages and Publics: Authority and Representation*. Manchester: St Jerome.

Galasinski, D. 1997 The making of history: Some remarks on politicians' presentation of historical events. *Pragmatics* 7: 55–68.

Gee, J. 1990 *Social Linguistics and Literacies: Ideologies in Discourses*. London: Falmer.

Giddens, A. 1984 *The Constitution of Society. Outline of the Theory of Structuration*. Cambridge: Polity.
    1998 *The Third Way: The Renewal of Social Democracy*. Cambridge: Polity.

Ginzburg, C. 1999 *The Judge and the Historian: Marginal Notes on a Late-Twentieth-Century Miscarriage of Justice*. London: Verso.

Goffman, E. 1974 *Frame Analysis: An Essay on the Organization of Experience*. New York: Harper & Row.

1981 *Forms of Talk*. Oxford: Basil Blackwell.

Goodwin, C. 1981 *Conversational Organization: Interaction between Speakers and Hearers*. New York: Academic Press.

1994 Professional vision. *American Anthropologist* 96: 606–633.

Graddol, D., Maybin, J., and Stierer, B. (eds.) 1991 *Researching Language and Literacy in Social Context*. Clevedon: Multilingual Matters.

Gramsci, A. 1971 *Selections from the Prison Notebooks of Antonio Gramsci*. (ed. Q. Hoare, and G. N. Smith). London: Lawrence & Wishart.

Grice, H. P. 1975 The logic of conversation. In Cole, M., and Morgan, J. (eds.), *Syntax and Semantics Vol. 3: Speech Acts*: 64–75. New York: Academic Press.

Gumperz, J. 1972 Introduction. In Gumperz, J., and Hymes, D. (eds.), *Directions in Sociolinguistics: The Ethnography of Communication*: 1–25. London: Blackwell.

1982 *Discourse Strategies*. Cambridge: Cambridge University Press.

1986 Interactional sociolinguistics in the study of schooling. In Cook-Gumperz, J. (ed.), *The Social Construction of Literacy*: 45–68. Cambridge: Cambridge University Press.

1992 Contextualization revisited. In Auer, P., and DiLuzio, A. (eds.), *The Contextualization of Language*: 39–53. Amsterdam: John Benjamins.

2003 Response essay. In Eerdmans, S., Prevignano, C., and Thibault, P. (eds.), *Language and Interaction: Discussions with John Gumperz*: 105–126. Amsterdam: John Benjamins.

Gumperz, J., and Cook-Gumperz, J. (eds.) 1982 *Language and Social Identity*. Cambridge: Cambridge University Press.

Gumperz, J., and Hymes, D. (eds.) 1972 *Directions in Sociolinguistics: The Ethnography of Communication*. London: Blackwell.

Gumperz, J., and Roberts, C. 1991 Understanding in intercultural encounters. In Blommaert, J., and Verschueren, J. (eds.), *The Pragmatics of Intercultural and International Communication*: 51–90. Amsterdam: John Benjamins.

Habermas, J. 1984 *The Theory of Communicative Action Vol. 1, Reason and the Rationalization of Society*. London: Heinemann.

1987 *The Theory of Communicative Action Vol. 2, Lifeworld and System: A Critique of Functionalist Reason*. London: Heinemann.

Haeri, N. 1997 The reproduction of symbolic capital: Language, state and class in Egypt. *Current Anthropology* 38: 795–816.

Hall, C., Sarangi, S., and Slembrouck, S. 1997 Moral construction in social work discourse. In Gunnarson, B.-L., Linell, P., and Nordberg, B. (eds.), *The Construction of Professional Discourse*: 265–291. London: Longman.

Hall, C., and Slembrouck, S. 2001 Parent participation in social work meetings: The case of child protection conferences. *European Journal of Social Work* 4: 143–160.

Hall, K., and Bucholtz, M. (eds.) 1995 *Gender Articulated: Language and the Socially Constructed Self*. London: Routledge.

Halliday, M. A. K. 1978 *Language as Social Semiotic: The Social Interpretation of Language and Meaning.* Baltimore: University Park Press.

Halliday, M. A. K., and Hasan, R. 1976 *Cohesion in English.* London: Longman.

Hanks, W. 1989 Text and Textuality. *Annual Review of Anthropology* 18: 95–127.

  1990 *Referential Practice: Language and Lived Space among the Maya.* Chicago: University of Chicago Press.

  1996 *Language and Communicative Practice.* Boulder: Westview.

  2000 Indexicality. In Duranti, A. (ed.), *Language Matters in Anthropology: A Lexicon for the Millenium*: 124–126. Special issue of *Journal of Linguistic Anthropology* 9/1–2.

Harris, R., Leung, C., and Rampton, B. 2001 Globalisation, diaspora and language education in England. *Working Papers in Urban Languages and Literacies* 17. London: King's College London.

Haviland, J. 1989 'Sure, sure': Evidence and affect. *Text* 9: 27–68.

  1996 Text from talk in Tzotzil. In Silverstein, M., and Urban, G. (eds.), *Natural Histories of Discourse*: 45–78. Chicago: University of Chicago Press.

Heath, S. B. 1983 *Ways with Words.* Cambridge: Cambridge University Press.

Heller, M. 1994 *Crosswords: Language, Education and Ethnicity in French Ontario.* Berlin: Mouton de Gruyter.

  1995 Bilingualism and Multilingualism. In Verschueren, J., Östman, J.-O., and Blommaert, J. (eds.), *Handbook of Pragmatics 1995*: 1–15. Amsterdam: John Benjamins.

  1999 *Linguistic Minorities and Modernity: A Sociolinguistic Ethnography.* London: Longman.

  2003 Globalization, the new economy and the commodification of language and identity. *Journal of Sociolinguistics* 7: 473–492.

Hewitt, R. 1986 *White Talk Black Talk: Inter-Racial Friendship and Communication among Adolescents.* Cambridge: Cambridge University Press.

Hill, J., and Hill, K. 1986 *Speaking Mexicano: Dynamics of Syncretic Language in Central Mexico.* Tucson: University of Arizona Press.

Hill, J., and Mannheim, B. 1992 Language and world view. *Annual Review of Anthropology* 21: 381–406.

Hinnenkamp, V. 1992 Comments on: Christian Heath, 'Gesture's discreet task, multiple relevancies in visual conduct and the contextualization of language'. In Auer, P., and DiLuzio, A. (eds.), *The Contextualization of Language*: 129–133. Amsterdam: John Benjamins.

Hobsbawm, E. 1983 Introduction: Inventing traditions. In Hobsbawm, E., and Ranger, T. (eds.), *The Invention of Tradition*: 1–14. Cambridge: Cambridge University Press.

  1986 *Nations and Nationalism since 1789: Myth, Programme and Reality.* Cambridge: Cambridge University Press.

  2000 *Bandits* 2nd edn. New York: The Free Press.

Hobsbawm, E., and Ranger, T. (eds.) 1983 *The Invention of Tradition.* Cambridge: Cambridge University Press.

Hodge, R., and Kress, G. 1988 *Social Semiotics*. Ithaca: Cornell University Press.

Hoffman, C. 1991 *An Introduction to Bilingualism*. London: Longman.

Hymes, D. 1966 Two types of linguistic relativity (with examples from Amerindian ethnography). In Bright, W. (ed.), *Sociolinguistics: Proceedings of the UCLA Sociolinguistics Conference, 1964*: 114–167. The Hague: Mouton.

1968 Linguistic problems in defining the concept of 'tribe'. In Helm, J. (ed.), *Essays on the Problem of Tribe*: 23–48. Seattle: American Ethnological Society and University of Washington Press.

1971 Sociolinguistics and the ethnography of speaking. In Ardener, E. (ed.), *Social Anthropology and Language*: 47–93. London: Tavistock.

1972 Models of the interaction of language and social life. In Gumperz, J., and Hymes, D. (eds.), *Directions in Sociolinguistics: The Ethnography of Communication*: 35–71. New York: Holt, Rinehart, and Winston.

1974a *Foundations in Sociolinguistics: An Ethnographic Approach*. Philadelphia: University of Pennsylvania Press.

1974b Ways of speaking. In Bauman, R., and Sherzer, J. (eds.), *Explorations in the Ethnography of Speaking*: 433–451. Cambridge: Cambridge University Press.

1975 Breakthrough into performance. In Ben-Amos, D., and Goldstein, K. (eds.), *Folklore: Performance and Communication*: 11–74. The Hague: Mouton.

1980 *Language in Education: Ethnolinguistic Essays*. Washington, DC: Center for Applied Linguistics.

1981 *In Vain I Tried to Tell You: Essays in Native American Ethnopoetics*. Philadelphia: University of Pennsylvania Press

1983 *Essays in the History of Linguistic Anthropology*. Amsterdam: John Benjamins,

1992 The concept of communicative competence revisited. In Pütz, M. (ed.), *Thirty Years of Linguistic Evolution*: 31–57. Amsterdam: John Benjamins.

1996 *Ethnography, Linguistics, Narrative Inequality: Towards an Understanding of Voice*. London: Taylor and Francis.

1998 When is oral narrative poetry? Generative form and its pragmatic conditions. *Pragmatics* 8: 475–500.

(ed.) 1969 *Reinventing Anthropology*. New York: Random House.

Irvine, J. 1989 When talk isn't cheap: Language and political economy. *American Ethnologist* 12: 738–748.

Irvine, J., and Gal, S. 2000 Language ideology and linguistic differentiation. In Kroskrity, P. (ed.), *Regimes of Language*: 35–83. Santa Fe: SAR Press.

Ivanic, R. 1998 *Writing and Identity: The Discoursal Construction of Identity in Academic Writing*. Amsterdam: John Benjamins.

Jacquemet, M. 1996 *Credibility in Court: Communicative Practices in the Camorra Trials*. Cambridge: Cambridge University Press.

2000 Beyond the speech community. Paper, 7th International Pragmatics Conference, Budapest, July 2000.

Jaffe, A. 1999 *Ideologies in Action: Language Politics on Corsica*. Berlin: Mouton de Gruyter.

Jakobson, R. 1960 Closing statement: linguistics and poetics. In Sebeok, T. A. (ed.), *Style in Language*: 350–377. New York: Wiley.

Jaworski, A., and Coupland, N. (eds.) 1999 *The Discourse Reader*. London: Routledge.

Johnstone, B. 1990 *Stories, Community, and Place*. Bloomington: Indiana University Press.

1999 Uses of Southern-sounding speech by contemporary Texas women. *Journal of Sociolinguistics* 3: 505–522.

Jupp, T. C., Roberts, C., and Cook-Gumperz, J. 1982 Language and disadvantage: The hidden process. In Gumperz, J., and Cook-Gumperz, J. (eds.), *Language and Social Identity*: 233–256. Cambridge: Cambridge University Press.

Kaye, H. 1984 *The British Marxist Historians*. Cambridge: Polity.

KCM (Koninklijk Commissariaat voor het Migrantenbeleid) 1989 *Integratie(beleid): Een Werk van Lange Adem*. 3 vols. Brussels: KCM/INBEL.

1993 *Tekenen voor Gelijkwaardigheid*. Brussels: INBEL.

Kress, G. 1976 *Halliday: System and Function in Language*. London: Oxford University Press.

1994 Text and grammar as explanation. In Meinhof, U., and Richardson, K. (eds.), *Text, Discourse and Context: Representations of Poverty in Britain*: 24–46. London: Longman.

1996 *Before Writing: Rethinking the Paths to Literacy*. London: Routledge.

Kress, G., and Hodge, R. 1979 *Language as Ideology*. London: Routledge.

Kress, G., and van Leeuwen, T. 1996 *Reading Images: The Grammar of Visual Design*. London: Routledge.

Kristeva, J. 1986 *The Kristeva Reader* (ed. T. Moi). Oxford: Blackwell.

1989 *Language, The Unknown. An Initiation to Linguistics*. New York: Columbia University Press.

Kroskrity, P. (ed.) 2000 *Regimes of Language*. Santa Fe: SAR Press.

Kulick, D. 1992 *Language Shift and Cultural Reproduction: Socialization, Self, and Syncretism in a Papua New Guinean Village*. New York: Cambridge University Press.

1998 *Travesti: Sex, Gender and Culture among Brazilian Transgendered Prostitutes*. Chicago: University of Chicago Press.

2000 Gay and lesbian language. *Annual Review of Anthropology* 29: 243–285.

Labov, W. 1966 *The Social Stratification of English in New York*. Washington, DC: Center for Applied Linguistics.

1972 *Sociolinguistic Patterns*. Philadelphia: University of Pennsylvania Press.

1984 Intensity. In Schiffrin, D. (ed.), *Meaning, Form and Use in Context: Linguistic Applications*: 43–70. Washington, DC: Georgetown University Press.

Laclau, E., and Mouffe, C. 1985 *Hegemony and Socialist Strategy*. London: Verso.

Leman, J. 1993 Het Belgisch migrantendebat revisited. *Ethische Perspectieven* 3: 131–139.

LePage, R., and Tabouret-Keller, A. 1985 *Acts of Identity. Creole-Based Approaches to Language and Ethnicity*. Cambridge: Cambridge University Press.

Levinson, S. 1983 *Pragmatics*. Cambridge: Cambridge University Press.

Lippi-Green, R. 1997 *English with an Accent: Language, Ideology, and Discrimination in the United States*. London: Routledge.

Lucy, J. 1985 Whorf's view on the linguistic mediation of thought. In Mertz, E., and Parmentier, R. (eds.), *Semiotic Mediation: Sociocultural and Psychological Perspectives*: 73–98. New York: Academic Press.

(ed.), 1993 *Reflexive Language: Reported Speech and Metapragmatics*. Cambridge: Cambridge University Press.

Martin, J. R. 2000 Close reading: Functional linguistics as a tool for critical discourse analysis. In Unsworth, L. (ed.), *Researching Language in Schools and Communities: Functional Linguistic Perspectives*: 275–302. London: Cassell.

Martin, J. R., and Wodak, R. (eds.) 2003 *Re/reading the Past: Critical and Functional Perspectives on Time and Value*. Amsterdam: John Benjamins.

Martin-Rojo, L. 1995 Division and rejection: From the personification of the Gulf conflict to the demonization of Saddam Hussein. *Discourse and Society* 6: 49–80.

Martin-Rojo, L., and Gabilondo-Pujol, A. 2000 Michel Foucault. In Verschueren, J., Östman, J.-O., Blommaert, J., and Bulcaen, C. (eds.), *Handbook of Pragmatics 2000*: 1–24. Amsterdam: John Benjamins.

Martin-Rojo, L., and van Dijk, T. 1997 'There was a problem, and it was solved!': Legitimating the expulsion of 'illegal' migrants in Spanish parliamentary discourse. *Discourse and Society* 8: 523–566.

Martiniello, M. 1995 *L'Ethnicité dans les Sciences Sociales Contemporaines*. Paris: Presses Universitaires de France.

Maryns, K., and Blommaert, J. 2001 Stylistic and thematic shifting as a narrative resource: Assessing asylum seekers' repertoires. *Multilingua* 20: 61–84.

2002 Pretextuality and pretextual gaps: On de/refining linguistic inequality. *Pragmatics* 12: 11–30.

Masquelier, A. 2002 Road mythographies: Space, mobility, and the historical imagination in postcolonial Niger. *American Ethnologist* 29: 829–856.

May, S. 2001 *Language and Minority Rights: Ethnicity, Nationalism and the Politics of Language*. London: Longman.

Mehan, H. 1996 The construction of an LD student: A case study in the politics of representation. In Silverstein, M., and Urban, G. (eds.), *Natural Histories of Discourse*: 253–276. Chicago: University of Chicago Press.

Mertz, E., and Yovel, J. 2000 Metalinguistic awareness. In Verschueren, J., Östman, J.-O., Blommaert, J. and Bulcaen, C. (eds.), *Handbook of Pragmatics 2000*: 1–26. Amsterdam: John Benjamins.

Meshtrie, R. (ed.) 2001 *Concise Encyclopaedia of Sociolinguistics*. Oxford: Pergamon Press.

Mey, J. 1985 *Whose Language? An Introduction to Linguistic Pragmatics*. Amsterdam: John Benjamins.

(ed.) 1998 *Concise Encyclopaedia of Pragmatics*. Amsterdam: Elsevier.

Milroy, J., and Milroy, L. 1985 *Authority in Language: Investigating Language Prescription and Standardisation*. London: Routledge & Kegan Paul.

Myers-Scotton, C. 1993 *Social Motivations for Codeswitching: Evidence from Africa*. Oxford: Clarendon Press.

New London Group 1996 A pedagogy of multiliteracies: Designing social futures. *Harvard Educational Review* 66: 60–92.

Ochs, E. 1990 Indexicality and socialization. In Stigler, J., Schweder, R., and Herdt, G. (eds.), *Cultural Psychology*: 287–308. Cambridge: Cambridge University Press.

1992 Indexing gender. In Duranti, A., and Goodwin, C. (eds.), *Rethinking Context*: 335–358. Cambridge: Cambridge University Press.

1999 (1979) Transcription as theory. In Jaworski, A., and Coupland, N. (eds.), *The Discourse Reader*: 167–182. London: Routledge.

Ochs, E., and Capps, L. 1996 Narrating the Self. *Annual Review of Anthropology* 25: 19–43.

Ochs, E., and Schieffelin, B. 1989 Language has a heart. *Text* 9: 7–25.

Pêcheux, M. 1982 *Language, Semantics, and Ideology: Stating the Obvious*. London: Macmillan.

Pennycook, A. 1994 Incommensurable Discourses? *Applied Linguistics* 15: 115–138.

Philips, S. 1998 *Ideology in the Language of Judges: How Judges Practice Law, Politics and Courtroom Control*. New York: Oxford University Press.

Phillipson, R. 1992 *Linguistic Imperialism*. London: Oxford University Press.

Prinsloo, M., and Breier, M. (eds.) 1996 *The Social Uses of Literacy: Theory and Practice in Contemporary South Africa*. Amsterdam: John Benjamins.

Psathas, G. 1995 *Conversation Analysis: The Study of Talk-in-Interaction*. Thousand Oaks, Calif.: Sage.

Rampton, B. 1995 *Crossing: Language and Ethnicity among Adolescents*. London: Longman.

1998 Speech Community. In Verschueren, J., Östman, J.-O., Blommaert, J., and Bulcaen, C. (eds.), *Handbook of Pragmatics 1998*: 1–30. Amsterdam: John Benjamins.

1999 'Deutsch' in Inner London and the animation of an instructed foreign language. *Journal of Sociolinguistics* 3: 480–504.

2001 Critique in interaction. *Critique of Anthropology* 21: 83–107.

2003 Hegemony, social class and stylisation. *Pragmatics* 13: 49–83.

Romaine, S. 1989 *Bilingualism*. London: Blackwell.

Romanucci-Ross, L., and De Vos, G. (eds.) 1995 *Ethnic Identity: Creation, Conflict, and Accommodation*. Walnut Creek: Altamira Press.

Roosens, E. 1989 *Creating Ethnicity: The Process of Ethnogenesis*. Newbury Park: Sage.

Ross, F. 2003 *Bearing Witness: Women and the Truth and Reconciliation Commission in South Africa*. London: Pluto Press.

Rossi-Landi, F. 1983 *Language as Work and Trade: A Semiotic Homology for Linguistics and Economics*. South Hadley: Bergin and Garvey.

Roulet, E. 1996 Polyphony. In Verschueren, J., Östman, J.-O., Blommaert, J., and Bulcaen, C. (eds.), *Handbook of Pragmatics 1996*: 1–18. Amsterdam: John Benjamins.

Sankoff, G. 1980 *The Social Life of Language*. Philadelphia: University of Pennsylvania Press.

1988 Sociolinguistics and syntactic variation. In Newmeyer, F. (ed.), *Linguistics: The Cambridge Survey, Vol. 4*: 140–161. Cambridge: Cambridge University Press.

Sapir, E. 1924 Culture, genuine and spurious. *American Journal of Sociology* 29: 401–429.

Sarangi, S. 1995 Culture. In Verschueren, J., Östman, J.-O., and Blommaert, J. (eds.), *Handbook of Pragmatics 1995*: 1–30. Amsterdam: John Benjamins.

Sarangi, S., and Slembrouck, S. 1992 Non-cooperation in communication: A reassessment of Gricean pragmatics. *Journal of Pragmatics* 17: 117–154.

1996 *Language, Bureaucracy and Social Control*. London: Longman.

Schäffner, C., and Anita Wenden, A. (eds.) 1995 *Language and Peace*. Aldershot: Dartmouth.

Schegloff, E. 1997 Whose text? Whose context? *Discourse and Society* 8: 165–187.

1999 (1991) Talk and social structure. In Jaworski, A., and Coupland, N. (eds.), *The Discourse Reader*: 107–120. London: Routledge.

Schieffelin, B., Woolard, K., and Kroskrity, P. (eds.) 1998 *Language Ideologies: Practice and Theory*. New York: Oxford University Press.

Scollon, R. 1998 *Mediated Discourse as Social Interaction: A Study of News Discourse*. London: Longman.

2001 *Mediated Discourse: The Nexus of Practice*. London: Routledge.

Scollon, R., and Wong Scollon, S. 2003 *Discourses in Place: Language in the Material World*. London: Routledge.

Scott, J. 1990 *Domination and the Arts of Resistance: Hidden Transcripts*. New Haven: Yale University Press.

Sidnell, J. 1998 Deixis. In Verschueren, J., Östman, J.-O., Blommaert, J., and Bulcaen, C. (eds.), *Handbook of Pragmatics 1998*: 1–28. Amsterdam: John Benjamins.

Silverstein, M. 1977 Cultural prerequisites to grammatical analysis. In Saville-Troike, M. (ed.), *Linguistics and Anthropology (GURT 1977)*: 139–151. Washington, DC: Georgetown University Press.

1979 Language structure and linguistic ideology. In Clyne, P., Hanks, W., and Hofbauer, C. (eds.), *The Elements: A Parasession on Linguistic Units and Levels*: 193–247. Chicago: Chicago Linguistic Society.

1992 The indeterminacy of contextualization: When is enough enough? In Auer, P., and Di Luzio, A. (eds.), *The Contextualization of Language*: 55–76. Amsterdam: John Benjamins.

1996a The secret life of texts. In Silverstein, M., and Urban, G. (eds.), *Natural Histories of Discourse*: 81–105. Chicago: University of Chicago Press.

1996b Monoglot 'standard' in America: Standardization and metaphors of linguistic hegemony. In Brenneis, D., and Macaulay, R. (eds.), *The Matrix of Language: Contemporary Linguistic Anthropology*: 284–306. Boulder: Westview Press.

1998 Contemporary transformations of local linguistic communities. *Annual Review of Anthropology* 27: 401–426.

2003a Indexical order and the dialectics of sociolinguistic life. *Language and Communication* 23: 193–229.

2003b *Talking Politics: The Substance of Style from Abe to 'W'*. Chicago: Prickly Paradigm Press.

Silverstein, M., and Urban, G. 1996 The natural history of discourse. In Silverstein, M., and Urban, G. (eds.), *Natural Histories of Discourse*: 1–17. Chicago: University of Chicago Press.

Skutnabb-Kangas, T. 2000 *Linguistic Genocide in Education – or Worldwide Diversity and Human Rights?* Mahwah, NJ: Lawrence Erlbaum.

Slembrouck, S. 1993 Globalising flows: Promotional discourses of government in Western European 'orders of discourse'. *Social Semiotics* 3: 265–292.

1995 Channel. In Verschueren, J., Östman, J.-O., and Blommaert, J. (eds.), *Handbook of Pragmatics 1995*: 1–20. Amsterdam: John Benjamins.

2001 Explanation, interpretation and critique in the analysis of discourse. *Critique of Anthropology* 21: 33–57.

2002 Intertextuality. In Verschueren, J., Östman, J., Blommaert, J., and Bulcaen, C. (eds.), *Handbook of Pragmatics 2002*: 1–25. Amsterdam: John Benjamins.

Sperber, D., and Wilson, D. 1986 *Relevance: Communication and Cognition*. Cambridge, Mass.: Harvard University Press.

Spitulnik, D. 1996 The social circulation of media discourse and the mediation of communities. *Journal of Linguistic Anthropology* 6: 161–187.

1998 Mediating unity and diversity: The production of language ideologies in Zambian broadcasting. In Schieffelin, B., Woolard, K., and Kroskrity, P. (eds.), *Language Ideologies, Practice and Theory*: 103–123. New York: Oxford University Press.

Stocking, G. (ed.) 1974 *The Shaping of American Anthropology, 1883–1911*. New York: Basic Books.

Street, B. 1995 *Social Literacies*. London: Longman.

Stroud, C. 2002 Framing Bourdieu socioculturally: Alternative forms of linguistic legitimacy in postcolonial Mozambique. *Multilingua* 21: 247–273.

Stubbs, M. 1997 Whorf's children: Critical comments on CDA. In Ryan, A., and Wray, A. (eds.), *Evolving Models of Language*: 100–116. Milton Keynes: Multilingual Matters.

Talbot, M. 1992 The construction of gender in a teenage magazine. In Fairclough, N. (ed.), *Critical Language Awareness*: 174–199. London: Longman.

Tannen, D. (ed.) 1984 *Coherence in Spoken and Written Discourse*. Norwood: Ablex.

Therborn, G. 1980 *The Ideology of Power and the Power of Ideology*. London: Verso.

Thibault, P. 1989 Semantic variation, social heteroglossia, intertextuality: Thematic and axiological meaning in spoken discourse. *Critical Studies* 1: 181–209.

Thomas, P. 2002 The river, the road, and the rural-urban divide: A postcolonial moral geography from Southeast Madagascar. *American Ethnologist* 29: 366–391.

Thompson, E. P. 1968 *The Making of the English Working Class*. London: Pelican Books.

1978 *The Poverty of Theory and Other Essays*. London. Merlin Press.

1991 *Customs in Common*. London: Penguin.

Thompson, J. B. 1984 *Studies in the Theory of Ideology*. Berkeley: University of California Press.

1990 *Ideology and Modern Culture*. Cambridge: Polity Press.

Thompson, N. 1996 Supply side socialism: The political economy of New Labour. *New Left Review* 216: 37–54.

Thornborrow, J. 1998 Playing hard to get: Metaphor and representation in the discourse of car advertisements. *Language and Literature* 7: 254–272.

Toolan, M. 1997 What is critical discourse analysis and why are people saying such terrible things about it? *Language and Literature* 6: 83–103.

Urban, G. 1996 Entextualization, replication, and power. In Silverstein, M., and Urban, G. (eds.), *Natural Histories of Discourse*: 21–44. Chicago: University of Chicago Press.

Van Dijk, T. 1987 *Communicating Racism: Ethnic Prejudice in Thought and Talk*. Newbury Park: Sage.

1991 *Racism and the Press*. London: Routledge.

1993a Critical and descriptive goals in discourse analysis. *Journal of Pragmatics* 9: 739–763.

1993b *Elite Discourse and Racism*. Newbury Park: Sage.

1993c Principles of critical discourse analysis. *Discourse and Society* 4: 249–283.

1995 Discourse analysis as ideology analysis. In Schäffner, C., and Wenden, A. (eds.), *Language and Peace*: 17–33. Aldershot: Dartmouth.

1997 What is political discourse analysis? In Blommaert, J., and Bulcaen, C. (eds.), *Political Linguistics*: 11–52. Amsterdam: John Benjamins.

1998 *Ideology: A Multidisciplinary Approach*. London: Sage.

Van Leeuwen, T. 1993 Genre and field in critical discourse analysis: A synopsis. *Discourse and Society* 4: 193–223.

1996 The representation of social actors. In Caldas-Coulthard, C., and Coulthard, M. (eds), *Texts and Practices: Readings in Critical Discourse Analysis*: 32–70. London: Routledge.

Van Leeuwen, T., and Wodak, R. 1999 Legitimizing immigration control: Discourse-historical analysis. *Discourse Studies* 1: 83–118.

VanZanten Gallagher, S. 2002 *Truth and Reconciliation: The Confessional Mode in South African Literature*. Portsmouth: Heinemann.

Verschueren, J. 1995 The pragmatic perspective. In Verschueren, J., Östman, J.-O., and Blommaert, J. (eds.), *Handbook of Pragmatics: Manual*: 1–19. Amsterdam: John Benjamins.

1998 *Understanding Pragmatics*. London: Edward Arnold.

1999 Whose discipline? Some critical reflections on linguistic pragmatics. *Journal of Pragmatics* 31: 869–879.

2001 Predicaments of criticism. *Critique of Anthropology* 21: 59–81.

Verschueren, J. (ed.) 1999 *Language and Ideology. Selected Papers from the 6th International Pragmatics Conference*. Antwerp: IPrA.

Verschueren, J., Östman, J.-O., and Blommaert, J. (eds.) 1995 *Handbook of Pragmatics: Manual*. Amsterdam: John Benjamins.

Voloshinov, V. N. 1973 *Marxism and the Philosophy of Language*. Cambridge Mass.: Harvard University Press.

Wallerstein, I. 1983 *Historical Capitalism*. London: Verso.

2000 *The Essential Wallerstein*. New York: The New Press.

2001 *Unthinking Social Science*. 2nd edn. Philadelphia: Temple University Press.

Walsh, C. 1998 Gender and mediatized political discourse: A case study of press coverage of Margaret Beckett's campaign for the Labour leadership in 1994. *Language and Literature* 7: 199–214.

Wetherell, M. 1998 Positioning and interpretive repertoires: Conversation analysis and post-structuralism in dialogue. *Discourse and Society* 9: 387–412.

Wetherell, M., and Potter, J. 1992 *Mapping the Language of Racism: Discourse and the Legitimation of Exploitation*. New York: Harvester Wheatsheaf.

Widdowson H. 1995 Discourse analysis: A critical view. *Language and Literature* 4: 157–172.

1996 Reply to Fairclough: Discourse and interpretation: Conjectures and refutations. *Language and Literature* 5: 57–69.

1998 The theory and practice of Critical Discourse Analysis. *Applied Linguistics* 19: 136–151.

Williams, R. 1965 *The Long Revolution*. London: Pelican Books.

1973 Base and superstructure in Marxist cultural theory. *New Left Review* 87: 3–16.

1977 *Marxism and Literature*. Oxford: Oxford University Press.

Willis, P. 1981 *Learning to Labor: How Working Class Kids Get Working Class Jobs*. New York: Columbia University Press.

Wodak, R. 1995 Critical linguistics and critical discourse analysis. In Verschueren, J. *et al.* (eds.), *Handbook of Pragmatics: Manual*: 204–210. Amsterdam: John Benjamins.

1996 *Disorders of Discourse*. London: Longman.

1997 Critical discourse analysis and the study of doctor–patient interaction. In Gunnarsson, B.-L., Linell, P., and Nordberg, B. (eds.), *The Construction of Professional Discourse*: 173–200. London: Longman.

(ed.), 1989 *Language, Power and Ideology: Studies in Political Discourse*. Amsterdam: John Benjamins.

(ed.), 1997 *Gender and Discourse*. London: Sage.

Wodak, R., and Reisigl, M. 1999 Discourse and racism: European perspectives. *Annual Review of Anthropology* 28: 175–199.

Woolard, K. 1985 Language variation and cultural hegemony: Toward an integration of sociolinguistics and social theory. *American Ethnologist* 2: 738–748.

1989 *Double Talk: Bilingualism and the Politics of Ethnicity in Catalonia*. Stanford: Stanford University Press.

1998a Simultaneity and bivalency as strategies in bilingualism. *Journal of Linguistic Anthropology* 8: 3–29.

1998b Language ideology as a field of inquiry. In Schieffelin, B., Woolard, K., and Kroskrity, P. (eds.), *Language Ideologies: Practice and Theory*. New York: Oxford University Press.

Zhukov, G. 1974 *Reminiscences and Reflections, Vol. 2*. Moscow: Progress.

Žižek, S. 1994 *Mapping Ideology*. London: Verso.

# Index